George Hudson:
The Railway King

Cover image– George Hudson in full Mayoral robes. Portrait by Sir Francis Grant (1847) (York Mansion House).

George Hudson: The Railway King

A New Biography

Matthew Wells

AN IMPRINT OF PEN & SWORD BOOKS LTD.
YORKSHIRE – PHILADELPHIA

First published in Great Britain in 2024 by
Pen and Sword Transport
An imprint of
Pen & Sword Books Ltd.
Yorkshire - Philadelphia

Copyright © Matthew Wells, 2024

ISBN 9781399057462

The right of Matthew Wells to be identified as author of this work has been asserted by him in accordance with the Copyright, Designs and Patents Act 1988.

A CIP catalogue record for this book is available from the British Library.

All rights reserved. No part of this book may be reproduced or transmitted in any form or by any means, electronic or mechanical including photocopying, recording or by any information storage and retrieval system, without permission from the Publisher in writing.

Typeset in INDIA by IMPEC eSolutions
Printed and bound in the UK on paper from a sustainable source by
CPI Group (UK) Ltd., Croydon. CR0 4YY.

Pen & Sword Books Ltd. incorporates the imprints of Pen & Sword Books:
After the Battle, Archaeology, Atlas, Aviation, Battleground, Discovery, Family History, History, Maritime, Military, Politics, Select, Transport, True Crime, Fiction, Frontline Books, Leo Cooper, Praetorian Press, Seaforth Publishing, Wharncliffe and White Owl.

For a complete list of Pen & Sword titles please contact

PEN & SWORD BOOKS LIMITED
47 Church Street, Barnsley, South Yorkshire, S70 2AS, England
E-mail: enquiries@pen-and-sword.co.uk
Website: www.pen-and-sword.co.uk

or

PEN AND SWORD BOOKS
1950 Lawrence Rd, Havertown, PA 19083, USA
E-mail: Uspen-and-sword@casematepublishers.com
Website: www.penandswordbooks.com

Contents

Introduction		7
Chapter 1	Who was George Hudson?	11
Chapter 2	1835 General Election	22
Chapter 3	Hudson Catches the Railway Bug	37
Chapter 4	Lord Mayor of York	52
Chapter 5	Railway Mania	69
Chapter 6	Hudson's Testimonial	83
Chapter 7	MP for Sunderland	90
Chapter 8	Reaching the Summit	101
Chapter 9	The Kingdom Unravels	110
Chapter 10	Hudson's Explanation	129
Chapter 11	Hudson's Last Hurrah	140
Chapter 12	James Richardson v Thomas Wodson	143
Chapter 13	In Chancery	164
Chapter 14	Hudson Goes Missing	179
Chapter 15	Exile	192
Chapter 16	The King Returns	203
Chapter 17	Final Days…	211
Chapter 18	What They Said	218
Chapter 19	Elizabeth Hudson	235

Appendix 1	261
Appendix 2	264
Appendix 3	266
Select Bibliography	279
Index	282

Introduction

In July 1847 *The Times* newspaper published an article in which the correspondent detailed how men such as George Stephenson (the 'father of the railways') and Rowland Hill (the inventor of the postage stamp) had made their mark in life despite their lowly beginnings but, *The Times* wrote, that there was one such man who stood out above all others as 'an instance of what may be achieved by well-directed energy and great clearness of perception.' That man was George Hudson, whose sobriquet of the 'railway king' showed that he had achieved 'the highest eminence in the most important modern element of national prosperity and civilisation [the railways].' Just two years later, following revelations that some of his business practices were less than ethical, Hudson's reputation went from hero to zero.

Hudson's fall from grace in early 1849 followed the bursting of the great Railway Mania bubble of the mid-1840s. Shrewd investors who sold their railway shares at the peak of the Mania walked away from the crash with huge profits. Unfortunately, there were many who were less astute who lost most if not all their money because, having been caught up by the Mania, they had invested in schemes never likely to succeed or, worse still, that never laid a rail. Those who had made a fortune kept quiet, but those who had lost money, or not made as much as they thought they should, wanted someone to blame and who better than George Hudson, the Railway King, who was seen at the time as the very embodiment of what was wrong with the headlong rush into railway shares during the Mania.

Hudson's misdemeanours were like manna from heaven, not just for those who had lost money, but also his detractors of whom there were many. As soon as the stories of his troubles broke, countless newspapers doubled down on his misfortune, blaming him for the Railway Mania and for the consequences of its collapse. Very prominent amongst these were the York based newspapers, the *York Herald* and *The Yorkshireman*, the former exclaiming Hudson was the 'most degraded' figure of the nineteenth century and describing the collapse of the Railway Mania as 'a sad lesson to a world of mammon worshippers.'

The nineteenth-century political and social commentator Thomas Carlyle described Hudson as a 'big swollen gambler' and even today, more than 150 years after his passing, Hudson is still often described as a 'fraudster', a 'charlatan' and even a 'crook.' Hudson's reputation goes before him – but are these insults a fair description of a man who, at the peak of his powers, was responsible for more than 25 per cent of England's early railway lines, the vast majority of which are still in operation today?

One of the most important books about the early history of railways in England is *A History of the English Railway,* by John Francis, published in 1851. Francis devoted two chapters of his book to George Hudson. Although later biographers criticised Francis's work as no more than an apology for Hudson's errors of judgment, Francis was clear that his approach would be to 'withdraw from all false and all favourable colouring' of Hudson's character. He would be dispassionate and judge Hudson calmly and consider his behaviours in the light of the feverish mania which possessed the world in 1845, rather than take a high moral tone. This is the approach I have adopted in writing this new biography of George Hudson. It is important to consider his behaviour against the backdrop of the world in which he found himself, particularly through the late 1830s and 1840s, and to avoid falling for the anti-Hudson hysteria of the time.

Hudson never wrote his own memoirs but following his fall from grace he did write detailed letters to his shareholders explaining the reasons for the actions he took on their behalf. He also gave numerous speeches in later life recalling the circumstances surrounding his fall.

In July 1850 he was questioned under oath at a libel trial between his close associate James Richardson and *The Yorkshireman* newspaper, a hearing for which he had no time to prepare. What he told the Court that day was probably the closest we will ever get to hearing what he had to say about himself and about his time at the helm of four different railway companies.

However hard Hudson tried to explain his actions, his critics only ever heard his explanations as excuses and not reasons for the decisions he made. As a result, his side of the story has become obscured in the fog of using him as a scapegoat for the national shame felt at the time for the pursuance of easy profits during the Railway Mania years. But, as John Francis put it in 1851, Hudson was 'not a tyrant because others were sycophants.'

For the purpose of this work, therefore, the emphasis has been on listening to Hudson's own words, accepting he would, on occasion, seek to justify what were at times quite unjustified and potentially unethical business methods. His words are balanced by what others said about him, both during and after his lifetime. By taking this approach it has been possible to get a deeper understanding of the man who was the most successful railway entrepreneur of the nineteenth century.

When he fell from grace, Hudson showed no outward signs of bitterness towards those who opposed him and who assisted in his downfall. There were many prominent members of society who benefitted from his time as the Railway King, but he never blamed anyone but himself for his misfortune. In later life he remained humble about his achievements. Recalling the old days, Hudson said his greatest misfortune was receiving a large inheritance from a distant uncle and using it to invest in railways. He would often reflect that he should he have stayed behind the counter of his York drapery shop and how, had he done so, he would have had a much less troubled life. But without Hudson, York would not have become the great railway city it became, nor would the east coast mainline have developed into one of Britain's premier railway routes. It has been said that during his career, Hudson was responsible for supporting maybe a million people through creating up to 100,000 jobs, not just on his railways, but in all the ancillary industries that supported them, from navvies and iron workers to engine makers and rolling stock builders and that is not accounting for all the other jobs created as a result of the coming of the railways in the mid-nineteenth century.

Hudson was much maligned in his own lifetime and his reputation has suffered ever since. I hope this new biography will help to bring a new appreciation to a man who was possibly England's greatest railway entrepreneur.

A first for any biography published about Hudson is a chapter dedicated to his wife Elizabeth who, during her lifetime and since, has often been subjected to unfair ridicule and criticism. But there was much more to Elizabeth than her supposed foibles. They say that behind every great man there is a great woman and this was very much the case for George Hudson.

I should like to acknowledge the help and assistance I have received from everyone who has helped to bring this work towards publication. These include Margery and David Hudson Smith who have kindly allowed the inclusion of some items from their family archive; Anthony Wells for his more than helpful advice on the draft manuscript; the staff of various museums and archives including York Reference Library, the National Railway Museum, the National Archives at Kew and Historic England; Ross Elliot, for guiding me towards sources of information I would not have found for myself. Also, mention must be made of various online resources which have proved invaluable, most particularly the British Newspaper Archive, without which this book would not have been possible, as well as Findmypast.co.uk and Familysearch.org. And finally, but by no means least, my wife Diane, who not only read through my drafts, but has had to listen all about George over the past three years!

Matthew Wells
October 2023

Chapter 1

Who was George Hudson?

By all accounts, George Hudson was not someone to whom others easily took a liking. He was straight talking, called a spade a spade and, like George Stephenson, did not stand on ceremony when it came to talking to anyone who thought that they were 'better' than him. In October 1845, when Hudson was at the peak of his railway career, an article describing his appearance and character was published in numerous newspapers across the country. For the first time, readers could learn more about the man who had recently been crowned 'The Railway King.' No longer did they need to ask themselves who was George Hudson and what was he like?

The article describes Hudson as being about five feet eight inches tall with a stout burly frame and a short bull neck 'surmounted by a head not conspicuous for intellectuality.' His smile, 'at first suspicious, is not ungracious and although his countenance is not attractive, his face attracts attention.' His voice was 'unharmonious' and his language, whilst not choice, was distinct and expressive and his views clear as he expressed them with conviction. Reflecting his lack of education, the writer describes Hudson's mind as 'uncultivated.' At first, the writer says, 'one dislikes him', but this impression was soon dispelled when he spoke and gave the 'why and wherefore for the faith that is in him.' Once you got to know him, Hudson became more agreeable and commanded respect and confidence. He seemed to be 'a good fellow.' Finally in this short description of his physical attributes, the writer tells his readers that from appearance, Hudson was about 55 years old (he was in fact only 45) and though he was fat, he had all the activity of youth.

Confirming some of these observations, John Francis wrote that there was nothing in his personal appearance to justify the excessive adulation he received. There was nothing in his elocution to warrant such raptures. He spoke rapidly and was somewhat thick in utterance (a reference to his broad Yorkshire accent). He affected no refinement of manner, no grace in delivery. He was plain and practical in speech, as master of his subject he spoke as briefly as possible. Physically he had a quick and shifting walk and keen grey eyes. During the day he had an almost slovenly appearance, indicative of most great speculators. At night he was distinguished by his expansive white waistcoat. His severe, even harsh, countenance did not indicate his nature until it was mellowed by a sweet and winning smile.

Hudson was the seventh of ten children born between 1788 and 1805 to John and Elizabeth Hudson of Howsham near York. He was born on 10 March 1800 and baptised five days later at St Peter and St Paul's church in Scrayingham, then the parish church for Howsham. Very little is known of his childhood, but one thing is certain; his early years were shrouded in tragedy. On 11 July 1805, when George was just five years old, he lost his youngest sister Elizabeth, who was only six months old. Then, just over two years later, on 3 September 1807, his mother Elizabeth died, aged 38, after contracting consumption. More tragedy was to follow 14 months later when his father John passed away on 22 November 1808, aged 52. Whilst not a rich man, it is evident from the bequests that he made in his Will that John had made a good living from his farming interests.

In his Will, John left his dwelling house and the family farm to his eldest son, also named John, who was shortly to reach the age of 21. John senior's Trustees were instructed to provide for the 'maintenance, education, and bringing up of my children until my son John reaches the age of twenty-one years.' Thereafter the Trustees were to ensure that each of John's other children received their not insubstantial inheritances on reaching the age of 21. Each son was to receive £1,000 and each daughter (three of them) were to receive £500 each. Despite the disparity in the amounts to be bequeathed to his daughters, it is remarkable for the time that they or his sons other than the eldest were to receive an inheritance. If any children should die before the age of 21, their share was to be allotted in proportion to the other surviving children. John also bequeathed various items of furniture and family silver in his Will. In lieu of receiving any furniture, George was to receive £20. He was also bequeathed two large silver spoons and two silver salt spoons. Bearing in mind that two of his sisters died before they could inherit (Philadelphia in 1815 and Ann in 1817), George is likely to have inherited around £1,100 when he reached age 21.

It is not known how the Trustees ensured that George and his siblings were educated. There were no formal schools in Howsham or the neighbouring villages of Crambe and Scrayingham at this time. It has to be assumed therefore that Hudson's early education was rudimentary to say the least. Such a lack of formal education would prove to be no barrier to his future success, although it would have the effect of adding fuel for those who would come to oppose him in later life. Being the second youngest of six boys, it was always likely that George would have to find a living away from the family farm and so it was that in 1813 he set out for York, where he became apprenticed to Bell and Nicholson, a firm of linen drapers in College Street.

One of George's biographers, A.J. Peacock, suggests in his biography (*George Hudson 1800-1871 – The Railway King*, 1988) that a possible reason for George leaving Howsham was that he had fathered an illegitimate child. Peacock's evidence for this is an entry in the 'Overseers' of the Poor' register for Howsham (dated 1815/16) which stated 'Received of George Hudson for bastardy 12 shillings and sixpence.' George always insisted that he left Howsham two years earlier, at the age of thirteen, but could he have been hiding a guilty secret? Peacock said a search of parish records revealed no other George Hudsons in Howsham. However, there were at least three other men of that name living in neighbouring villages at the time. There were two George Hudsons born in Crambe (in 1783 and in 1785) and another who was born in Barton le Willows in 1796. There is no mention of such an incident by his first biographer Richard Lambert, (*The Railway King*, 1934) nor was it alluded to at any time during his lifetime, not even at the time of his fall when he was subjected to all sorts of vitriol and abuse.

It is likely that a distant relative of the Hudson family, wealthy York resident called Matthew Bottrill (of whom more later), helped to find George his apprenticeship at Bell and Nicholson. The drapery shop was founded by William Bell in around 1810 and not long afterwards he was joined by Richard Nicholson, the business becoming known as Bell and Nicholson. In April 1813, William married Richard's sister, Rebecca, but sadly William passed away just eight months later, leaving Richard and his sister Rebecca to jointly run the business with their younger sister, Elizabeth. It is possible that when William and Rebecca married, they knew he was ailing and so decided that they should seek another pair of hands to help in the shop. Enter young George Hudson.

By all accounts, George excelled in his work and helped to make Bell and Nicholson one of the most successful small businesses in York. In February 1821, just a month before his twenty-first birthday, George was made a partner in the business. There are various tales of how much money he contributed to the partnership. One source quotes £6,000 but this is highly unlikely, as George would never have had access to such a sum. York diarist J.A. Knowles (his collected notes are available in the Knowles Family Archive at York Reference Library) recalled that when they became partners in the business in 1821, George and Elizabeth each contributed £1,000. This is likely to be nearer the truth as George was due to inherit £1,000 (maybe a little more) from his father's Will when he reached the age of 21.

Elizabeth was five years older than George, and some have suggested that George showed an interest in marrying her to pursue his aspirations at Bell and Nicholson. As with the bastardy story above, it is perhaps a little disingenuous to jump to such a conclusion. It is more likely their relationship grew from the fact that when George arrived in York at age 13, Elizabeth, then aged 18, took it upon herself to look after the boy from the country and that their closeness grew from there. The couple married not long after they became partners in the business, on 15 July 1821 at Holy Trinity, Goodramgate, York. The witnesses included Richard Nicholson and Mary Hudson, George's only surviving sister.

George and Elizabeth began married life living above the shop in College Street and were soon blessed with their first child, James Richard who was born on 15 April 1822. Sadly, James died just three weeks later on 3 May. A second son, Richard Nicholson (named after Elizabeth's brother), was born on 27 September 1824. A third son was born on 21 June 1827 and was named in honour of George's uncle, Matthew Bottrill, who had passed away the previous month. Sadly, Matthew junior died in infancy, on 9 January 1828. The couple would go on to have four more children who were all more long-lived: George (1829-1909); Ann, their only daughter (1831-74); John (1832-57); and William (1834-76); tragically Richard, born 1824, died on 5 March 1834, aged just 9.

George settled well into family life, continuing to develop the drapery into one of York's most profitable and prestigious businesses. Then came an event that would change his life for ever, the substantial legacy left to him by his uncle, Matthew Bottrill, who died on 25 May 1827. Bottrill's Will was dated 21 April 1827 and inevitably some of Hudson's critics have seized on the closeness of these two dates to suggest that he somehow influenced Bottrill on his death bed. Peacock, for example, remarks that there is 'certainly a prima facie case that George exerted influence' on Bottrill. But before jumping to such a conclusion, it is worth considering the facts surrounding the Will.

It was not at all unusual at the time for Wills to be written by the dying in their last days 'before it was too late.' With this in mind, the date of Bottrill's Will is not entirely unreasonable. It might have been had it been written even closer to his date of death. As for Hudson's influence over the Will, there is no evidence to suggest that there was any undue influence. The Will was not contested, which indicates that those who were interested parties were not taken by surprise by its contents. Maybe Hudson's relationship with his great uncle was much closer than some might care to admit.

As already mentioned, Bottrill was probably instrumental in George being apprenticed to Bell and Nicholson and it is not unreasonable to suggest that George met with Bottrill after he arrived in York, particularly as it would seem that Bottrill had no close family. When unwell in his final days, both George and Elizabeth will, no doubt, have visited Bottrill and provided support. During these visits, the question of what to do with his fortune would have arisen and George, by now an aspiring businessman with ambition, may well have made certain suggestions to Bottrill. With such an opportunity in front of him, Hudson would have been foolish not to have pursued the possibility of inheriting from his great uncle. Examining Bottrill's Will in detail, it is possible to see how Hudson benefitted compared to others who also inherited.

Bottrill's personal effects, cash, investments, chattels etc (personalty) were valued at £10,000. Out of this sum Peacock mentions that there were various bequests of £500 and that overall, legacies totalling £4,500 were left to beneficiaries other than George. As the residual legatee, Hudson also inherited Bottrill's land and property. Hudson is reputed to have inherited a fortune worth £30,000, which means that the property assets he inherited were worth around £25,000. However, there is no evidence of the value of these assets and it is not inconceivable that they were worth a lot less (or a lot more!). Perhaps the most important issue is that this sum was not in cash. More crucially, is the fact that Hudson did not attempt to liquidate all these assets, a fact confirmed at a hearing he attended in the House of Commons in July 1835 (see Chapter 3), when he stated that he had a 'landed estate' comprising property in York and the North and East Ridings of Yorkshire. It is very unlikely that he bought more property at this time, suggesting that, until 1835 at least, he had kept much of the land that had been left to him by Bottrill.

Thus, although he is reputed to have inherited a fortune of £30,000, the reality is that, in cash terms, he inherited a lot less.

Amongst the property George inherited was 44 Monkgate, York and shortly after inheriting, George moved his family there from the flat above the shop in College Street. He then bought the neighbouring property, No 42, and combined the two houses to make one large family home. The property was described by Bill Fawcett (*George Townsend Andrews of York "The Railway Architect"*, North Eastern Railway Association, 2011) as being part of a two acre 'deer park' alongside the River Foss, something which is very hard to imagine today. It is little known that in their days at Monkgate, George and Elizabeth had an interest in gardening. In October 1832 it was reported that Mr Hill, their gardener, had successfully grown a Syrian white grape vine, which the *Yorkshire Gazette* reported had been planted only eighteen months previously. It produced two bundles of grapes, one weighing seven pounds and the other five pounds. At this time George was involved in the York Agricultural Society and it seems he also took an active part in the York Horticultural Society. For example, in August 1840 the *York Herald* reported that he and his gardener, by then a Mr Johnson, won numerous prizes at the Annual Show, including first prize for their pine fruits, cucumbers and celery and third prize for their fuchsias, balsam and melons.

With his small fortune behind him and now living in one of York's grandest town houses, George's thoughts turned to considering how he could develop a political career and establish himself amongst the city's elite. His entry on to the political stage would prove to be a catalyst for reinvigorating York's stagnating economy.

In the early years of the nineteenth century, the industrial revolution was taking hold of many towns and cities in the north of England, but York was missing out as it was nowhere near any of the principal sources of wealth such as coal or iron ore. Between 1800 and 1840 the population of York increased by 71 per cent, which seems a lot, but the population of Leeds had increased 300 per cent and that of Bradford by 400 per cent in the same period. York badly needed new blood in its ruling corporation to inspire and encourage new industry and revive its stagnating economy. Cometh the hour, cometh the man and for York – cometh George Hudson.

To pursue his political ambitions, Hudson began raising his profile in the city, showing a particular concern for improving the welfare of ordinary citizens. For example, in February 1829 the *Yorkshire Gazette* reported that he and his drapery business partner, Richard Nicholson, each donated £21 to the York County Hospital. Other initiatives followed, including support for the passing of the Factory Act in 1833, which banned the employment of children aged under 9 and restricted the working day in textile mills to eight hours a day for children aged between 9 and 12 and to twelve hours a day for children aged 13 to 17. He contributed generously to subscriptions for the poor in York and supported the work of the York Bluecoat School, the York Subscription Library, the Yorkshire School for the Indigent Blind and the Central Diocesan Society for the Education of the Poor in York; the latter was recorded in February 1834 as teaching as many as 350 boys and 200 girls at two schools in York.

During this time Hudson also served on the Grand Jury of York Quarter Sessions held each spring and autumn. The Grand Jury was a committee of prominent local men called together by the Crown to decide if there was sufficient evidence to prosecute someone suspected of a crime.

All these good works did Hudson's reputation no harm at all, but it was his work with the City's Board of Health during the cholera outbreak of 1832 that really established his reputation for doing good in the city. In May 1832, he had been one of eleven new additions on the City's Board of Health. Others included his close friend and local solicitor James Richardson, as well as Samuel Tuke, a Quaker philanthropist and mental health reformer, and Joseph Rowntree, also a Quaker, who was a York shop keeper and educationalist. Rowntree was father of Joseph Rowntree, of Rowntree's chocolate fame, and renowned philanthropist whose work continues to this day under the various Rowntree Trusts. The newly formed York Board of Health soon had work to do.

In the summer of 1832, an outbreak of cholera in York affected at least 450 people out of a population of around 26,000 and resulted in 185 deaths. The outbreak was part of a national pandemic which affected 85,000 people across 431 towns in Britain. Countrywide, over 31,000 people would lose their lives to the disease. In his role as a member of the York Board of Health, and without regard for his own safety, Hudson made many visits to afflicted households, providing help and support as best he could. These visits did not go unnoticed and his popularity amongst the people of York, particularly the poor, increased hugely.

The government of the day decreed that burials of cholera victims should take place within twelve hours of the time of death and that graves should be six feet deep to avoid the possibility of further infection. Across much of the country, especially in the newly industrialising towns of the north, existing burial grounds were becoming overcrowded. It was a similar story in York. A solution to the problem was needed and local politicians soon became embroiled in arguing where the dead should be buried. Several different sites were suggested, including using York's old moats and ramparts. During his house visits, Hudson became acutely aware of the distress being caused by the council's dithering. He vigorously berated the corporation and their leaders, including Joseph Rowntree, for their insensitivity and disrespect for the dead and for the delay in finding a suitable site for the burial of the victims.

The site eventually chosen was a piece of land just outside the city's north wall. The arguments about the burial site did not end with this decision. Parish burials were allowed in perpetuity, but the York Council favoured a time limit, after which what would happen to the bodies of those buried was uncertain. Relatives were understandably upset by this plan. The council was split along party lines. The Whig majority voted to let the land to the church for just sixty years, with the

Archbishop paying a peppercorn rent. Hudson, by this time a leading Tory in the city, disagreed and argued strongly that, as the land had been consecrated, it should remain a burial ground in perpetuity. He led a successful appeal to the Judges of the King's Bench in London to confirm this decision. As a result of this early political success the burial ground remains intact to this day on what is now known, appropriately enough bearing in mind future events, Station Road.

To pursue his political ambitions in the city, Hudson had decided to back the Tory party. The reasons for his decision are not known. The Whigs were already well established in York and it would have been no surprise had he decided to join them. His reasoning for joining the Tories might have been based on the fact that, having lived and worked in York for the past fifteen years, he was well aware that the Whigs, who had been in control of the city for a number of years, had done very little, not just for the poor, but for the city itself which by the early 1830s was rapidly becoming a backwater, left behind by the rapidly growing and increasingly prosperous towns of the West Riding such as Bradford, Leeds, Huddersfield and Halifax.

The Whig Party was to evolve over the nineteenth century to become the Liberal Party and assume a more centrist role in British politics. At this time, in the 1830s, the Whigs were educated men representing the landed elite and the upper classes and were in expectation of being the rightful ruling class in York. As far as they were concerned, Hudson was just a tradesman, the owner of a drapery business. Worse, after his inheritance, he would have been considered nouveau riche. Hudson did himself no favours amongst the Whigs by splashing his cash around, for example when he extended his home at 44 Monkgate.

By deciding to join the Tory party, Hudson would soon find a formidable group of opponents in the Whig party ranged against him, men such as Harry S. Thompson, Charles Heneage Elsley, George Leeman, Robert Henry Anderson and James Meek. All were educated men and all were well established members of the York hierarchy; Thompson and Elsley had landed interests, Leeman and Anderson were prominent York solicitors, whilst Meek was the owner of the York Flint Glass Company, York's largest employer at the time. They would not have been at all impressed by someone they will have looked on as an uneducated and uncouth 'plough boy', whose broad Yorkshire accent some of them may have found hard to understand. In other words, there was a class difference between Hudson and his Whig adversaries and, no doubt, considerable jealousy that he should have inherited a large estate which enabled him to stand shoulder to shoulder with them. Hudson was not like them. Not like them at all.

Chapter 2

1835 General Election

The Great Reform Act of 1832 gave the vote to householders such as Hudson and his brother-in-law Richard Nicholson. Their first opportunity to vote came at a general election in December of the same year. Hudson campaigned on behalf of the true-blue cause and attended a meeting at the George Inn in Coney Street in late August to discuss putting forward a candidate at the election. Hudson, who by now was treasurer of the Tory Party in York, spoke in support of and seconded the candidature of John Henry Lowther.

In those days polling was held over a number of days and candidates were confirmed at an open-air meeting. At such a meeting held on 10 December, John Lowther was selected as the Tory candidate. At the meeting, Lowther was shouted down amidst extremely riotous behaviour on the part of the Whig supporters and during the poll there was more violence with two public houses that supported the Tory party, the Kings Arms in Fossgate and the Punch Bowl in Stonegate, being 'attacked in a most ferocious manner' (according to the *Yorkshire Gazette*) by Whig supporters. It is evident from these stories of violence that there was no love lost between the two parties in York and it was similarly between Hudson and his opponents in York all of whom were Whig supporters.

At the election Edward Petre (Whig party, with 1,505 votes) and Samuel Bayntun (Tory party, with 1,140 votes) were elected. Not elected were Lowther, who came third with 884 votes, and Thomas Dundas, another Whig candidate, who received 872 votes.

Samuel Bayntun tragically died, aged just 28, of scarlet fever in October 1833, causing a by-election to be held the following month.

Hudson provided his full support for John Lowther, but again was on the losing side. Lowther polled 554 votes to Thomas Dundas' 953. It would not be long before the next general election was held in January 1835. Although by this time the Whig Party was losing some of its popularity, it still managed to win the election, albeit with a reduced majority. In York, Hudson once again backed Lowther and, on the back of a national Tory resurgence, Lowther succeeded in becoming one of York's two MPs, along with John Dundas (the younger brother of Thomas Dundas). Lowther secured 1,499 votes against Dundas' 1,301. The third and losing candidate, Charles Francis Barkley, a nominally independent radical but in reality a second Whig candidate, polled 919 votes.

Having finally succeeded in securing his election as an MP, Lowther's supporters arranged a victory celebration at the George Inn in Coney Street, York. The *Yorkshire Gazette* reported that around 100 guests assembled to enjoy a 'wine and dessert' party. It is quite likely that Hudson, having given much support to Lowther during his election campaign, was behind the idea of a party. His wife Elizabeth was the subject of a toast towards the end of the evening's proceeding, suggesting it was she who organised and arranged the evening's entertainment. As the wine flowed and desserts were eaten, many toasts were raised, including to the King (William IV), the Queen (Adelaide) and the Princess Victoria and of course to their 'worthy champion' Mr Lowther, who was not actually present at the celebration as he was attending a family gathering in Malton. Music was provided by the Cathedral Choir and apart from the National Anthem and *Rule Britannia*, they sang over a dozen other songs, most of which are lost to us in 2023, but one that still endures is the love song *Sally in our Alley*, which was written by Henry Carey in 1725.

Hudson addressed the party to propose thanks to Thomas Barstow, the chairman of Lowther's election committee. Hudson said that, as the Duke of Wellington had presided over his excellent troops, so had Mr Barstow presided over the 'blue committee.' Barstow responded by proposing a toast to Hudson for his zeal and indefatigable exertions in the blue cause which had not been exceeded by anyone. In his reply, Hudson said he was hugely gratified that he was he able to help promote so glorious a cause, adding that his politics were to love the King and the constitution. Another speaker, Hawley Graham, alluded to some accusations of bribery that had been made against Lowther during his campaign and he rejected them with scorn:

> Mr Lowther was not returned by money but by the free hearts [of the voters] and by the smiles of the ladies. The bribery was on the other side and facts have come to my knowledge which are sufficient to hurl Mr [John] Dundas from his seat ten times over!

Late into the evening, after numerous others had left the party, Hudson assumed the chair of the gathering and shortly after 11pm, the final guests began leaving. It is not hard to believe the correspondent when he wrote that everyone present at the party would remember the evening for a long time.

Despite Graham's assertion that there was no question of bribery on the part of Lowther's election campaign, there were strong rumours that this was not the case. *The Yorkshireman*, then a recently established local newspaper (in March 1834) that favoured the Whig party, wrote that 'gold' had turned the election and that never 'in the annals of electioneering' did 'drunkenness, bribery, and treating hold up their hands and stalk through our streets.'

Not long after the election, the defeated candidate Charles Barkley considered petitioning the House of Commons requesting an inquiry into alleged illegal practices, including the payment of bribes by Lowther's election committee during the campaign and at the election itself. When Barkley discovered that it might cost upwards of £3,000 to do so, he abandoned the idea. Although he had stood at the election as an independent radical candidate, Barkley was an active member of the Society for the Diffusion of Political Knowledge which was founded by Whig MP Henry Brougham in 1826. The aim of the Society was to provide 'useful knowledge' to those who did not have access to formal education. George Leeman and Robert Anderson were members of the York branch of the Society.

Shortly after Barkley decided not to go ahead with his petition, those who had voted for the Tories started to receive anonymous payments through the post, two sovereigns for those who had voted solely for Lowther (plumpers) and one sovereign for those who had also voted for Dundas (split voters). At this time voters could vote for one or two candidates, but could not vote twice for the same candidate. The promise of such a payment, although technically unlawful, but seemingly common practice at the time, is most likely the 'gold' to which *The Yorkshireman* referred.

When these payments came to light, George Leeman and Robert Anderson decided to revive Barkley's petition proposal. That these two should combine to make such a move was the more surprising because in June 1834 they had a public spat about similar payments being promised by the Whig party at the 1832 election. The *Yorkshire Herald* reported that in an 'anonymous' letter to the *York Courant* in June 1834, Leeman had described how Edward Petre's election had not been a victory for the independence of the voter because, he alleged, 800 of Petre's supporters had voted for him on the basis that they had been promised a payment as 'messengers' for doing so. Anderson was apoplectic about this revelation. In a handbill published shortly after Leeman's letter was published, Anderson wrote that this information had been given to Leeman 'in confidence' and that the letter was 'received with the suspicion of a habitual trickster, the culminator and the man of malice' and that for his misrepresentation, the writer should blush as 'deep as scarlet.' As would be expected, Leeman did not allow such comments to go unanswered. In his reply, which was co-signed by Josh Allan (another member of Petre's election committee), Leeman wrote that Anderson's claims were 'False as Hell.' Anderson, they wrote, should prove his assertions or be content to stand convicted as a 'wholesale dealer in falsehood.'

Nevertheless, Anderson joined Leeman in preparing a petition to ask the Commons to investigate the Tories' alleged unlawful behaviour in the 1835 election. The petition referred to the increase in Lowther's vote between the 1832 election, when he received 884 votes, and the 1835 election, when he received 1,499 votes. This increase in votes, the petition said, was due entirely to the fact that those who said they would vote only for Lowther were promised a payment of £3, and those who split their vote between Lowther and another candidate would receive £1. The petition also alleged that liquor was made widely available by Lowther's committee during the campaign, resulting in the worst drunkenness seen in York for over ten years. It was alleged also that some voters who were eligible to vote in the concurrent North Riding election were promised a payment of three shillings and sixpence if they voted for a Tory candidate in that constituency.

The petition claimed that such behaviours were a violation of the law and if allowed to continue would perpetuate a disgraceful system of bribery and prevent the free exercise of the vote in York. They called on the Commons to discover and punish those who were responsible. With Leeman and Anderson quite aware that Hudson would be one of the leading witnesses (because he was treasurer of Lowther's committee), their intent was clear. The *Yorkshire Gazette* commented that the petition represented a 'most surprising degree of impudence', bearing in mind that the Whig party had behaved similarly during the same election. The petition was signed by sixty-three citizens of York.

Taking account of the fact that this Whig inspired petition was aimed at attacking only the Tory party, Joseph Rowntree drew up a second petition which spoke more generally about the prevalence of corrupt and illegal practices at the election; that some voters were promised 'future reward' for their vote and that many voters were intoxicated when they voted. Rowntree's petition called on the government to pass legislation to make such 'disgraceful practices' illegal. Rowntree's petition received forty-four signatures.

Leeman and Anderson's petition was presented to the House on 29 June by Henry Aliongby, the Whig MP for Cockermouth who was a long-time campaigner for the secret ballot which he felt would put an end to bribery and corruption at a general election. Aliongby presented Rowntree's petition two weeks later, on 11 July. MPs considered the subject of the two petitions so serious that they decided immediately to establish a Select Committee to investigate the allegations being made. They called not just George Hudson and James Richardson as witnesses, but some fifty others from York, including many who had voted and received payments, as well as post office clerks, letter carriers, messengers and various others who they considered might be able to shed light on what had occurred. It would have been a phenomenal effort for all these witnesses to go to London in the pre-railway age. As might be expected, Hudson and Richardson travelled by the mail coach, the first class travel of its day. The mail coach may have been faster than an ordinary stage coach, but, even so, the journey to London would have taken around 24 hours, with only a few short breaks. It is tempting to think of Hudson and Richardson making small talk about how much quicker it would be to travel on a new-fangled railroad!

The Select Committee began interviewing witnesses on 5 August 1835. George Leeman, Robert Anderson and a Mr Parkes were the solicitors for the petitioners, whilst Hawley Graham and James Richardson were solicitors for the defence. Each side had Counsel present; Mr Hill for the petitioners, and Digby Wrangham for the defence. Charles Barkley sat with the petitioners' solicitors.

One of the first witnesses to be called was George Seymour, the Under Sheriff for York. The petitioners must have been mortified when, at this early stage of the inquiry, Seymour told the committee that it had been common practice for many years for both parties, 'orange and blue', to pay for votes. Out of 2,800 voters in the constituency, Seymour said that some 800 might be influenced by payments ranging from £1 to £3 but, he said, Charles Barkley had not made any payments.

George Hudson followed Seymour. He confirmed that he was treasurer of Lowther's election committee in 1832 and that £3,240 had been made available for the election campaign by Lowther's father, Sir John. Hudson declined to answer when he was asked whether any payments had been made following the 1832 election, saying that he feared he might incriminate himself should he also be asked if *he* had made the payment. The committee insisted that he answer the question and Hudson again refused, saying simply that he did not know. Surprisingly the committee did not pursue the question, but instead moved on to ask Hudson about a cheque for 1,000 guineas paid to Mr Harwood, a member of Lowther's election committee. Hudson explained that this sum was to cover the expenses of messengers and runners who had been employed during the election campaign. He admitted that £3 had been given to 'plumpers' and £1 to those who had split their vote between Lowther and another candidate. Asked why there was a difference in the amount paid, Hudson said he supposed that it was to encourage voters to 'plump' for Lowther at a future election. The session was adjourned for the day at this point. Hudson had been questioned for over an hour, but his time as a witness was not yet over. He was back the following day to answer more questions.

In a foretaste of his future cavalier attitude to keeping accounts, when asked the whereabouts of the accounts for the 1832 election, Hudson at first replied that he did not know, but then said he had given them to Sir John Lowther who had returned them and that he (Hudson) had since destroyed them. Asked about the 1835 election, Hudson said the funding for that campaign had again been provided by Sir John Lowther and that he had accounted for the expenditure by word of mouth to Mr Lowther. Although he said he had not kept any papers, Hudson was able to give the committee a summary of the expenditure incurred at this election:

	£
Bandsmen and Bannermen	300
Lawyers	250
Publicans	500
Printing	250
Bodyguards	170
Messengers etc	110
Sheriff	55
Committee rooms	70
Charities	50
Out voters chairs and cabs	160
Balls to wives of Blues	150
Miscellaneous	100
Total	2165

In addition to these payments, Hudson said that he had charged his lunch expenses to this account and that a further £60 had been spent on dinners for voters for the two days of polling and a further £130 had been made available to bodyguards. Lowther had a personal bill at the George Inn of £190.

The Committee then turned its attention to the issue of the sovereigns that were sent to some of Lowther's voters after the 1835 election. Hudson told the Committee that he could not remember if he had heard about the letters before or after he had settled the election account with Lowther. He was shown some of the letters, but said he did not recognise any of the handwriting. He expressed surprise that the letters had been sent out, as he had not promised any money to voters nor had anyone else. It was surprising that the Committee did not press Hudson on this issue. As treasurer of Lowther's election committee, it would have been entirely reasonable to have expected Hudson to have had some knowledge of these payments. Who else could have authorised the payments and had local knowledge as to where to send them? Maybe the Committee drew its own conclusion. Asked about payments to bodyguards, Hudson explained that bodyguards were needed to protect Lowther's supporters from 'orange violence.'

He was then asked about the petitions themselves and replied that he thought them uncalled for and shameful. He added that, whilst some who had signed them did not know what was in them, others would have been aware that Whig voters for both Dundas in 1835 and Petre in 1832 had received payments for their votes. Having endured another long session of questioning, Hudson was allowed to stand down as the inquiry adjourned until the following morning, when his interview would continue.

Hudson began his third day of questioning by setting out what payments had been made at the 1832 election. Presumably he found this summary in his papers overnight, as he had previously said he destroyed all the records from that campaign. The questioning then returned to the two petitions. He told the Committee that all the signatories of the first petition were known to him. They were not as respectable as those who had signed the second petition. He took aim at James Meek who, Hudson said, had not signed either petition because he knew his hands were not clean. Meek admitted as much when he later told the Committee that he had refused to sign either petition because the Whig party 'was none too pure.' Hudson added that Jonathan Gray, a prominent York solicitor, had told him he had not signed because he knew one party was as bad as the other when it came to making payments.

Hudson's time in the witness chair had begun with him being slightly nervous and unsure of himself, but as the questioning went on, he seemed to become more self-assured and gave the impression that he was thoroughly enjoying the opportunity to freely attack his political opponents. On more than one occasion he had taken the opportunity to identify George Leeman, as the leader of a mob that had attacked the Tory committee rooms in 1832 and who had also led the riot that occurred on Stonegate in 1835. It is unclear whether it was due to his increasing confidence or if it was due to the Committee having heard enough from him that, to bring his interview to an end, the record says he was 'ordered to retire' by the Committee. His appearance in front of the Select Committee was the first occasion that Hudson had been subjected to such close questioning. It would prove to be a formative experience for him for the future, not just in the political circles of York but in his future careers as a railway mogul and as an MP.

During James Richardson's interview, Mr Hill, the petitioners' KC, complained that when Robert Anderson had approached Hudson for copies of Mr Richardson's and Mr Gold's accounts from the York Union Bank (which Hudson had founded in March 1833), Anderson had been given a 'very warm welcome' by Mr Hudson, who used language that could not be repeated. Mr Hill said the Committee should not be deprived of seeing any accounts just because of Hudson's insolence. Mr Wrangham (for the defence) objected, saying Hudson had agreed to hand over his own accounts at the time as he was present when asked, but the others were not present. Wrangham said Hudson had behaved without the least *mala fides* (bad faith) in refusing to hand these two customers' accounts to Mr Anderson. In the event, it was agreed that copies of both Richardson's and Gold's accounts would be produced to the Committee.

In response to a question about the need for bodyguards at the election, Richardson told the Committee that George Leeman had led a mob that rioted in Stonegate and that Whig supporters had broken into the George Inn where a Tory Party meeting was being held. As a result of these events, Lowther had fled York in fear of his life. It was essential, Richardson said, to pay bodyguards to protect voters from this type of behaviour. He agreed that bodyguards were employed by both parties during the election.

Charles Barkley told the Committee that he had been promised 1,000 votes for the election. He had spent £300 but, he said if he had spent £2,000, he would now be in parliament and not Lowther.

Other notable interviewees were John Simpson, a Whig Alderman, and James Meek. Both had voted for Dundas at the election. Simpson told the Committee that he had been involved in elections since 1820 and that it had always been the practice for voters to be 'set-down' (that is, asked to commit to voting for a particular candidate) at the start of an election campaign. He said he was opposed to the practice but that it was essential to secure votes for a particular candidate. He had not signed either petition because he was directly involved in the election, but he believed all the signatories of the petition were respectable men, as was Mr Hudson.

Henry Bellerby, the owner of the *Yorkshire Gazette*, told the committee that at the 1832 election there had been great violence in the city. George Leeman, he said, had led a mob that attacked the Punch Bowl public house and Mr Hudson's house had also been attacked. Messengers had been employed as bodyguards and paid £3, which Bellerby thought was too low, bearing in mind the risks that those men took. The petitions, he said, had been driven by vindictiveness; had two Whigs been returned as MPs, he said there would have been no petitions. Another witness, a Mr Pashley, was asked about Leeman's involvement at the Punch Bowl. He said he thought he saw Leeman was present but that he did not take part in the riot, which had been started when a servant girl had thrown a brick out of a window. Nevertheless, Pashley added, there was a popular local song which had praised Leeman for leading the mob, which Leeman had disclaimed.

James Meek admitted that he considered setting-down a great evil, but there was a two-fold reason for making payments to voters who did set-down. Firstly, the services of those involved were needed as bodyguards and, secondly, to secure their votes. He did not know exactly how many voters set-down for Dundas, but he believed it was in the region of 500.

Thomas Benson, who had voted for Dundas and Barkley, told the Committee that Meek had given him money to buy bread and cheese for voters and that after the election Meek had helped him recover his expenses from the Whig party. He said he also bought 3 gallons of beer on behalf of Charles Barkley at Wilkinson's public house in Swinegate and that Barkley had told him to go to other public houses to offer potential voters a quart of ale. Benson added that he had been shown a ticket in George Leeman's handwriting to buy drink in another public house. He said that buying drink for potential voters was a common practice by the Whig party at election time.

Another witness, a Mr Hanson, who had seconded Dundas for the election, agreed that 'setting-down' was fatal to the purity of an election, nevertheless it did 'a great deal of good for the poor fellows' (the Freemen). Hanson said the present system could not be abolished until there was a secret ballot and that, following this investigation, he would not get involved in paying voters at any future election.

Robert Ellison, a voter at the election, said he had received a letter with two 'bad pennies.' When he asked Hudson about it, Hudson declared he knew nothing about it, but a few days later Ellison received a letter with two sovereigns. The inference being that Ellison's comment to Hudson had not been in vain! Ellison also told the Committee he had received a sovereign from 'the yellows' as he had split his vote between Lowther and Dundas. Robert Dixon, the oldest interviewee at age 85, told the Committee that he had received a letter with two sovereigns but had received no promise beforehand. In previous elections, Dixon said he had voted for the 'oranges' and received one guinea for a split vote and two guineas for a 'plumper.' In 1832 he had received a guinea from each party as he had split his votes between Lowther and Petre.

Overall, the Committee spent four weeks steadfastly interviewing fifty witnesses. Apart from those mentioned above, they called a number of Post Office clerks and letter carriers to question them about the 'sovereign' letters that they delivered. They also called numerous voters who had received a letter and others who had received other payments as messengers or runners, and some who had received similar payments from the Whig party. By interviewing so many witnesses from across the political divide in York, the Committee discovered that the Whig party was just as guilty of any wrong doing as the Tory party. Even Robert Anderson, one of the instigators of the first petition, was forced to admit that the Whig party had made payments to voters. The Committee completed its inquiry on 3 September 1835.

In their report, the Committee noted that at the 1835 election it was apparent that many leading members of the Whig party 'were also implicated in illegal pecuniary transactions' and that these payments had been authorised by Mr Dundas's agent, James Meek. They found that it had 'long been the practice at York that after an election the members [elected MPs] should pay a small gratuity to their respective supporters in the poorer class of freemen.' Such practice, which they noted had also occurred in other parts of the country, was not consistent with the 'purity' of an election. They did not consider they had been provided with any evidence of liquor being made freely available by Lowther, or that there was unusual drunkenness during the election, although some voters were intoxicated when they voted. They agreed there had been systematic intimidation of Mr Lowther's supporters during the 1835 election campaign which was 'wholly inconsistent with the freedom of election.'

Concluding their report, the Committee noted that, although the payment of gratuities after the 1835 election did not influence the result, current legislation was insufficient to discourage such behaviour. The Committee said it could have recommended partial disenfranchisement for the city (that is removing the vote from the freemen), but instead they would rely on the fear of such a consequence to deter such practices in the future. If any penalties were required, it would be for parliament to decide. In the event, parliament took no further action, most likely because such practices were rife in other boroughs across the country and too many MPs were reluctant to stop them, as to do so could result in them losing their seat.

The Select Committee's rather vapid conclusion leads to a question as to whether the time and expense of the four-week inquiry was of any value either to parliament or the Whig party. For Hudson however, his reputation was, if anything, enhanced by the manner in which he had conducted himself during his inquisition. The *Yorkshire Gazette* noted he had received the 'unqualified approbation' of the Committee for the 'straightforward manner' in which he gave his evidence. Perhaps the last words on the petitions should be left to the *Yorkshire Gazette* which, at the conclusion of a long article reflecting on the inquiry, wrote that the petitions were a ridiculous failure, 'whether to blacken Mr Lowther, whitewash Mr Dundas, or gild Mr Barkley, the petitioners have most confoundedly bespattered and besmirched their own shoulders.'

There is some irony in the fact that Leeman and Anderson's plan to embarrass the Tories and Hudson should fail largely because their side was just as guilty of bribery and treating. However, despite such behaviour being essentially unlawful, it was endemic at elections across the country. With this in mind, it is not surprising that Hudson and his supporters and those of the Whigs should have indulged in such practices to get their candidates elected. It was not so much the case they were acting immorally but that they were acting according to the standards of the time. And before we today get too indignant over such behaviour, we should bear in mind that such practices are still in play today as large donations to political parties are made often in the hope that the receiving party will be sympathetic to the donors' interests should they win the election. One thing that is starkly evident from this episode is that Hudson's life-long rivalry with George Leeman started well before a rail was laid in York.

Finally, a note about 'Freemen.' Before the 1832 Reform Act, only Freemen could vote at a general election. These were men who had a hereditary right to vote. Many of them were not wealthy and were often the target of bribery during an election campaign. The 1832 Act widened the franchise to include all male householders whose property had an annual rental value of more than £10. The *Yorkshire Gazette* suggested that the aim of the first petition was an attempt to disenfranchise the Freemen. It quoted the *Morning Advertiser* (a Whig supporting newspaper) as asking how long was the country to be disgraced by such venal practices (bribery and corruption) and how long would the Tories in the Commons and the Lords 'defend hereditary rights of Freemen'? This might, in part, explain why the Select Committee took the petitions so seriously. Although at the centre of the inquiry, it was not all about Hudson.

Chapter 3

Hudson Catches the Railway Bug

While establishing himself in York's political circles, Hudson had shown little to no interest in the new railway technology that was beginning to spread itself across the north of England. However, this was to change when it became apparent that, if York was to prosper in the future, consideration should be given to linking the city to the coal fields of the West Riding of Yorkshire by railway. The idea was first raised in 1833 by one of Hudson's Whig rivals, James Meek, who owned the York Flint Glass Company, which was consuming upwards of 1,000 tons of coal annually. At the time, coal for the glass works came from the West Riding and was delivered to York via the Aire and Calder Navigation, the Selby Canal and the River Ouse. Meek realised that if York was connected by railway to the coalfields of the West Riding, not only would the cost of transporting coal be much reduced, but supplies would arrive more speedily.

While many people were making money from investing in new railway companies, such as the Liverpool and Manchester Railway and the Stockton and Darlington Railway, there were many who were investing in less worthy schemes and not making any money at all. In 1834 Richard Cort published a long treatise, warning potential investors about the dangers of investing in new railway schemes. Not only was his book long, so was its title. It was called *Railroad Impositions Detected; or facts and arguments to prove that the Manchester and Liverpool Railway has not paid One Per Cent Nett Profit and that the Birmingham, Bristol, Southampton, Windsor and other Railways are, and must forever be, only Bubble Speculations*. However, such dire warnings did not deter investors and the mid-1830s saw a mini railway mania with numerous new lines being proposed and built. Among these were the London and Birmingham (Act passed 1833), Great Western (1835), London and Southampton (1834), London and Greenwich (1833), Newcastle and Carlisle (1829), the Grand Junction Railway between Manchester and Birmingham (1833), not forgetting the Leeds and Selby (1830) and the Whitby and Pickering railway (1833).

A meeting to consider the railway options that could work for York was held at Mrs Tomlinson's Hotel at 89 Low Petergate York on 30 December 1833. James Meek was unanimously elected chairman. At this meeting, three possible routes were discussed. Firstly, from York to Selby, to meet the Leeds and Selby (requiring capital of £70,000); secondly, York to South Milford, again on the Leeds and Selby (£120,000); and thirdly, a direct route to Leeds (£250,000).

A provisional committee was formed to consider the options going forward. Initially this comprised twenty-one members and included Meek and Hudson. It was agreed that no one subscriber would be allowed to apply for more than 100 shares in the new railway company and that no one holding fewer than 20 shares could be a director. The shares would be issued at £50 each. Remarkably, between 400 and 500 shares were subscribed for that evening by those present, each paying a ten-shilling deposit for each share. Bearing in mind later events, it is not without some irony to learn that Hudson was appointed Treasurer of the new venture.

Despite this initial surge of enthusiasm, the committee took its time to decide its next step. The principal reason for this hesitancy was that, in early 1834, a proposal had been put forward by a newly formed company called the Grand Northern Railroad (GNR) to construct a new railway from London to York via Cambridge, Lincoln and Selby. The prospect of being linked directly with the capital, with a junction at Selby for Leeds, was an extremely attractive proposition for the York railway committee and, if it came to pass, would obviate the need for them to build their own railway.

Elsewhere in Yorkshire at the time, George Stephenson was working as line engineer for a new railway between Whitby and Pickering. Construction of this line began soon after its Act of Parliament was obtained in May 1833. Although Stephenson was the line engineer, he left much of the day-to-day work to his assistant, Frederick Swanwick. However, Stephenson often visited Whitby to check on progress and it was during one of these visits that, with Hudson also in town on business connected with his property interests, the two men were first introduced. The 'father of the railways' and the future 'railway king' are alleged to have got on famously, with Stephenson encouraging Hudson to get involved with developing York's railway ambitions. As a direct result of their introduction Stephenson was invited to attend the next meeting of the York railway committee, which was held on 23 September 1834 at the Merchant Adventurers Hall in York.

James Meek was once again in the chair. He advised the meeting that the committee appointed at the December 1833 meeting had walked the route of the proposed railway between York and South Milford, where it would join the Leeds and Selby Railway (which had opened the previous day, 22 September 1834). Meek said the committee had also been keeping a check on progress, or rather lack of progress, on the proposed lines to Scarborough, to Bridlington and from Malton to Pickering. He added that he had recently sourced a new supply of coal in the West Riding, which he intended to transport to Selby via the newly opened Leeds and Selby Railway and then by barge up the River Ouse to York. He said that if this new supply of coal 'found favour' in York, it would be an important factor in deciding the future of the committee's railway proposals. Meek told the meeting that the railway would be of incalculable benefit to the city, and promised every effort would be made to pursue the project – 'although the plan might appear to be now asleep, it is far from our intention for it to be an eternal sleep.'

The York committee had employed George Stephenson's great rival George Rennie to survey the proposed route. Henry Newton, one of the committee's joint solicitors (the other was a Mr Ord), reported that Rennie had suggested that operation of the line by horse power would be far more cost effective than by steam locomotion. Rennie estimated the comparative capital costs as £177,000 for steam locomotion, with annual costs of £19,000, whilst for horse power the respective costs would be £105,000 and £11,400. George Stephenson begged to differ. He advised the meeting that in his opinion, locomotive power was the future of railways. He added that, in time, steam locomotion would prove to be as cheap as horse power. He suggested that four engines would be sufficient for the traffic proposed. As engineer of the Whitby and Pickering Railway, Stephenson said he was very keen for York to be connected to the growing railway network and that, with this in mind, he had already surveyed two routes from Pickering to York, one via Malton and the other via Easingwold. The committee listened attentively to Stephenson's advice and were appreciative of his enthusiasm and support for York to be connected to the railway network.

The meeting was made aware that their decision was much awaited by those who were thinking of opening lines to Scarborough, Bridlington and Knaresborough. There was also much discussion about the possibility of finding different supplies of coal, as the new railway would pass by many new collieries, and whether these new supplies would be acceptable to York customers.

Despite the committee's desire to get York connected to the railway network, Henry Newton and George Hudson counselled against proceeding too quickly. Newton said the delay would allow the public in York to judge the usefulness of the projected railway and allow time to decide the best route, whether via South Milford or direct to Leeds. Hudson concurred, saying he did not think it prudent to put a bill before parliament with the information currently available. More detailed and accurate knowledge was needed before taking this step. There was also the question as to whether the proposed GNR line would go ahead. The meeting supported a delay, but only for a short while, as they were determined to have York connected to the railway network as soon as possible. At the close of the meeting, Hudson thanked George Stephenson for his 'kindness, urbanity and intelligence' regarding the questions he was asked and for responding to them so satisfactorily. There appears to be more than just a hint here that Hudson, having been enthused by Stephenson when they met in Whitby, was keen to keep Stephenson on board with York's railway endeavours.

In his biography of Hudson published in 1934, Richard Lambert asserted that Hudson begged Stephenson to make York not Leeds the northern terminus of the North Midland Railway's line from Derby (see below) and to "mak all t'railways cum t'York". By giving this phrase double quotes, Lambert infers that Hudson actually uttered these words and ever since it has been assumed that he did, but that was not the case. Hudson would have been well aware that there was never any question that the North Midland would terminate anywhere other than Leeds. Lambert was simply trying to give emphasis to Hudson's ambition, but it is very unlikely that Hudson would have had any such thoughts as his approach towards railways at this time was very cautious, a fact confirmed by George Stephenson in a speech he gave during the opening ceremony of the York to Scarborough railway on 7 July 1845. Stephenson said that when he first met him in Whitby, Hudson had shown little interest in railway 'speculations' and that, even though he would go on to become thoroughly convinced of the need for railway communication, at the time Hudson 'looked coolly at those undertakings.'

A week after the York committee's meeting on 23 September, the Grand Northern Railroad convened a meeting in York to provide an update on progress with their line. The meeting was attended by, amongst others, the Lord Mayor (William Cooper), George Hudson, James Meek, Samuel Tuke, Thomas Price and Joseph Rowntree. The chief line engineer of the GNR, Nicholas Cundy, explained to the meeting that it was proposed to construct a railway from Whitechapel in east London to 'near Micklegate Bar' in York via Bishop's Stortford, Cambridge and Lincoln, with branches to various other towns including

Norwich, Sheffield, Leeds, Hull and Nottingham. He said the first two phases of construction would be the sections from Whitechapel to Cambridge in the south and between York and Selby in the north. Much enthusiasm was expressed by those present for the proposals and, after much discussion, resolutions were passed acknowledging that the proposals were 'deserving of the utmost attention' and that they would be of 'great public utility' to York and its neighbourhood. It was agreed that a committee would be set up in York to liaise with the GNR. In seconding a motion of thanks to Mr Cundy at the end of the meeting, Meek remarked that, although not by him, the project might be 'viewed with jealousy by those connected with the project of a railroad from York to Leeds.' This barb was possibly aimed at Hudson who, it would seem, was none too enthusiastic about the GNR's plans.

In a very detailed newspaper report of the meeting there was no mention of Hudson having anything to say either for or against the GNR's proposals. For Hudson to have nothing to say at such a meeting is quite unexpected, but he had hitherto shown little or no enthusiasm for the GNR scheme, not even with projected dividends of 7 per cent to 10 per cent. His lack of enthusiasm was probably not down to jealousy, but a realisation that what was being proposed was extremely ambitious and unlikely to come to fruition. It is perhaps the first evidence of Hudson's uncanny knack of knowing what would make a successful railway. His reservations about the GNR scheme were seemingly justified when it became apparent that the company was finding it difficult to raise funds in London for its scheme. Not only that, the York committee set up to oversee progress of the GNR scheme later discovered that some of Cundy's claims were untrue. For example, he had claimed that the government, via the General Post Office, was to provide some of the funding for the railway, but this claim was found to be completely false. Cundy was pressed further for assurances that the GNR had financial support for its proposal, but the committee received no response. It turned out that this was due to the fact that Cundy had been replaced as chief line engineer by Joseph Gibbs.

The change in engineer had the effect of re-invigorating the GNR. Three new committees were set up, in London, Norwich and York, to oversee progress. The York committee comprised twenty-three members, including John Lowther MP, John Dundas MP, the Lord Mayor and George Hudson. It should be noted, however, that Hudson was on the committee simply as a representative of York Council and that he had no executive or promotional role in the proposed new railway.

Gibbs made some minor changes to Cundy's proposed route and presided over a change of name of the project from the 'Grand Northern Railroad' to the 'Great Northern Railway.' It had been hoped to put a new GNR bill before parliament for the 1835 parliamentary session, but the company was nowhere near raising sufficient capital, nor were its plans complete. In March 1835 the GNR began placing advertisements in the press about its plans but, despite the change of chief line engineer, the company was still finding it difficult to raise the financial backing needed. This lack of support was almost certainly due to the fact that what was being proposed was the most ambitious railway scheme yet seen in England, seeking to raise capital of £3.5million in shares of £100 each. The company's financial difficulty was of sufficient concern to the York committee for them to resolve that, if sufficient funds could not be raised by the GNR, then they would pursue the formation of the northern end of the railway between York and Selby.

Over the next few months, the Great Northern Railway continued to experience problems with raising capital and finalising its planned railway. As a result, the York railway committee was unable to press ahead with its plans to join the railway network. But then, in the Summer of 1835, an event occurred that would shake the committee into action. A proposal was put forward to construct a line between Derby and Leeds, to enable the latter to be connected to London via the Midland Counties route from Derby to Rugby and by the London and Birmingham Railway, which was then under construction. George Stephenson was commissioned to survey the route for the new railway company, which was to be called the North Midland Railway (NMR).

At this stage the new railway was still very much just a paper proposal (the NMR would not be incorporated for another year, in July 1836) but, on hearing of George Stephenson's involvement, the York committee was certain that the project would go ahead and they did not want to be left behind. The committee called a meeting on 13 October 1835 to discuss progress with the faltering GNR proposal and the developments happening in the West Riding.

In a report read out by Robert Davies (York's Town Clerk) it was confirmed that some of the claims made by Nicholas Cundy at the October 1834 meeting had been fallacious and misleading, including that the government was going to help fund the railway. The meeting also heard that Joseph Gibbs, Cundy's replacement as chief line engineer, was finding it difficult to secure the necessary funds. In discussion, it was becoming apparent to the committee that there was not sufficient support for the GNR project.

The committee was in no doubt that the NMR under the guidance of George Stephenson, and with the full support of influential parties in Leeds, would go ahead speedily. Thus, with the ongoing delays and uncertainties surrounding the GNR, the York committee resolved to resurrect its plan to construct a railway as the 'readiest' way of connecting York not just to the 'opulent' town of Leeds, but also to London. The resolution was proposed by Charles Elsley and enthusiastically seconded by James Meek, who once again took the opportunity to extol the virtues of bringing new coal supplies by railway to York and the North and East Ridings. Thomas Price proposed the new railway company be known as the York and North Midland Company (YNM) and that a capital sum of £200,000 should be raised by way of 4,000 shares of £50 each. The resolution was seconded by George Hudson.

Meanwhile, with the prospect of a railway from London reaching York, proposals were drawn up for a new line connecting York to the north of England and Newcastle. Appropriately called the Great North of England Railway, the GNER counted amongst the fifty-five members of its provisional committee numerous luminaries from

York including James Meek, John Dundas MP, John Lowther MP and George Hudson. Richard Nicholson, Hudson's brother-in-law, was also a member of the provisional committee. Hudson's involvement with the GNER indicates his growing interest in the new phenomenon of railways. In just a few years, he would have a lot more to do with GNER and its successor companies. He was catching the railway bug.

A meeting of the new YNM company was held on 27 October 1835 to appoint the company's secretary, solicitors and bankers. George Baker was appointed company secretary, with Henry Newton, James Richardson and John Blanchard appointed as joint solicitors. Newton was proposed by Meek and seconded by Hudson; Blanchard and Richardson were proposed by Thomas Price and seconded by Samuel Tuke. Meek's York City and County Bank and Hudson's York Union Bank were appointed as the company's joint bankers. The shareholders present also gave full powers to the committee appointed at the 13 October meeting to push the company's Act through parliament and to pursue putting its plans into effect. In the same week as this meeting, Frederick Swanwick, George Stephenson's trusted assistant, arrived in York with a team of surveyors to survey the intended route between York and South Milford, where the railway would join the Leeds and Selby Railway. Swanwick, who was apprenticed to George Stephenson aged 19 in 1829, oversaw many of Stephenson's projects including the construction of the Whitby to Pickering (W&P) line and the NMR.

In November 1835, the YNM, the Great North of England Railway and the Great Northern Railway, which had been stung into action following the resolve of the York committee to go ahead with their own scheme, each submitted their proposed bills for parliamentary consideration.

The GNR expressed great confidence that their Act would be obtained with minimal opposition and at comparatively small expense. But the company's confidence was misplaced for in April 1836 the Commons rejected their bill, on the grounds that the plans submitted with their proposal differed substantially from those submitted to the various local authorities along the route of the line. In addition, whilst acknowledging that many landowners supported the projected railway, MPs were concerned that, to protect landowners from speculators on the Stock Exchange, the proposal should have been 'better digested and considered.' In essence the House was saying the GNR's promoters should have been better prepared before taking their bill to parliament. As if to prove parliament's point, the company was dissolved soon after the bill failed. Those investors who had paid deposits of £2 on their shares of £100, were refunded 14 shillings per share. It should be noted that this company has no connection with the similarly named Great Northern Railway, which was authorised in June 1846.

On 12 April 1836, a draft petition was put before York Council making reference to the importance of the YNM forming part of 'a great Line of Railway from London to Edinburgh' and that it would be highly advantageous to the City of York and other places that it passed. The petition was proposed by George Hudson and was signed by over 260 people including Sir John Simpson (York's Lord Mayor at the time), James Meek, Samuel Tuke, Thomas Backhouse, Charles Elsley, George Crawshay, Robert Hudson (George's older brother), Richard Nicholson, Thomas Price, Joseph Rowntree and James Walker (of Sand Hutton).

It was practice at the time for an MP representing the area in which a projected railway was based, to chair the Parliamentary Committee set up to consider a proposed Bill. In the case of the YNM this was John Lowther, whom Hudson helped to get elected in the 1835 election. Hudson was a member of the team that represented the YNM at the parliamentary committee hearings in London, along with James Meek and Thomas Backhouse. George Stephenson, Frederick Swanwick and Thomas Grainger were the engineers cross-examined in support of the Bill.

In May 1836, the *Yorkshire Gazette* reported a meeting at which John Lowther MP provided an update on the progress of the YNM Bill's passage through parliament. Lowther mentioned there had been some petitions against the railway, including from the Leeds and Selby Railway and various landowners, but the promoters of the YNM had made 'amicable arrangements' to satisfy these objector's concerns. It was normal practice for a nascent railway to pay compensation for the land they took from a landowner. The amount of compensation paid was often disputed by both parties but, in order to get a project over the line, sometimes a larger inducement had to be agreed. For example, all was going well with the YNM's draft bill until Lord Howden, over whose estate the railway would pass, made an about turn and withdrew his support and decided to oppose the bill. Howden's action could have put a brake on the bill going through parliament, so the YNM had to act fast. Urgent discussions took place with Howden and soon an agreement was in place whereby, provided he withdrew his opposition to the bill, the company would pay him £5,000 within six months of the company's bill receiving its Royal Assent. The agreement also provided that Howden would receive £100 per acre for any land taken by the railway. In the event the company decided to alter the railway's route so that it did not encroach on Howden's land. The company no doubt thought that by doing this, they would save themselves £5,000.

However, when the six month period expired in December 1836, Howden demanded payment of the £5,000 that had been agreed. The company refused on the grounds that the payment was only to be made if the railway crossed his land. Howden threatened legal action and the company sought an injunction to prevent him from taking them to Court. Howden appealed this decision and in November 1838 the case was heard by the appeal judges of the Queen's Bench in London. The appeal judges found in favour of the company, on the ground that the agreement had been concealed from parliament.

Howden decided to appeal the judgment and this was heard before Lord Chief Justice Tindal on 18 June 1839. To the company's dismay, Tindal reversed the Queen's Bench decision on the basis that the three grounds of objection were untenable. These were that: the agreement was kept secret from other landowners; the agreement was kept secret from parliament; and it was void because it placed Lord Howden in a position where his duties to the public were placed in opposition to his personal interest as a private individual.

But that was not the end of the matter, as the company sought and obtained, leave to take an appeal to the House of Lords. It would be an extraordinary three years to the day of Tindal's judgment, before the Lords considered the appeal. Both parties waited for the Lords' decision, but it was Lord Howden who celebrated, when it was announced that the Lords had upheld Tindal's decision. The company were liable to pay £5,000 to Howden.

It would be easy to speculate that Hudson, as the YNM's treasurer, was behind the idea of offering Howden £5,000 as an inducement to dropping his opposition to the YNM's bill, but this event occurred when James Meek was chairman. Meek, of course, was probably keener than Hudson about the railway at the time. In addition, the company's representative at each of the court hearings was Sir John Simpson, another director of the company and a former Lord Mayor of York. There can be little doubt therefore that, in this instance, the decision to offer such a vast, and ultimately unnecessary inducement to Howden was by no means Hudson's alone. Whoever was responsible for the idea, it was a salutary lesson to the company and one which Hudson certainly learnt from as, going forward, he always drove a hard bargain when it came to compensating landowners.

At the meeting of the YNM held in May 1836, John Lowther reported that the parliamentary committee had agreed that the capital of the new company would be £370,000 raised in shares of £50 each. So far, 320 individuals had paid a £1 deposit for a total of 5,926 shares. Thirty-six of these individuals had subscribed for forty shares or more. A list of the company's directors who had bought shares was provided along with a list of those who had subscribed for forty or more shares. The table below is a list of those with the highest number of shares:

	No. of Shares	Value (£)*
George Hudson (York)	200	10,000
James Meek (York)	150	7,500
Benjamin Honor (York)	100	5,000
William Routh (London)	100	5,000
George Crawshay (London)	100	5,000
John Roskill (London)	100	5,000
Thomas Backhouse (York)	90	4,500
Rt Hon John Simpson (Lord Mayor)	75	3,750

*Value of fully paid-up shares. All who had subscribed at this point will have paid just £1 deposit per share.

It is not known how Hudson intended to pay for his shares, but most likely he would have borrowed the sum from his York Union Bank. Other notable subscribers from York included Hudson's brother Robert Hudson (30 shares), his brother-in-law Richard Nicholson (50), Joseph Rowntree (30), Charles Elsley (25) and Samuel Tuke (50). Another prominent shareholder was G.T. Andrews (50) who would become the YNM's leading architect, designing many of the company's buildings including the original York station (1841).

Lowther said the parliamentary committee was satisfied that the proposed railway posed no difficulties for its construction and that it would benefit both commerce and agriculture. It would be particularly beneficial to the community, by providing a much-needed link in the line of railways between the north and south of the country, and between east and west. Lowther's confidence was not misplaced. On 21 June 1836, the YNM bill received Royal Assent. The company was authorised to raise £370,000 of share capital, much of which it was hoped would be raised locally. It was recognised that funds would need to be raised in London via the London Stock Exchange in Capel Court and at Exchanges around the country. In his role as Treasurer to the

YNM and as a director of the York Union Bank, Hudson set about trying to raise these funds, a role that he would come to relish as his railway empire expanded. A month after the YNM Act was passed, the GNER Act was passed by parliament. The GNER's success, coupled with that of the YNM and the failure of the GNR bill, confirmed Hudson's growing prowess for recognising a successful railway opportunity when he saw one.

At a meeting of YNM shareholders held on 10 August 1836, 12 directors were elected:

The Lord Mayor (Sir John Simpson)	422 votes
George Hudson	421
James Meek	412
Thomas Barstow	400*
Robert Davies	392
Thomas Backhouse	379
James Richardson	339
Alderman John Hotham	339
Richard Nicholson	338
William Cooper	319
James Walker	290
George Dodsworth	262

*estimated, figure unclear in source used (BNA copy of *Yorkshire Gazette*)

At the same meeting Alderman Wilson proposed that £300 in silver plate be presented to Sir John Simpson, George Hudson, James Meek and Thomas Backhouse for their 'unwearied exertions' in getting the YNM bill through parliament. The motion was seconded by Alderman Hotham and was carried unanimously. James Meek proposed that grateful thanks should also be passed to John Dundas MP and John Lowther MP for their support of the Bill in parliament. This motion, which was also carried, was seconded by Hudson. At a further meeting of shareholders on 24 August, George Hudson was voted unanimously as chairman of the company and James Meek elected deputy chairman. Meek remained a director of the company until July 1839, when he resigned due to a disagreement about the railway carrying passengers on Sundays (he was a strict Methodist).

Three years after showing minimal interest in the railway coming to York, Hudson was now on the cusp of an extraordinary railway journey but, for now, his ambitions lay elsewhere.

Chapter 4

Lord Mayor of York

Before 1835, local government in England and Wales had been dominated by what were essentially cliques of local worthies, elected by a very limited electorate. York, like many other towns and cities in England, was in effect a closed corporation dominated by the Whig party with little possibility of the Tories having any involvement. In February 1833, a parliamentary select committee reviewed the system of local government in England and Wales and following their findings, a Royal Commission was established to make recommendations for reform. The result was the Municipal Reform Act of 1835, which provided for regular elections of local councillors and the extension of the electorate to all male ratepayers with at least three years qualification. One such ratepayer was George Hudson, who made full use of the Act to further his political ambitions in York.

Under the Act, York Council would have forty-eight councillors. The city would be divided into six wards, with six councillors elected for each ward. Those thirty-six councillors would be voted for by the electorate, then twelve aldermen would be elected by the elected councillors, the latter arrangement perhaps being a nod to the previous system, allowing council members to appoint who they considered worthy of joining the council. Finally, the Lord Mayor would be elected by the council from the pool of elected aldermen.

Hudson was determined to seek political change in York, to end years of stagnation under the Whigs, and enable the city to reap the benefits from the ongoing industrial revolution. At the first local election following the passing of the Act, he put himself forward as a candidate for the Tory party in Monk Ward, where James Meek was also standing for the Whigs. Meek came top of the poll. Although Hudson came third, he still qualified for election to the council. Following the election, the Whig party maintained overall control of York Council, winning twenty-one seats to the Tories' fifteen, but change was on its way.

The new council met on 31 December 1835 to discuss the appointment of twelve aldermen. James Meek put forward a motion that each councillor should put forward twelve names to be voted for in secret. Hudson opposed Meek's suggestion saying that 'nothing like secrecy should be resorted to.' Supporting his argument, Hudson referred to the fact that the Speaker of the House of Commons was not elected in secret – the candidates were proposed and then the MPs voted for their choice. He said to have lists prepared in secret would be unfair, as those elected would be imposing their decisions on the minority (Tory) party who represented a large number of electors who should not have aldermen 'thrust down their throat.' Hudson did not take kindly to Whig councillor Hanson when the latter laughed out loud at this remark, insisting that he be treated 'as a gentleman in this assembly', as he had always treated Hanson. There were loud shouts of 'hear, hear!' from those present in support of Hudson. Hanson apologised and explained he had not meant anything personal or offensive to Hudson, but he was concerned that lists of potential candidates had been drawn up by the Tory party prior to the meeting, an accusation Hudson denied.

Twenty-two names were put forward for election as aldermen. Each councillor had twelve votes. The twelve candidates who received the most votes would be appointed. After the vote was taken, ten candidates, all Whigs (including James Meek) received between twenty and thirty-five votes and were selected immediately. The next four candidates, Hudson (Tory), Jonathan Gray (Tory), Thomas Backhouse (Whig) and Mr Watkinson (Whig), each received eighteen votes, resulting in a vote-off for the remaining two aldermanic appointments. Hudson and Gray were fortunate that there were some Whigs on the council who placed their deciding votes with them, rather than with their Whig colleagues. Hudson and Gray were also both appointed to the council's new Finance Committee, whilst Hudson was also appointed to the Council's Ouse Navigation Committee, which oversaw the operation of the River Ouse as the major transport artery between York and Selby.

Fourteen of the Council's thirty-six seats came up for re-election in November 1836. The Tory party, under Hudson's guidance, won eight seats to the Whigs' six. George Leeman, for the Whig party, was elected to the council for the first time, as a representative of Castlegate Ward. Inevitably there were accusations of skulduggery as each side sought to attract votes to their respective parties. The Whig supporting *York Herald* congratulated the Whigs on the election of their six candidates who, they wrote, would be more active and carry more weight on the council than all the miserable Tories 'as have slipped in by [their] dishonourable trickery.' Meanwhile the *Yorkshire Gazette*, not unknown for its Tory bias, praised the Conservative party (note the name now being given to the Tory party) for its forbearance under the circumstance of provoked 'injustice and insult.' The *Gazette* described numerous nefarious practices adopted by the Whigs, including the use of false voter forms and votes made on behalf of qualified voters who were absent from York at the time. There were also accusations of bribery, treating and other inducements offered to voters by both parties. It would seem that no lessons had been learnt from the saga of the 1835 general election.

Although the Tory party now had a majority of councillors on the council (19-17), the Whigs still held sway by virtue of the fact that they had the majority of Aldermen (10-2). At the first meeting following the election, held on 9 November 1836, James Meek was unanimously elected to be the next Lord Mayor of York, whilst Hudson was reappointed to the Finance Committee and the Ouse Navigation Committee.

Similar accusations about electoral improprieties were made during the council elections the following year, in November 1837, when fourteen seats were up for re-election. At this election, the Tories gained sufficient seats to give them an overall majority on the Council (23-13) and they were now in a position to select their own candidate for York's next Lord Mayor (which was, and still is, an annually elected office). Prior to the council meeting held on 8 November 1837, it was rumoured that John Wolstenholme, a longstanding Tory stalwart, would be selected as Lord Mayor, as he was not unfavourable to the Whigs and would likely have been elected without any opposition. However, Hudson, and many members of his party who recognised his tireless efforts to secure the position they now found themselves in, had different ideas.

In proposing George Hudson as a candidate for Lord Mayor, Tory Councillor John Swann said that despite his strong political opinions, Hudson would discharge his duties with the strictest impartiality, to the benefit of all citizens of York and that any objection to his appointment would simply be on the grounds he was a conservative. Hudson, Swann said, had demonstrated his suitability by attending council meetings with great regularity and through his exertions in the business of the City of York. Hiding any disappointment he may have felt at not being selected himself, John Wolstenholme 'heartily' seconded Swann's proposal. The meeting was asked if there were any other candidates to be proposed. The Whigs could think of no one who could challenge Hudson and he was elected unanimously. He was 37 years old and one of the youngest ever to have served as Lord Mayor of York.

His election to Lord Mayor was something Hudson had dreamed of since he first began to involve himself with the Tory party ten years prior. When he stood to give his acceptance speech, he was rapturously applauded and cheered by his Tory colleagues. He told the meeting he would discharge his duties in an impartial and honest manner and that he would endeavour to promote the best interests of his fellow citizens and the City of York. To loud cheers he called on his opponents to unite with him to achieve these aims. He said his conduct would be open to scrutiny and if he erred, it would be due to an error of judgment as his intention would always be to do that which was right.

At this time there were four newspapers published in York, the *Yorkshire Gazette* and *York Chronicle,* which both favoured the Tories, and the *York Herald* and *York Courant,* which both favoured the Whigs. There were some in York, however, who felt the *Herald* and *Courant* were not radical enough and that a stronger voice was needed to counter the influence of the *Gazette* and the *Chronicle.* Thus, a fifth title, *The Yorkshireman,* was founded in 1834. This new newspaper would prove to be no friend of Hudson and an early example came in the paper's reaction to Hudson's appointment as Lord Mayor, when it wrote that though it found no fault with Hudson as a private individual, they considered that putting the representation of York in his hands was 'a thing most monstrous.'

As Lord Mayor, Hudson advocated a tight lid on council spending, to keep the cost to ratepayers to a minimum. Such a policy might seem at odds with the lavish entertainments that he and the Lady Mayoress provided at York Mansion House, the official residence of the Lord Mayor. However, these events were not funded out of the public purse because, as Lord Mayor, Hudson was expected to provide them at his own cost.

His spending on balls and banquets did Hudson's reputation in York no harm at all. On 24 May 1838, to celebrate the new Queen's nineteenth birthday, Hudson had the Mansion House lit up by a vast number of gas lamps, courtesy of the York Union Gas Light Company, which he had founded two years previously. A month later, on 28 June, Queen Victoria's Coronation took place and this provided another glorious opportunity for Hudson to splash his cash. He provided a feast for upwards of 14,000 of York's citizens that day, and more was to follow. On the occasion of the opening of the Summer Assizes in York on 12 July, the *Hull Packet* reported that a Grand Ball had been held at the Mansion House for 200 of the nobility and gentry of York, 'dancing was kept up with great hilarity till an early hour the following morning.'

In late October, right at the end of the mayoral year, another Grand Ball and supper was held in honour of the York Hussars. Describing the event, the *Leeds Intelligencer* recorded that the Lady Mayoress was 'at home' to nearly 500 of Yorkshire's elite, including the 2nd Earl de Grey (the Hussars' Colonel), Sir Maxwell Wallace and John Lowther MP. Guests were received by the Lord and Lady Mayoress. Dancing commenced at 10 pm, with 'Mr Hardman's quadrille band in attendance.' At midnight the ballroom presented 'a very busy and animated scene' and at half past midnight the guests descended the grand staircase of the Mansion House and walked under a covered way to the Guildhall, to enjoy a sumptuous banquet laid on by the Lady Mayoress and the Lord Mayor.

The Guildhall was decorated with seemingly no expense spared. At one end of the hall was 'a brilliant device in gas light presenting an imperial crown and the letters V.R.' During supper, the Lady Mayoress had Earl de Grey seated to her right and John Lowther MP to her left. As they and the other guests enjoyed their supper, the band of the 5th Dragoons provided a musical background. After supper, the guests filed back to the Mansion House, where dancing resumed 'with increased vigour' and continued until the early hours of the morning. Although this would not prove to be George Hudson's last mayoral event (he was already planning a second successive year in office), it most certainly seemed like it, as it was probably the largest and most extravagant Ball and Supper that he and Elizabeth hosted during their year in office.

Hudson had reached the end of his year as Lord Mayor at the peak of his popularity in York. His banquets, balls and hospitality had gone down well with the citizens, particularly those from the wealthier classes, but poorer people did see some benefits too, for example the feast provided for 14,000 to celebrate Queen Victoria's coronation. There was also the reflected glory of living in a city run by one of the most charismatic Lord Mayors York had ever known.

When appointed Lord Mayor in November 1837, Hudson was no doubt hopeful that the York railway towards Leeds would be completed by the end of his mayoralty, giving him the opportunity to preside over its opening as Lord Mayor. As 1838 progressed, it became increasingly clear that the railway would not be ready until at least mid-1839 and that he would miss out on that honour, unless of course he stood for re-election as Lord Mayor for the following year. To do so he faced two major obstacles, the first being that it was quite unprecedented for a Lord Mayor to serve two successive years and the second, his eligibility to stand as a candidate for the post.

The order of mayoral and aldermanic elections was laid down in the Municipal Corporations Act of 1835. Although not entirely clear, the intention of the Act was to provide that mayors of boroughs should be selected from existing aldermen before the election or re-election of new aldermen. Unfortunately for Hudson and his supporters, his initial three-year term as an alderman had expired at the end of October 1839, which meant that technically he was ineligible to stand for re-election as Lord Mayor. But his Tory colleagues on the council, and no doubt himself, were desperate for him to be re-elected. He had had a very successful year at the Mansion House and had been far and away the most charismatic and popular Lord Mayor York had ever witnessed and the Tories – and the citizens of York – wanted more, especially with the new railway due to open in 1839. The question was how to get round the terms of the Act of Parliament?

In the days before the Council meeting held to elect the new Lord Mayor and aldermen, it became clear that the Tory councillors would vote to hold the aldermanic elections before the Lord Mayor was elected. The *Morning Advertiser* commented 'it is to be feared that the Tories will complete their triumph and degrade the old Whig City of York.' The paper expressed the hope that if the Liberals remained united and active, they could foil the Tory plan, but acknowledged it was likely that Hudson would be re-elected as Lord Mayor, particularly as amongst his party it would be difficult to find a better candidate.

At the annual Council meeting held on 9 November, Hudson reported that he and Robert Davies (the Town Clerk and a Whig who, somewhat surprisingly, backed Hudson), had taken the opinion of Sir Frederick Pollock (the Attorney General under Sir Robert Peel in

1834 and 1835, and thus a highly respected lawyer) who had advised that it would be lawful to hold the aldermanic elections before the appointment of a new Lord Mayor. The Whigs, particularly George Seymour, George Leeman and James Meek, were outraged. Seymour called Sir Frederick's advice 'decidedly contrary to the plain meaning of the Act of Parliament.'

Following a request from George Leeman, James Richardson read out the advice from Sir Frederick in full. In summary, Richardson said the advice left no doubt as to the legality of proceeding with the election of the aldermen before the election of the Lord Mayor. Seymour put forward a motion calling on councillors to elect the Lord Mayor first. Richardson countered this with an amendment to the effect that the councillors move directly to the election of the aldermen. As Chairman of the meeting (he was still Lord Mayor until the election) Hudson rather needlessly, but perhaps to stir up his opponents, said he would not be bound by any decision of the Council, whatever they chose to do. Leeman retorted that he hoped Hudson would be bound by the express words of the Act of Parliament. Affronted by the suggestion, Hudson told Leeman that there was no justification to accuse him of acting unlawfully.

The arguments raged on, with Leeman asking how anyone who had read the Act of Parliament could be bold enough (though he knew the Lord Mayor was a bold man) to suggest that aldermen should be elected before the Lord Mayor. Leeman said if this happened, then those elected would be as unqualified for election as Lord Mayor as any man on the street, as they would have been illegally elected. Meek agreed, saying the Act specifically stated that at the first quarterly meeting of a new council 'the first business shall be the election of the Mayor.' However, Meek admitted that Sir Frederick's opinion was very strong and, being such an eminent lawyer, asked would he sacrifice his reputation by giving an opinion which was not borne out by the law? Leeman said the only reason the Tories wanted to vote on the new aldermen before voting for a new Lord Mayor was to re-elect Hudson. The Tories could not deny that was the case.

Hudson claimed he would have preferred his name not to have been mentioned as, even though Mr Seymour had some kind words for his tenure as Lord Mayor, he thought there was an insinuation that maybe he had gone beyond a fair line of conduct. Seymour denied this was the case. Hudson accepted the apology and, in an effort to show some humility, said he would very much like to be relieved of the office of Lord Mayor, it was not his ambition, nor gratifying to his feelings to be nominated once again. It is very unlikely, however, that this is truly what Hudson thought considering the lengths to which he and his party went to ensure he could stand for re-election.

After a long and at times tortuous discussion and whether lawful or not, the election of the new aldermen went ahead as the first item on the meeting's agenda. Hudson, as Chairman of the meeting, declared that he, Robert Cattle, John Swann, John Hotham, William Matterson and William Clark had all been duly elected.

There then followed the election for the office of Lord Mayor. Hudson was proposed by Alderman Clark, who described Hudson as a man of long standing who had filled his role of Lord Mayor conspicuously. He was a man of the strictest integrity and of unbounded liberality. It was of the utmost importance that York should have a man to sway the sceptre of power; a firm defender of the institutions of the country, in Church and State. Clark said that in the whole course of his life he had never proposed any resolution which gave him greater satisfaction. Edmund Roper said he was proud to second the motion, saying that Hudson had been very popular during the previous year. The people of York should be very pleased that Hudson had agreed to have his name put forward for nomination.

For the Whigs, Henry Smales and Alderman Wilson opposed Hudson's candidacy on the grounds that he was ineligible to stand. Smales said the only reason Mr Roper proposed Hudson was because of the hospitality that Hudson had lavished on the city during his term as Lord Mayor. Roper denied this and said it was because Hudson had conferred great benefits on the city. Alderman Wilson, also opposing

Hudson's appointment, commented that if the Queen's Bench (Appeal Court) were to hear an appeal against his candidacy, his election would not hold good. James Meek, while praising Hudson for acting in an honourable and independent manner during his year as Lord Mayor, also agreed he was not eligible to stand.

Even though they knew he had little chance of success against Hudson and his Tory supporters, the Whigs proposed alderman Gregory as their candidate, but he was unable to overcome Hudson, who as expected won the election, polling twenty-five votes against Gregory's fourteen. It was a measure of Hudson's achievements as Lord Mayor and his increasing popularity in York that, despite the Whig opposition to him and the questions over his eligibility to stand, he succeeded in securing an unprecedented second successive term. It was a notable landmark in his burgeoning political career.

In his acceptance speech, Hudson attempted to soothe those who had opposed his candidacy saying, tongue firmly in cheek, that it was well known he wanted to retire from the office of Lord Mayor, but the sense of duty which he felt he owed to his fellow citizens induced him to again occupy the chair. He said when he was first asked about standing again, it was extremely inconvenient for him to do so. He would have been happy if someone else had been asked to serve, but he was not a man to shrink from the requirements of his party. He said he did not have a personal ambition to be Lord Mayor again, adding that he felt the office would be extremely burdensome, and very painful to him, if he did not get the support of all parties across the council. Hudson said he understood the question of his eligibility could go to appeal and if that should decide against him, he would be sorry, but he would retire with pleasure into the bosom of his family. He thanked Meek for being very supportive during his first term in office and said he would always serve him (Meek) to the best of his ability. This acknowledgement shows there was a deal of mutual respect between the two men who, as directors of the YNM, were working very hard at the time to bring the railway to York. To Smales' criticism of his hospitality, Hudson said that the citizens of York were always proud to see the Mansion House respectably and hospitably maintained. Hospitality should be kept up and, responding to the claim that only rich men could afford to do so when in office, Hudson suggested the Council should vote the Lord Mayor a handsome income to do so.

Hudson then recalled he had come to the city penniless and friendless and that he had followed a lucrative business and felt himself obliged to make some sacrifice. He had spent his money on behalf of the city and had done so cheerfully and despite the sneering of others as to his motives. In his concluding remarks, Hudson expressed gratitude for the kindness he had always received from his fellow citizens and assured them it was his aim to promote science and, of far higher importance, the cause of religion, remarks for which he received much applause from all in the room. With that, Alderman Clark, the Mayor's 'squire', placed the Mayoral cap on Hudson's head. Finally, Clark took the gold chain from Hudson's neck and immediately replaced it, indicating that Hudson was to continue as Lord Mayor. Hudson might not yet be a king, but he had reached the very pinnacle of his political career in York, to serve a second time as Lord Mayor.

The highlight of Hudson's second term was undoubtedly the opening of the York and North Midland railway between York and the junction with the Leeds and Selby railway at South Milford. Opening day was 29 May 1839. On a bright and sunny morning, a breakfast for 400 guests was provided at York Guildhall and at 12.30pm these guests set off for the station, which at this time was a temporary building just outside the city walls. They boarded the celebratory first train, which was topped and tailed by the *Lowther* and the *Leeds and York* steam engines, which had both been built by Robert Stephenson & Co of Newcastle. The journey to South Milford took 36 minutes and the return journey 46 minutes. After their return, a dinner for selected guests, including George Stephenson, was provided at the Windmill Inn, Blossom Street, York. In the evening, Elizabeth Hudson, as Lady Mayoress, organised a Ball at the Mansion House at which guests danced until 4am (having enjoyed a 'supper' at midnight). The *Yorkshire Gazette* commented that when guests left the Mansion House, they gave the impression that 'the day had been one of great and uninterrupted pleasure.' The Hudsons and their guests certainly enjoyed a good party.

When a Lord Mayor's year of office came to end, it was usual practice that a vote of thanks would be moved at the annual meeting at which the succeeding incumbent was appointed. Normally such a vote would be passed unanimously and not split on party lines. However, when the vote of thanks was moved at the November 1839 meeting of the Council, the controversial circumstances of Hudson's appointment once again came to the fore. For his Tory party colleagues there was no issue. Hudson was a hero for them, and they had no doubts about such a vote. For the opposition Whigs however, they were still adamant that Hudson had been ineligible to stand for election as Lord Mayor for a second term. During the debate many Whig councillors took the opportunity to vent their spleen about a man they disliked with a passion.

George Leeman led the way saying that he was 'greatly delighted' that Hudson's second term had come to an end, particularly as his candidature had been unlawful and that during his second term he had only served his party not the city. In the long debate that followed Hudson was subjected to a tirade of criticism, much of it petty, such as when one councillor complained he had never been invited to one of Hudson's lavish banquets at the Mansion House. Another said he had not even been invited to a dinner there, although he subsequently admitted that he had been invited but had decided against attending. Alderman Wilson complained Hudson had insulted him by calling him a 'virulent and personal man.' Hudson did not deny saying this and judging by the virulence of the abuse he received from Wilson's party colleagues during the debate, one cannot help but think that maybe Hudson had a point.

At the end of the debate the vote of thanks was taken. Twenty-four councillors voted in favour of the motion and thirteen against.

Somewhat surprisingly, but perhaps because they had worked closely together on York's new railway, James Meek voted in Hudson's favour, whilst another prominent Whig, Robert Anderson, abstained. After the vote, Hudson rose to several rounds of applause, but he was in no mood to be conciliatory. He spoke with a forthrightness and an honesty which took his opponents by complete surprise. He began by saying that he had listened with considerable pain and annoyance to the debate, nevertheless he had feelings of pleasure and gratitude to the large body of members who had voted in his favour. He said his opponents had been motivated by a disgraceful littleness of feeling. He strongly refuted the allegation that he had insulted Alderman Wilson, even though the Alderman had been venomous towards him (to which Wilson cried 'no, no'). Hudson explained why Councillors Simpson and Hanson had not been invited to the Mansion House – 'Why should they', he barked, when they, particularly Hanson, had been 'so offensive towards me'? He said he had been accused of party partiality and asked Simpson and Wilson for a specific charge. He said his opponents had criticised him for his election but he felt obliged to continue as Lord Mayor as no other successor could be found. It was not his fault that the Whig candidate standing against him at the election (Alderman Gregory) was not up to the mark. Addressing Henry Smales' sneers about the hospitality provided at the Mansion House, Hudson said he had not exceeded his income on hospitality. In a snipe at Wilson's pride at being born and bred in York and never having visited anywhere else, Hudson said he (Wilson) should visit other towns and cities and see the public spirit which exists in them. As for George Leeman, Hudson accused him of sailing close to the wind with his remarks and expressed the hope that he would reflect that he had no right to throw out his insinuations. Hudson said his conscience was clear. The law imposed a duty on him, and he had carried it out to the manner he believed to be right. Who was Leeman, or anyone else, to judge his motives? His speech was, as one might imagine, subject to constant interruption, jeers and cheers, but Hudson was unfazed. He told his hecklers their interruptions would just mean they would have to listen to him for longer. In expressing his 'hearty, sincere and cordial thanks' to those who had voted in his favour, he said he could spare the approbation of the gentlemen opposite – he supposed he should call them honourable gentlemen – as he had received numerous marks of regard and esteem from gentlemen of all grades of politics – Whigs or Conservatives – in his role as Lord Mayor. Lastly, he told his opponents they had not got rid of him. He would continue to take an interest in council matters and take part in debates. He sat down amidst loud cheers (and jeers) and applause.

The *Yorkshire Gazette* expressed its contempt for the Whig's behaviour in the debate, drawing out special criticism for Henry Smales, who had complained about Hudson's 'profuse hospitality.' The paper said that, had Smales been Lord Mayor, he would have turned the Mansion House into a pigsty; as for Leeman, the paper said he had acted like little David throwing stones at Hudson, the York Goliath. It was rash of him to do so as the giant crushed him 'as he would a spider' – a 'lemon' would never be so completely squeezed! And 'if Mr Lemon had a little more spirit, he would have been an excellent "punch" but there was a little too much of the acid.' The paper gave similar treatment to Sir John Simpson, a previous Lord Mayor, who had said he could not give thanks to Hudson as he had never been invited to the Mansion House for dinner. The paper joked that Simpson would go down as a 'pie-ous man, a good liver'! In its editorial, the *Gazette* could not hide its glee at how Hudson had completely discomfited his Whig opponents, who, the paper said, had been utterly defeated, routed and put to flight by:

> Hudson's nervous, eloquent and justly indignant speech which caused his puny adversaries to shrink within the narrow compass of their own littleness and hide their faces in shame and self-convicted malice, meanness and depravity. His assailants marched to the field in battle array but he smote them hip and

thigh and slew them with a mighty slaughter. Away ye yelping curs, slink to your kennels and there bark and howl in secret but show not your teeth again in the face of day for fear of the beadle's whip – you have bearded the lion in his den and you have felt his paw!

Although this editorial was most likely penned by Henry Bellerby, the owner of the paper and a close friend of Hudson, there is little doubt his words reflected how the citizenry of York felt at this time regarding Hudson and the Whig opposition to him. The Whigs were the old guard, completely out of touch with how popular Hudson had become in York. He and his Tory party had been a breath of fresh air since they came to power in the city after years of Whig domination.

As they had threatened to do, the Whigs had submitted an appeal in late 1838 to the Queen's Bench in London concerning Hudson's eligibility to stand for re-election as Lord Mayor. The case took its time to go through the legal system and it was not until May 1840 that the Judges came to a decision. They concluded that, although the election of the new aldermen should not have taken place before the election of a new Mayor, outgoing aldermen were eligible to be elected Mayor. Thus, Hudson's election as Lord Mayor in November 1838 had been quite lawful.

In appreciation of Hudson's two years as Lord Mayor, in July 1840 a subscription was raised as a testimonial for his service. £650 was raised, a phenomenal sum at the time for such a purpose, but one which reflected the enormous esteem Hudson held in the city at the time. The silver plate purchased with this money and presented to Hudson included a candelabrum with 'six massive branches' and a 'richly ornamental vase for fruit and flowers.' The centre stem was decorated with chased foliage and wreaths of oak and laurel, surrounded by three figures representing Justice, Truth and Civic Hospitality. The base included the arms of both the city of York and of Hudson. Also included were two smaller candelabras. The base of the candelabrum was suitably inscribed reflecting the 'deep sense of his munificent hospitality, his strict impartiality in the administration of justice and his unwearied and successful exertions for the benefit of the city.'

The Lord Mayor (William Clark) gave the presentation speech. Amongst the more than 150 guests present were John Lowther MP and George Stephenson. In his very fulsome address, Clark told Hudson that his career in the life of the city of York had been 'marked by unexampled prosperity' and that he was presenting Hudson with the 'most ample tokens of munificence and of friendship that was ever given to any individual, however exalted, within the walls of this noble and splendid city.' Clark said the pieces were a mark of 'public respect for your public and private character', adding that he hoped Hudson and his 'amiable partner', his wife Elizabeth, would enjoy the pieces for many years to come.

In his response, Hudson said it was a difficult task for him to express his feelings on such an occasion, but he assured all those present that he would continue, as he had done for the past twenty-five years, to devote his energies to promoting the prosperity of York. He noted that Clark had referred to the hospitalities of the Mansion House during his tenure and said that this compliment was more due to the one person to whom he owed the position he had attained in York – his wife, Elizabeth. Unfortunately, Elizabeth was not feeling well enough to attend the presentation, but if she had been present, Hudson said she would have been gratified to have heard the kindly manner in which he had been spoken of. In his speech, Clark had alluded to the criticism that Hudson had faced during his time as Lord Mayor, saying that it was impossible to steer through life and obtain the good opinion of everyone. 'To that truism, I fully assent', Hudson said, adding that he would endeavour to conciliate the good opinion of all citizens, regardless of their class or grade in society. He expressed the hope that any ill feeling which may have existed or arisen in the city would be done away with and that the unanimity and kindly feeling would 'regain its wonted seat in our ancient city.' Hudson said he wanted to express to every lady and gentlemen present, and to all citizens, subscribers and non-subscribers to his testimonial, how much he was flattered by the testimonial. He would proudly cherish the memory of the day as one of the proudest and happiest of his life. When he resumed his seat there were loud cheers and plenty of applause before Clark asked for three cheers 'which were most enthusiastically given.'

In serving his successive terms as Lord Mayor and having overseen the opening of the YNM, Hudson had reached a new peak in his political career in York. He would continue to be interested in York politics and would again serve as Lord Mayor in 1846/47. For now, however, his career would take a different path. His determined and single-minded character, much despised by the Whigs, would take Hudson to heights even he could not have imagined.

Chapter 5

Railway Mania

Prior to 1837, new railway companies were required to say they could raise half their proposed share capital before their Bill could go to a second reading in the Commons. However, there was no certainty that the capital could be raised. In addition, this requirement often resulted in some dubious companies being formed to raise funds for new lines that had no prospect of going ahead. To deter such speculation, and the rush to raise cash that might not be utilised, this rule was changed in 1837, so that each new railway company had to raise 10 per cent of their capital and put it on deposit with the Bank of England, or invest an equivalent sum in government securities, before a project would be considered by parliament. The intention was to oblige promoters to raise at least 10 per cent of the expected capital expenditure from their committed supporters. All well and good in theory, but in practice a new company could simply borrow the 10 per cent from another bank, which rather negated the purpose of the exercise which was to ensure that, as far as possible, the proposal being put forward was serious and that the promoters could raise the necessary sums to build their railway if it received parliamentary approval.

When a new railway company was proposed, a subscription list would be opened encouraging investors to reserve a share or shares and to pay a deposit of one or two pounds to secure each share they wanted to buy. Railway shares were not cheap. They often ranged in price between £25 and £100. Having paid their deposit, the prospective shareholder would, at a given date, be 'called' to pay the balance of the share or shares they had reserved. This was usually at the time the new company received its authorisation via an Act of Parliament. These deposits were known as 'scrip' (basically share 'subscriptions' or share promissory notes). Trading in scrip often took place on the fringes of the Stock Exchange before an Act of Parliament was received by the company concerned. These were known as 'kerb' deals because such trades often took place quite literally on the pavement, hence various cartoons of the day showing pandemonium outside the London Stock Exchange.

Kerb deals would have been avoided by anyone with any sense, because there were numerous unscrupulous dealers who would set up a fake company advertising a railway from A to B, promising big profits and high dividends and inviting the unwary to buy scrip. By the time these unfortunate investors realised they had been duped, it was too late, they had lost their money. Hudson never involved himself in any such schemes. He was only ever involved with bona fide companies that were created to build and operate a profitable railway. However, because he was seen as the embodiment of the greed to make money during the time of the Railway Mania, the responsibility for such scams taking place was often unfairly put upon him.

In 1851, the railway historian John Francis wrote that the opening of the York and North Midland line to South Milford in May 1839 had been due to Hudson's energy and perseverance and that when the first train ran from York to London (via Leeds and Derby), Hudson was almost content with what he had achieved and that 'he gave no thought to the morrow.' If only for Hudson's sake that statement had been true, and he had stopped there. But, on the contrary, as Francis again noted, from this moment Hudson 'did not allow himself a pause!'

Under his direction, the YNM extended its line to Normanton in July 1840, which enabled through services from York to London via the North Midland Railway between Leeds and Derby. Shortly afterwards, in November 1840, the YNM through Hudson, leased the Leeds and Selby Railway, thereby reducing competition for York to Leeds traffic and boosting YNM receipts. In December 1841 he formed the Newcastle and Darlington Junction Railway following the failure of the Great North of England Railway (GNER) to complete their line between York and Newcastle. The GNER had been authorised by Act of Parliament in July 1836 to construct a line between Newcastle and Darlington, followed by another Act in 1837 for a line between York and Darlington. but the company ran out of money and by March 1841 their line had reached no further than Darlington. Hudson, seeing an opportunity to extend his railway interests, formed the NDJ to complete the line from Darlington to Newcastle. So confident was he of this line's future success that he subscribed for five times as many shares in the company as anyone else. The NDJ was authorised by Act of Parliament in June 1842 and construction began almost immediately.

Around this time the investing public was beginning to take notice that railway shares were a solid investment, capable of producing good dividends. With more new railways being planned and with investors seeing the benefits that were accruing to towns and cities that already had a connection, the conditions were ripening for what would become known as the Railway Mania. Hudson took full advantage of these favourable economic conditions, expanding his railway empire as quickly as funds would allow. He may not have been responsible for the Railway Mania, but he certainly took full advantage of the public enthusiasm for railway investment.

Hudson's success was due as much as anything to solid hard work as he planned and promoted each of the companies' various extensions and branch lines through parliament. In 1844 he was responsible for guiding five railway bills through parliament and for opening three new lines; in 1845 these figures rose to twelve bills and eight openings; in 1846, thirty-nine bills and five openings; in 1847, twenty bills and eleven openings and in 1848, six bills and thirteen openings.

But Hudson was not the only one promoting new railways. Between 1844 and 1847, parliament approved no less than 650 new railway schemes. In 1844, 805 miles of new railway were approved, in 1845, 2,700 miles and in 1846 an incredible 4,538 miles. Thereafter the mania for new railways declined sharply with just 371 miles approved in 1847, falling to just 50 in 1850. From a base of 100 in 1827, the railway sector share index rose to 200 in 1841 and to 400 in June 1845, when the Stock Market peaked. By December 1845 it had fallen back by 20 per cent. In contrast, railway shares only fell 14 per cent. The reason railway shares held up was probably because the Railway Mania was still in full swing with new companies promoting and building new railway lines. With more shares on the market and now selling at a discount, rather than the premium of a few months earlier, there was still public demand for the shares, which were still seen as a safe investment even though the size of dividends had reduced.

Francis commented that every class and every household succumbed to the temptation of buying railway shares, although in truth railway shares were very expensive and in practice were available only to the wealthier middle and upper classes. Considering there had been a mini boom in railway shares in the mid-1830s which had left a lot of investors poorer once the boom subsided, it is somewhat difficult to understand why, just ten years later, the public should rush into railway shares again, this time with even more alacrity than in the 1830s.

Under the terms of their Act of Parliament, railway companies could compulsorily purchase land, but they still had to pay for it. An Act authorising a new railway did not set any guidance about the price to be paid. This was for negotiation between the landowner and the railway company and each would bargain as hard as possible to get the best price for their respective interest. Where the parties could not agree a price, the issue would go to arbitration. It is evident that Hudson enjoyed these battles and would often involve himself directly in such negotiations.

The Dean and Chapter of Durham Cathedral were bitterly opposed to the NDJ crossing their land and Hudson was involved in a battle about the level of compensation to be paid. John Francis recorded that Hudson was resolute in pursuing the cause of the railway and that it was 'to his honour and their disgrace' that he 'obtained the land for something like twenty-five per cent of the sum they had demanded.' Hudson would no doubt have been very proud of himself for paying only a quarter of the price demanded by the Church, but this was by no means an isolated case. With landowners setting high prices, and others refusing to sell, battles erupted all across the country as landowners attempted to extract the highest price possible from railway companies.

When Hudson set about purchasing land at Selby for the YNM's line from Selby to Market Weighton, he became embroiled in a row with a landowner who believed that Hudson had originally offered a higher price for the land than the owner eventually received. Hudson resolutely refused to increase the railway's payment. He was a businessman first and a railway promoter second and he safeguarded his company's expenditure as though it was his own money. As his career progressed, this trait came more and more to the fore and to such an extent that it seems he got to a stage where he could not see the difference between his own money and that of 'his' railway companies. Although in time such behaviour would be held against Hudson, he was by no means the only example of a chairman who behaved in such a high-handed way.

Herbert Spencer, in his book *Railway Morals & Railway Policy* published in 1855, strongly criticised railway boards for being less than democratic. Spencer no doubt had Hudson in mind when he wrote that, although shareholders elected directors (who in turn elected the Chairman), they (the directors) were habitually re-elected without opposition, the board eventually becoming a 'closed' body. Directors did not consider themselves 'servants' of shareholders, nor did they take kindly to þeing dictated to by them either. Often, any criticism or objections to a Board's decisions would be met with a chairman tersely saying if the shareholders did not like what their board was up to, they should elect a new board. In practice this was quite impracticable, not least because of the detrimental impact such a move might have on the company's share price.

An example of such behaviour was an occasion when the NMR was facing some financial difficulties. Hudson, who had become a director of the NMR in November 1842, proposed the company should reduce its running costs from £40,000 to £22,000 by reducing its employees' wages. Although his fellow directors opposed the move, Hudson was not to be deterred. He pressed home his proposal and Francis wrote that because Hudson had 'perfect mastery over the detail', he often won the argument. Six of the company's nine directors resigned, but Hudson's decision was justified by the effect it had on the company's share price, which rose significantly. The move greatly enhanced his reputation as a man who knew how to make profit and he was appointed chairman of the NMR in September 1843.

Another example of Hudson's resolute leadership came when he proposed amalgamating the three companies that served Derby (the Midland Counties Railway, the NMR and the Birmingham and Derby Junction Railway). He contended the amalgamation would deliver efficiencies that would save £25,000 per year between the three companies in running costs and add £20,000 in additional traffic. The proposal was heavily opposed by his fellow directors and by the shareholders of each company. However, Hudson 'answered all their questions and met all their objections' and carried his project through stormy opposition to create the Midland Railway on 10 May 1844. In its first month of operation, the new company increased its receipts by £2,500. In February 1845 the Midland under Hudson took over the running of the Birmingham to Gloucester and the Bristol to Gloucester lines and in 1846 the line from Nottingham to Lincoln was added.

But his policy of amalgamations was not limited to the Midland's operations. In July 1846 he brought together a number of railway companies that were under his control to form the York and Newcastle Railway company. These companies included the NDJ, the Brandling Railway, the Durham Junction Railway and the Great of North of England Railway. Then in August 1847, he merged the York and Newcastle with the Newcastle and Berwick Railway to form the York, Newcastle and Berwick Railway (YNB). He also oversaw the expansion of the YNM. The Leeds and Selby Railway, which had been leased by the YNM since 1840, was fully absorbed in May 1844, whilst the lines from Seamer to Filey and Hull to Bridlington were taken over in 1845.

Hudson's policy of amalgamations was subsequently adopted by many other railway companies of the time, most notably the Great Western Railway, and his successors at the YNM (Harry Thompson) and YNB (George Leeman) who merged their two companies to form the North Eastern Railway in 1854.

The years of the Railway Mania proved to be very busy for Hudson with many of the railways he promoted being opened during these tumultuous years and numerous others being absorbed into his companies. One of his pet projects was the branch from York to Scarborough. There had been some concern amongst his fellow directors about building this line but, with Hudson now in full control of the YNM, he made the decision for the railway to be built. It was opened throughout on 1 July 1845 along with a branch from Rillington to Pickering, where it joined the existing Whitby and Pickering railway which had been formally taken over by the YNM the previous day.

But Hudson was not alone when it came to a chairman or a set of directors going against the wishes of their shareholders. One example involved the directors of the London and South Western Railway (LSWR) who studiously ignored the wishes of their shareholders and decided to double the Railway's lines between Dorchester and Exeter and between Dorchester and Southampton. They also went ahead with the Exeter to Yeovil line despite shareholders' opposition. Reflecting such attitudes, Herbert Spencer wrote that such behaviour was common, as many directors used the property of shareholders as if it were their own. To give some credit to the LSWR directors, their decisions were heavily influenced by the threat of the Great Western Railway (GWR) moving in on their 'territory.' Such defensive behaviour was employed by many early railway company directors, including Hudson. The York to Market Weighton and the Selby to Market Weighton lines were principally built by the YNM to safeguard the Yorkshire Wolds from rivals that may have attempted to build lines from West Yorkshire to Hull, Scarborough or Bridlington.

Hudson often counselled against companies building competing lines between towns and cities. Despite the understandable desire by new and existing companies to build new lines and branches, he said that many such lines would have an adverse impact on existing railways. John Francis noted that, in 1844, Hudson declared that 'all competing lines which had no traffic were unworthy of the support of parliament' and added, he 'would not be connected with any line which competed with an existing railway.' He refused his sanction to many new railway companies because he did not think they would pay, though his name would have sent their shares to a premium. Bearing in mind the many misconceptions of Hudson, such a stance might be considered out of character, but his argument is perhaps best understood by the fact that if a duplicate line was built, not only would the profits of the existing company be diluted, but so would those of the new company. His insistence on only supporting profitable schemes that produced good dividends for shareholders enhanced his reputation as a sound railway businessman.

Objections to a rival line on the grounds of competition with an existing line was no argument against a new scheme being approved by parliament. For example, not even the influence of George Hudson, who by then had become MP for Sunderland, could prevent the sanctioning of the new Great Northern Railway (GNR) in 1846. The GNR would provide direct competition to Hudson's Midland Railway for traffic between London and York. In his role as chairman of the Midland Railway, which had its own route to London via Derby, Hudson inevitably opposed the GNR even though the new railway would provide a more direct (and therefore quicker) route between his home city and London. His opposition to the new line was criticised at the time – and since – by some biographers as being myopic, but bearing in mind the new line would directly affect the profitability of his existing railway, it is hardly surprising he opposed it. In time, Hudson would come to accept the new railway and eventually agreed it could share 'his' existing station in York. The alternative would have been a new station and the possibility of thwarting his ambition of taking his railway empire north of York to Newcastle and eventually Edinburgh.

In October 1845 a proposal was put forward to construct a new railway in the East Riding to link the port of Hull with the coal fields of north east England. This line would require 20 miles of new railway between Driffield and Malton. It was proposed to link this new line with the Thirsk and Malton railway, then under consideration by the Newcastle and Darlington Junction Railway. The Malton and Driffield Junction Railway (MDJR) as it became known, would cut through the very heart of the East Riding 'territory' that Hudson had fought hard to defend from incursion by railways from the West Riding.

A group of directors of the MDJR, led by their chairman Lord Morpeth, met with Hudson and other directors of the YNM, to seek help with the cost of constructing their line. It would not have been a surprise had Hudson said no, as the MDJR was proposing to impinge on his territory. However, quite the contrary, he was very supportive and at the half-yearly meeting of the YNM, in January 1846, he asked shareholders to agree to subscribe for 800 shares at £50 each. By October 1849 the YNM had met calls on these shares totalling £20,000. However, construction of the MDJR was majorly disrupted by Hudson's fall, which caused delays not only to the to the MDJR but also the Thirsk and Malton line. Both lines eventually opened in June 1853.

George Carr Glyn, a partner in Glyn Mills Bank and London agent for Hudson's York Union bank, was a leading force in providing finance to railway companies and was chairman of the NMR and the London and Birmingham Railway. Glyn recognised the importance of bringing railway companies together to ensure they developed a standard system of fares and charges. He warned that otherwise parliament might impose legislation to force them to do so. Glyn encouraged the development of ideas for a regulatory body that would set out various rules and regulations which each railway would be required to abide by, including the fair allocation of revenue of fares and charges received by companies for passengers and goods that travelled over the lines of different companies.

In the days of the stage coach, if a passenger went on a long journey, for example from London to York, they would likely have to change coaches more than once and often on to a coach operated by a different company. The coaching companies had developed a system whereby the passenger paid one fare and received a single ticket for their complete journey and each coach provider received a fair allocation of the fares charged. However, no such system existed on the railways. Instead, where the starting and final station of a journey was on a different railway, passengers often had to re-book their tickets at the junction station where they changed trains. Where through booking was possible, the receipts collected by the initial company had to be divided between that company and the other companies' railways over which the passenger had travelled, but there was no agreed standard for doing this, which often resulted in disputes over what was paid to each company. Glyn suggested a system similar to that operated by the stage coach companies.

For Glyn, it was essential that Hudson was on board because at this time Hudson controlled such a large proportion of the railways in the Midlands and the north. Initially, Hudson was dubious. He was concerned that what Glyn was proposing was a body that could adversely affect his companies' income by apportioning receipts to other companies. However, he came round to the idea when he realised that, of course, the system would work both ways and that his companies would most likely benefit, particularly as the YNB and YNM were on the then existing route between London and Scotland. With Hudson fully on board, in January 1842 Glyn established the Railway Clearing House (RCH). Hudson's full support for the creation of the RCH proved to be one of his most significant and enduring achievements and one that is often overlooked. At first the clearing system was used by just nine companies, but eventually all railway companies took part. The Railway Clearing House remained a key regulatory body right through to the nationalisation of the railways in 1948.

In 1843 Hudson became aware that a new company called the North British Railway was proposing to construct a line between Edinburgh and Berwick. Recognising the opportunity for York to be connected to the Scottish capital, Hudson set up the Newcastle and Berwick Railway, to link the North British line with that from York. It was proposed to route the Newcastle and Berwick line north of Alnmouth close to land owned by Earl Grey, the former Prime Minister. However, Grey opposed the idea and sought a deviation. Although an altered route might have satisfied the Earl's concerns, George Stephenson and Hudson dismissed the idea, saying any change to the planned route would be too costly.

Taking into consideration that parliament would be unlikely to refuse a new line on the basis of a landowner's objection, the two Georges kept to their original plan. Grey's son, Viscount Howick, agreed that parliament would be unlikely to pay much heed to his family's objection, so he formed a new company, the Northumberland Railway, with the intention of building a line between the two towns, but far enough away from his family's estate. Howick employed Isambard Kingdom Brunel as his line engineer. Brunel at this time was very much interested in the use of atmospheric propulsion as an alternative to steam locomotion and he recommended that the Northumberland Railway adopt this new system for its railway. Atmospheric propulsion did not require a steam locomotive to haul trains. Instead, a pumping engine was built at each end of the railway to provide a steam vacuum in a cast iron metal pipe laid the length of the line. The pipe was sealed at each end and along the top was a hinged metal strip covering a slit in the pipe. A piston attached to a carriage was placed in the pipe and was pushed along by vacuum.

The rival schemes were considered by parliament in 1845 and, unfortunately for Howick, parliament considered his proposed line to be much inferior to that proposed by Stephenson and Hudson, not least that it was intended to use atmospheric propulsion rather than steam locomotion. Recognising that his proposal was unlikely to find favour with parliament, Howick withdrew his bill, leaving the NBR to receive its Act of Parliament on 31 July 1845. Brunel, however, was undaunted by parliament's rejection of atmospheric propulsion and went on to develop the system for the South Devon Railway (SDR).

The SDR opened the first 14 miles of its railway, between Exeter and Teignmouth, in May 1846, with construction ongoing for the next 13 miles to Totnes. Despite the SDR Directors and Brunel's unequivocal support for the atmospheric system, there were doubts amongst the company's shareholders from the very start and these doubts increased as the cost and delays of putting the system into operation grew. It was with this in mind that Hudson was invited to address a shareholders' meeting in August 1847, when a motion to delay any further expenditure on the atmospheric system was to be discussed. Brunel was also at the meeting, which would prove to be one of the rare occasions that these two hugely influential railwaymen would meet in the same room.

Hudson was not impressed with the idea of atmospheric propulsion, a view he made very clear during a reception hosted in London by the Marquis of Northampton (the President of the Royal Society) in March 1846, at which he was introduced to Prince Albert. The two men were said to have shaken hands very heartily and remained in conversation for some time, something that was quite unheard of when it came to a commoner conversing with such a senior royal. But, of course, Hudson was no ordinary commoner, he was the Railway King! During their conversation Prince Albert asked Hudson for his thoughts on the ideas put forward by Brunel for atmospheric railways. Hudson reputedly replied, in his broad Yorkshire voice, 'I think they're a 'umbug, Your Royal 'ighness.' Albert was allegedly much amused by Hudson's bluff reply, but Hudson's views on atmospheric railways were in no doubt. It was no wonder, therefore, that the *Western Courier* reported that there was much excitement at the fact that George Hudson was to address the SDR shareholders' meeting.

Hudson attended the meeting in his capacity as chairman of the Bristol and Gloucester Railway. Before he spoke, Brunel reported that, due to problems with the standing engines, there had been further delays in operating the system. However, he said, an experimental service had operated successfully. Brunel said he understood the impatience at the delays, but the new railway should only open when it was ready. It was unlikely that the more sceptical shareholders present would have been impressed by Brunel's assurances.

When Hudson rose to speak, he was greeted with considerable applause. He said he had visited the route of the SDR and was convinced that with good management it would pay a fair dividend. But, he added, it was not a railway that was capable of spending too much on experimental projects, a statement for which he was cheered by much of his audience. As chairman of the Bristol and Gloucester Railway, he regretted that the SDR had decided to adopt the atmospheric experiment. However, as the company had gone so far with it, then it was owed to all concerned that it should be fairly and properly tested, to establish whether the system could be considered superior to the steam locomotive. However, he considered the expenditure so far on the system at £10,000, per mile to be high and told his audience that he had sought a pledge from the SDR chairman to commit no further expense until the system had proved itself. He concluded by saying that he would be delighted to support the expansion of the system if he believed it to be in the interests of the shareholders. A resolution was passed at the end of the meeting to the effect that no further expenditure would be committed to the system beyond the 27 miles already agreed (between Exeter and Totnes). This resolution effectively sealed the fate of the SDR's atmospheric railway experiment. In March 1848 the SDR board instructed Brunel to suspend all work on the stationary engines west of Totnes and at a company meeting held on 29 August 1848, it was decided to suspend the system for good. The last train powered by the atmospheric system ran on 9 September 1848.

Hudson was foremost an entrepreneurial businessman. Nevertheless, his pursuance of profits and high dividends has often been derided by his critics, especially by those who, when the Railway Mania bubble burst, held him single-handedly responsible for society's worship of Mammon. But without profits there would be no future investment and no dividends; without profits there would be liquidations and closures. None of Hudson's companies failed as a result of his tenure, either at the time of his fall or afterwards. In October 1845 the *Nairnshire Mirror* observed that Hudson had said:

> I am not connected, and never will be connected, with any line that I don't believe to be for the public advantage; and I would be ashamed of myself, and would not deserve or receive so much confidence as is placed in me by the proprietors of the various lines with which I am connected, if I were so selfish to forget the public good in my desire for private gain.

Hudson's foresight and judgment in the railway schemes that he promoted is evidenced today by the fact that the vast majority of the railways he promoted are still in operation, despite the ravages of road competition and the impact of Dr Beeching. The only lines of note that have closed are the YNM routes between York and Market Weighton and between Selby and Market Weighton. The line between Malton and Grosmont closed in March 1965, but much of that line is now part of the North Yorkshire Moors heritage railway. On the Eastern Counties Railway, the lines from March to Wisbech, March to St Ives, St Ives to Cambridge and Maldon to Witham have closed, whilst the line between Wymondham and Dereham is now part of the Mid-Norfolk heritage railway. Nottingham to Mansfield was closed in October 1964 but, as if to vindicate Hudson's original judgment, was re-opened by British Rail in November 1995.

Chapter 6

Hudson's Testimonial

On 12 July 1845, the Midland Railway (MR) held a special shareholder's meeting to discuss the joint leasing of the GNER by the Midland Railway (MR), the York and North Midland Railway (YNM) and the Newcastle & Darlington Junction Railway (NDJ). Towards the end of the meeting, Hudson said that at the forthcoming general meeting of the MR, he would propose a form of testimonial for George Stephenson, to whom, Hudson said, the world owed a debt of gratitude for all that he had done in respect of railways. The suggestion was met with strong support from those present, but Colonel Blaine (a shareholder) suggested that if a testimonial was to be raised for Mr Stephenson, then the energy and talent of the Midland's chairman should also be rewarded, 'if a tribute was due to Mr Stephenson, then one was equally due to Mr Hudson.'

At a subsequent general meeting it was agreed that the MR would join with the YNM, the NDJ and the Newcastle and Berwick Railway, in contributing to a fund for the erection of a statue to George Stephenson on the proposed bridge over the River Tyne in Newcastle, and to a presentation of silver plate, in recognition of the work Stephenson had done for each of the railway companies. The MR would contribute £2,000 towards the cost of the statue and the silver plate. After this motion was passed, Hudson was asked to leave the room. Vice Chairman John Ellis then took the chair and proposed that a testimonial should also be raised for Hudson in recognition of his 'able and efficient services' on their company's behalf. The motion was passed unanimously.

In August 1845, the *York Herald* reported that at a recent meeting of the NDJ, it had been agreed the company would support a testimonial for George Stephenson as well as a testimonial for George Hudson. In moving the proposal, Thomas Barstow said that George Hudson deserved to be considered alongside Stephenson bearing in mind his 'active and unwearying energy in railway matters' which had produced so much good. The motion was passed unanimously. Similar motions were proposed and passed at meetings of the YNM and the Newcastle and Berwick Railways.

The *Herald* remarked that both Stephenson and Hudson merited recognition for what they had achieved. Stephenson for his ingenious work as a railway engineer and Hudson for his bold and unflinching direction of getting railways built. Referring to a proposed statue for Stephenson and a 'mere' testimonial for Hudson, the paper commented that the two men deserved equal honour, particularly as one could not have achieved so much without the help of the other, 'ingenious discovery could have drooped on the sod where it originated, had not talented effort nursed it in its infancy and carefully trained it to the perfection of maturity.' The paper added that if the Tyne Bridge was to bear a statue of Stephenson, then it should also bear a statue of Hudson. Even though it considered Hudson's politics objectionable (the *Herald* was a Whig supporting newspaper), the *Herald* said it recognised that he had particular talents when it came to promoting railways. He was always straightforward and honourable, even though to say so might 'not quite accord with the views of men who are blind to merit in an opponent, or may excite in others the envious objections of little minds.'

The proposal for a statue for Stephenson caused some merriment in some quarters, with a number of papers carrying a syndicated humorous article about a statue for the man who 'first made boiling water to run upon a rail'! The article quipped that statues were usually erected for kings and queens and made of the most 'unfeelingness metal', or of conquerors who, because they are in uniform, carried on quite lawfully creating mangled bodies, misery, housebreaking and wickedness of all sorts. But Stephenson's statue would 'look kindly and sweetly about him – he will know that he has carried comfort, and knowledge, and happiness to the doors of millions! He has brought men together, that they might know and love another.' In the event, despite being proposed by the four railway companies under Hudson's control, the proposal for a statue of Stephenson was lost in the attention which was subsequently given to raising funds for Hudson's testimonial.

Inevitably, the idea of a testimonial for Hudson was subject to much comment from the press and many criticised the idea for rewarding someone who was already very rich. Not only that, many people considered Hudson's path to those riches, successful railway speculation, as immoral. The *Perthshire Advertiser* lamented the 'deference for wealth is a widespread national vice.' Letters to the press suggested Hudson should use the money raised to benefit the poor. As with the proposal for Stephenson's statue, there were some light-hearted suggestions, including that the money raised could be used to build alms houses for those 'persons ruined by railway speculations.' Several newspapers carried a story saying it was gratifying to know that the testimonial would not just be the 'lucky gamesters clubbing together to express gratitude to him who had taught them the trick of the game [railway speculation]', but would be used to build alms houses for railway workers (though it is unclear where this idea came from).

Raising testimonials for people who it was considered had served their community well was common practice throughout the nineteenth century and Hudson (and others) had benefitted previously. For example, in February 1835, Hudson and fellow director Alderman Cooper were presented with 'very elegant 18 inch rose and lily scroll edged round silver salvers' by the shareholders of the York Union Banking Company. The salvers, which had a value of 50 guineas, were presented as 'tokens of esteem and gratitude for their valuable service as Directors.' In August 1836, Hudson, James Meek, Sir John Simpson and Thomas Backhouse had each been presented with silver plate valued in total at £300 by the board of the YNM as a token of their efforts in respect of successfully guiding the YNM bill through parliament and then, in December 1839, Hudson was presented with a service of silver plate to mark his two years as Lord Mayor.

The testimonial subscription was formally launched in September 1845. John Ellis, vice-chairman of the Midland Railway, was appointed Chairman of the Subscription Committee. In a letter dated 1 September 1845 sent to very many prominent people across the country, Ellis said the Committee had concluded that the best way of acknowledging Hudson's eminent services would be to raise a fund by individual subscription rather than by grants of money from the public stock of companies. Ellis wrote that the Committee considered it unnecessary to attempt to impress the powerful claim of Hudson to the gratitude and respect of not just shareholders of the companies with which he was connected, but to the public generally. Ellis added that Hudson's pre-eminent services were universally appreciated and acknowledged; his commanding intellect enabled him at once to comprehend and carry out the principles of railway business and grapple with the practical details in all their minutiae and that his self-devotion was unparalleled and that his zeal, energy and perseverance was beyond all praise. Hudson, Ellis continued, had for several years devoted his time and talents to the advancement of railways and every shareholder had experienced the success of his labours. Ellis concluded his letter by saying there were none who would not seize the opportunity with alacrity, to show their respect for Hudson personally and their deep and grateful thanks for what he had done for them individually and for the public at large.

The letter was accompanied by a list of thirty-six people who had already subscribed £100 or £200 to the fund. The list included John Ellis, James Richardson, Thomas Barstow, Robert Davies, Sir John Simpson, Nathaniel Plews, Richard Nicholson, George T. Andrews, George and Robert Stephenson (all of whom contributed £100). Sir John Henry Lowther was one of three subscribers shown to have contributed £200 (the others were Alexander Dunlop of Largs, Ayrshire, and Graham Hutchinson of Glasgow). The fund grew rapidly with contributions of all sizes, from ten shillings to £100, coming from all across the country. On 11 October, the *Yorkshire Gazette* noted the fund had reached £13,000. Two weeks later, the figure had exceeded £17,500 and by mid-November, £18,280.

Predictably there were elements of the press that felt raising a Testimonial for Hudson was unnecessary and inappropriate. He was already a wealthy man and not in need of financial support. There were many other people, it was argued, who were more deserving, such as Samuel Wilderspin, an educationalist who had founded over 2,000 schools based on the principle that the early years of a child's life were their most important; or Thomas Gray, the early proponent of a national railway system through his book *Observations on a General Iron Railway* published in 1823; or maybe Rowland Hill, the social reformer best known perhaps for introducing the modern postal system. The *Dundee, Perth and Cupar Advertiser* made a case for Thomas Waghorn, an English explorer who in 1830, established a new overland route between Britain and India, via Egypt, which had reduced the journey time between the two countries from between three and six months (via the Cape of Good Hope), to just thirty days. The *Advertiser* said that, whilst Waghorn had added to the glory and grandeur of England, Hudson would never do anything so great for his country and exclaimed, 'Blush, ye Mammon worshippers of George Hudson! Let your ears tingle ye ungrateful recipients of the matchless services of Thomas Waghorn!'

In a further attempt to discredit Hudson, *The Yorkshireman* published an article in December 1845 claiming that a fall in the share price of the Newcastle and Berwick Railway, from £20 to £6, was due to Hudson recently selling 3,000 shares. *The Yorkshireman* inferred that Hudson had done this so that he could repurchase the shares at a lower price. The article was carried by numerous other newspapers, including the *Leeds Times*, which commented that this action would severely shake Hudson's standing as many subscribers had contributed to his Testimonial in the belief that he always kept faith with the shareholders of the various lines of which he was chairman. The *Leeds Times* said

Hudson's action had led to some people refusing to pay their promised subscription to his Testimonial, adding it would not be a surprise if Hudson's 'former ardent admirers might be changed into bitter opponents.' The veracity of *The Yorkshireman*'s article is unknown but, as a bitter opponent of Hudson, it is not beyond the realm of possibility that it was an attempt by the paper to stymie contributions to Hudson's Testimonial.

The *Leeds Times*, like *The Yorkshireman*, had a history when it came to criticising Hudson. In September 1845, it published a long article in which it said Hudson might one day be made a saint, such was the country's worship of Mammon. But, it continued, Hudson was notoriously an object of fear. His talents and indomitable resolution might enlist respect, but his manners repelled anything like love or attachment to him. He was uneducated, imperious and vain. In a different life he would have been a despotic sovereign, a scourge to those over whom he ruled. In manner he was singularly abrupt, indeed insolent and naturally impatient of control. The *Leeds Times* said Hudson had become accustomed to unlimited command, and occasionally said and did things which would subject other and more responsible men to the severity of rebuke, but no one thought of questioning the demeanour of the Railway Monarch. There was, the paper said, a very erroneous and exaggerated opinion about his powers of oratory. Voluble, he might be, but he had the 'loquacity of a country ploughboy excited by potations.' He was as rough in words as he was inelegant in style, blundering and stuttering through speeches with an air of the most imposing confidence. He endured no interruptions, nor answered any questions. 'You must accept what he says as "gospel".' The paper's concluding remark, that Hudson's ardent admirers would turn from him at a time of trouble, would prove remarkably prescient.

The Yorkshireman and the *Leeds Times* articles may have had some effect, as between November 1845 and January 1846 the Testimonial fund increased by just £350, but still to a remarkable £18,631.

Contributors during this time included a donation of £2 from Alfred Dickens (Charles Dickens' brother), who at the time was working as a railway engineer on the York to Scarborough line) and £100 from Lord Feversham of Duncombe Park. Other known contributors to the Testimonial included the Brontë sisters (Anne, Emily and Charlotte) who each subscribed £1, Francis Frith (the well-known Liverpool photographer) £25, and Colonel Cholmley of Howsham £100.

Strangely, after January 1846 news about the Testimonial and what the funds would be used for dried up and questions began to be voiced about what had happened to the money. In a letter to *Herepath's Railway Journal* in March 1846, a correspondent describing themselves simply as 'Candour', asked if any readers could say what had been done with the reputed £20,000 that had been raised; had it been presented to Hudson, or been put to another use, or was the subscription list still open? As so much time had passed since anything had been heard about the Testimonial, Candour said the committee responsible should let the world know what was happening. As 'an admirer of Mr Hudson', he was anxious to know, but Candour's question was never answered, either at the time, nor since. Subscriptions were sent to John Close; a friend of Hudson's and it is presumed that he deposited the money into Hudson's bank account at the York Union Bank. How Hudson used the money has never been revealed but it is perhaps no coincidence that in January 1846 he bought No. 1 Albert Gate, for a sum believed to be just short of £14,000.

No. 1 Albert Gate was one of a pair of houses built by Thomas Cubitt in 1844. They were the largest houses in London at the time and were often referred to as 'Malta' and 'Gibraltar' because they were so big, 'they never would be taken.' With a nod to the memorial raised in 1830 in honour of the Duke of Wellington (which originally had Wellington sitting on a horse on top of the arch) in nearby Hyde Park, a cartoonist of the day suggested the Testimonial could be spent on a statue of Hudson sitting astride a railway locomotive on top of the Albert Gate houses.

Chapter 7

MP for Sunderland

As the British economy began to show signs of recovery from the economic slump of the early 1840s, William Gladstone, the President of the Board of Trade, fearing another railway mania bubble similar to that which occurred in the mid-1830s, established a Select Committee to review railway legislation. He was particularly concerned to ensure that future railway schemes were properly planned and avoided unnecessary competition. He was also concerned about the monopolistic impact that companies had over fares for passengers and the carriage of goods. In Britain, unlike many other countries around the world, there was no state control or direction in the planning and building of new railway lines. Gladstone believed that some state direction was needed if a new railway mania was to be avoided. To discourage opponents of any future regulation, Gladstone said any recommendations the committee made would not apply to existing railway companies, nor to schemes that had received parliamentary approval but not yet been built.

Hudson, along with many of the most prominent railwaymen of the day, including George Carr Glyn, Charles Saunders (Great Western Railway), Mark Huish (Grand Junction Railway), Captain John Laws (Manchester and Leeds Railway), Edward Cardwell (South Eastern Railway) and Rowland Hill (London and Brighton Railway) gave evidence to the committee. The Committee's principal recommendations were that the Board of Trade could, after a period of fifteen years, buy out a new railway company or revise all its charges if it made substantial profits. 'Substantial' was defined as declaring an annual profit of more than 10 per cent for three successive years. New railways would be obliged to provide third class carriages on one train per day at the rate of 1d per mile. The carriage would have to have seats and be protected from the weather and each passenger would be allowed to take up to 56lbs of luggage before any additional charge could be made. Children aged between 3 and 12 would be charged half the full fare and under-threes would be free of charge. New railways would also be required to convey military and police personnel, at the rate of 1d for privates and 2d for officers, and carry the mail at a 'reasonable cost.'

Inevitably, Hudson and his railway colleagues were completely opposed to the first provision, which in effect meant the railways could be nationalised, that is taken over and controlled by the government. Hudson, with Glyn and Saunders met with Prime Minister Robert Peel and Gladstone but were unable to persuade them to change their minds on the issue. Not daunted, the three railwaymen along with others set about a public campaign in which they argued that parliament's existing willingness to allow competing lines disproved that railways were monopolistic, that the average low dividends showed their charges were not extortionate and nothing the government had done had shown they would be good railway managers.

In response to the campaign, the government compromised by increasing the initial period from 15 to 21 years. Otherwise, the Act, best known for its introduction of the 'parliamentary train', received its Royal Assent on 9 August 1844.

Hudson's experience in front of Gladstone's committee brought home to him the power the government could exert over the railway industry and that perhaps his interests might be better served by exerting his influence within the corridors of power rather than without. So it was that, in 1845, his thoughts turned to becoming a Member of Parliament. There is little doubt that he would have liked to have represented York as a Tory MP. However, firstly John Lowther and then John George Smyth were both popular Tory MPs in the city and neither would be likely to give way to him to have a run at becoming the city's MP. He would have to find another constituency.

In the summer of 1845, the Tory party in Sunderland was looking for a candidate to take part in a by-election caused by the resignation of Viscount Howick, who had become the 3rd Earl Grey upon the death of his father in July 1845. Sunderland at the time was in a period of economic depression and the local Tory party thought Hudson might be the man to improve the towns fortunes, just as he had done for York and Whitby. The Anti Corn Law League saw Sunderland as an opportunity to get their candidate, Colonel Perronet Thompson, elected but they knew Hudson would be a formidable opponent. Referring to Hudson's potential influence on the voters of Sunderland and his 'undetectable' powers of corruption, Richard Cobden, the radical Liberal MP, wrote that if Thompson stood, he would be well beaten – 'I would rather face any man than Hudson in a contest for Sunderland.'

Hudson visited Sunderland on 27 July 1845 to begin his election campaign. There was a mixed response from the press to his reception in the town. The *Bolton Free Press* recorded that, although Hudson had arrived in the town to much 'pomp and parade', his speech was a 'lamentable affair', full of foolish predictions regarding Free Trade which had been 'spouted from the mouths of a thousand quack prophets.' The paper concluded by saying that Hudson might have proved himself as a potentate of the railways but he was no political economist and as such lacked the necessary qualities to qualify him as an MP. The *Leeds Times* decried Hudson as the railway 'Napoleon', adding that he had arrived in the town in a sixteen-coach train with men from York and Newcastle, including an 'organised corps of bribers kept for the York Elections.'

The *Yorkshire Gazette* was more enthusiastic about Hudson's visit. It reported that a large crowd had gathered at the Monkwearmouth Station to greet him and his entourage from York. From the station, Hudson travelled to the town centre in a coach led by four grey horses, his procession accompanied by hundreds of supporters and four marching bands. In the town centre he was met by a crowd estimated by the *Gazette* to be 30,000. The procession stopped in the High Street which was crowded with spectators. Every house he passed was filled with enthusiastic supporters, the ladies waving blue handkerchiefs from the windows to show their support for Hudson and the Tories. Hudson was quoted as saying he had never seen anything like the welcome he received in Sunderland.

Hudson and his close supporters made their way to a first-floor window at the George Inn. His chief sponsor and political agent, Joseph Wright, began the speeches by saying that he was supporting Hudson for election as he was convinced that he would advance the interests of Sunderland, adding that Hudson had acquired all the great power and dignity of a king. When people asked what he would do for the town, Wright said he would do what he had done for York and other towns in the north of England such as Derby, Thirsk, Northallerton and Darlington. Hudson was not a man who promised everything and delivered nothing.

When Hudson began his own speech, he was greeted with much cheering from his supporters, mingled with some minor heckling from his opponents. Although he was standing as a Tory party candidate, Hudson told the crowd he had come to Sunderland as an independent, bound to no party and that he was a friend of improvement, not reckless change for changes sake. He said he did not talk about the poor, he acted for the poor. As an example, he said his railway enterprises had provided employment for all classes particularly the poor. He supported the Corn Laws because he believed they were beneficial to everyone. If repealed, they would lead to land being taken out of production and swathes of the countryside becoming a desert. He said that if it could be shown that repeal would benefit the poor, he would support their repeal immediately. When he finished speaking, he was greeted with 'loud and reiterated cheering.'

Two weeks later, a crowd estimated at between 10,000 and 15,000 turned out for the nomination meeting held on 13 August 1845. Each side paraded banners. Referencing his support for abolishing the Corn Laws, Thompson's banners included 'Give us this day our daily bread', whilst another harked back to Nelson's rallying call before the Battle of Trafalgar and proclaimed, 'England this day expects every man to do his duty.' Hudson's supporters had simpler messages such as 'Hudson for Ever', 'Speed and Power' and 'Hudson and prosperity.' Supporters of both candidates mingled before the meeting and inevitably fights broke out. In the ensuing mayhem, banners on both sides were brought to the ground and torn to shreds and poles broken and used as weapons. Two of Hudson's 'bullies' were arrested, another suffered a broken arm and others suffered 'contusions to the hand and face.'

Hudson was accompanied to the nomination meeting by his wife Elizabeth, daughter Ann and one of his sons (most likely William). They viewed the proceedings from the safety of a window in the upper floor of the Saddle Inn, opposite the Sunderland Exchange. When Thompson and Hudson were called on to speak to the crowd, they were both met by groans and hisses, with Hudson's words all but drowned out by Thompson's supporters. Hudson said he would not complain about his reception as he believed in free speech. The main reason for his noisy reception was his support for the Corn Laws, which many saw as being a direct cause of poverty amongst the poorer classes. Hudson, however, was resolute in saying the Corn Laws helped to protect the rural poor by ensuring that landowners had sufficient means to pay their labourers' wages, which were higher in England than in many other parts of Europe. He told the crowd he would not give them any 'clap trap' nor would he make any assertions which might misguide or mislead. He knew he had the support of the shipowners of Sunderland, and all connected with the port. He admitted he was an untried candidate, but he would do all he could to ensure the rich provided employment to the poor.

After Hudson had finished speaking, a show of hands was taken to allow the crowd to show their preferred candidate. They voted overwhelmingly in favour of Thompson. There is little doubt that Hudson's support for the Corn Laws would not have gone down well with the vast majority of the crowd, few of whom could vote at this time. In the election all that mattered to Hudson was that, out of around 1500 who were qualified to vote, 497 voted for Thompson and 627 for him. It had been a short, gruelling battle, but he came through and was now one of two MPs representing Sunderland (the other was David Barclay, a Whig).

It has been said, and with some justification, that Hudson did not have an illustrious parliamentary career. However, he started as he meant to go on, making twenty-five contributions in the Commons during his first year. His first came on 26 January 1846. The government, or perhaps more specifically the prime minister, Sir Robert Peel, was concerned about the large number of railway Bills that the House would have to deal with in the 1846 session.

In his introduction to the debate, Peel said that in 1844, forty-eight Bills had been approved authorising expenditure of £14.78million. In 1845 there were 118 Bills with authorised capital of £56million. He said that generally it was the case that railways took three years to build. With this in mind the actual expenditure on railway construction would be £23.5million in both 1846 and 1847 and £18million in 1848. Peel said these amounts were a huge drain on the capital of the country. At present, he said, there were 606 new proposals for England and Wales, 121 for Scotland and 83 for Ireland. These schemes amounted to 20,687 miles of new railway which would require an estimated capital of £350million. Such a sum would be a major disruption for the country, and he asked the House what, in the light of these figures, should be the principles for the approval of new railways? Such a task would be too much for the usual committees of the House, hence he was proposing a new Select Committee to consider how parliament should govern railway legislation.

Hudson was clearly of the mind that Peel's proposal could, following on from the 1844 Railway Act, be another way of the government trying to wrest control of railway development. Admitting that he was not a disinterested party in the matter, he suggested that before any proposed scheme was considered, the Committee would need to decide whether the promoters of a scheme were in a proper position to carry out their proposal and whether they had a sufficient deposit of money before they could pass through the Standing Committee process. Not to do so, he said, could result in the new Committee recommending schemes promoters would be unable to carry out, which in turn could result in other beneficial schemes being rejected.

Hudson said he was not alarmed at the amount of money required. It would not be going out of the country, he said. One fifth would go to landowners and a large proportion would go to manufacturers of the hardware needed to build the new railway. He said the prime minister wanted to limit the amount spent on railways, but who was to decide which schemes should proceed? For example, if a new 70-mile railway in Yorkshire could be shown to be justified to get produce to market, and the money was available to invest in such a line, then that should be sufficient. He thought that the number of schemes coming before the House would be much less than the figure Peel quoted and with this in mind and the fact that railways in general take three years to build, there would be no derangement of the economy. In an aside, with reference to the Corn Laws, he said if there should be large imports of corn, then it would be necessary to 'button up our pockets' – but that time had not arrived yet. He was concerned that the new committee would use powers it did not possess to prevent schemes from going ahead. He added that, although at times he had been greatly aggrieved by some of the decisions of the House, he had 'on cool reflection' considered the decisions of Select Committees to be right and he would abide by the decisions of this new Committee. He said his purpose in rising to speak was to make the suggestion that until companies were in a position to pursue their Bills – 'many plans are duplicates, many are imperfect' – it would be useless for the new committee to consider such schemes and report to the House which are most eligible.

In his speech, Hudson seemed to have understood Peel's proposal as being a threat of increased government control over railway development.

However, the proposal was not to set up a committee to examine new proposals in any detail, but to consider the principles that should govern the process. Indeed, the following speaker, Charles Russell (the Tory MP for Reading) suggested as much, saying the proposal was not to investigate the merits of a line, but to consider if a principle could be established whereby only railways that were justified could be considered for approval and perhaps to spread the proposals to protect capital expenditure. The aim was to discount 'every bubble scheme.'

A month later, on 17 February 1846, Hudson took part in a debate about one of the most important political topics of the time, the proposed repeal of the infamous Corn Laws. Legislation had been passed in 1815 to protect producers of home-grown cereals from the impact of cheap foreign imports. Essentially, the domestic price of corn had to reach the high price of 80 shillings per quarter (28lbs) before any corn could be imported. The policy was extremely controversial as in years of shortages the price would rise making it very difficult for the poor to buy corn to make bread. In reality the only beneficiaries were wealthy landowners. Bearing in mind his comments about supporting policies to help the poor before the Sunderland election, it seems odd that Hudson should support the retention of the Corn Laws.

Noting that he was a newcomer to the chamber, Hudson began his speech by seeking the indulgence of the House for the fact that although he was used to making public speeches, he was about to speak on a question of great importance in a place where he was not yet familiar with its practices. He began by deeply deploring the 'calamity' that had taken place in Ireland (the famine – and one of the drivers for the repeal of the Corn Laws). He believed the situation could be met by special measures of relief. He felt, however, that this should not be met by a measure that could adversely affect the greater interest of the country. He felt deeply for the wretchedness that had befallen the people of Ireland and called on the prime minister to provide for the emergency. Such measures would have widespread support but, he added, these should not include the repeal of the Corn Laws.

Hudson was concerned that, by allowing free trade in the import of corn, much of the country's money would be spent abroad and not be available for investment at home. For example, in 1841 he said he had sought capital for a new railway but it was not forthcoming because so much money had been spent abroad on corn imports. However, when the home harvest improved in 1842, and corn was not being imported, capital became more freely available again. The potential shortage of money in the economy was partly what Peel was referring to in the railway debate, when he expressed his concern about the amount of money being spent on railway investment.

Hudson went on to say that Peel had suggested British cereal producers should compete with producers in the wider world but that this argument took no account of the reality that British producers had a range of expenses, such as poor rates, land taxes, highway rates and other expenditures that foreign producers did not incur in their own countries.

Although Peel had changed his mind (Peel had previously been in favour of the Corn Laws), Hudson said he would not overthrow those principles which had led to a state of prosperity in the country not seen in the history of the world. If the repeal went ahead and landowners suffered a loss of income from lower prices for their corn, why not spread the burden of protecting the poor to other sectors of the economy such as Consolidated Fund holders or why not suggest to manufacturers that they could not make a product unless they had paid a tax for the benefit of the state? The burden of supporting the poor should not be on landowners alone. Hudson expressed the hope that the country would not suffer if repeal went ahead, adding that currently farm labourers in the country were receiving between 12s and 14s per week, whilst their counterparts in Poland and Prussia were receiving only 4s or 5s a week. He feared wages at home would fall to these levels if the Corn Laws were repealed. He again implored the government to give its immediate attention to the situation in Ireland rather than to repeal of the Corn Laws.

Hudson soon found that speaking in the House was not like speaking to his shareholders. Unlike his shareholders, MPs would not be afraid of tackling anything he said. In a subsequent debate on the Corn Laws, Viscount Duncan, the Whig MP for Bath, rebuked Hudson on a number of points in the latter's speech, particularly his comments relating to the situation in Ireland. Duncan said that Hudson had dismissed the 'potato disease' as 'a mere matter of small moment' – Hudson interjected loudly, 'that is not what I said' – but Duncan disagreed and went on to criticise Hudson for suggesting the situation in Ireland could be solved by raising a public subscription and for defending agricultural interests, when he had so often cruelly invaded those turnpike trusts and rural solitudes [with a railway] which were once the pride and the boast of the country gentlemen of England. Duncan's tirade continued, berating Hudson for his comments about capital being hard to come by in 1841, a period of expensive corn and a time of great distress, and then explaining that the prosperity in 1842 was not caused by the Corn Law tariffs, but by low prices, owing to an overproduction of English corn. Duncan also criticised Hudson's comments on labour costs, saying that the removal of the tariff would not affect labourers' wages. These would be determined by the normal rules of supply and demand.

Hudson was understandably enraged by Duncan's assertions. In his response he appealed to all who had heard him to say whether any expression of his warranted the construction put upon it by Viscount Duncan. There were cries of 'No, no' from the chamber. Hudson said he had stated that it was the duty of the government to immediately provide for the distresses of Ireland, and that he would be ready to give his support to any measures that were brought forward to immediately afford relief to the Irish people. Hudson had heard Sir Robert Peel say 'Hear, hear' when Duncan spoke and, clearly mortified, said he begged most distinctly to say that he did not and would never treat lightly the distresses of the sister country. Viscount Duncan said he apologized if he had overstated Hudson's meaning and added that he was 'delighted' to hear Hudson's expression of sympathy with the Irish people. In the event, parliament repealed the Corn Laws in May 1846.

Taking account of the fact that he had become MP for Sunderland in 1845 and his propensity for micro-managing his railway businesses, one can only be in awe of the amount of work Hudson committed himself to at this time. He was truly a workaholic. Two verses from a popular song published at the time, appropriately titled *The Railway King*, reflected how hard Hudson worked, as he went from meeting to meeting up and down the country:

> King Hudson committees at York at nine
> At twelve [he] committees at Newcastle Tyne
> Committees at Rugby at half past seven
> And then committees in Town at eleven
>
> At twelve p.m. committees the Commons
> At 1.54 steams a speech at short summons
> At four old Morphus lets off the steam
> And Old King Hud, committees in a dream

Chapter 8

Reaching the Summit

Despite his new found career in the Commons, Hudson was still hard at work building up his railway empire and receiving plaudits for his achievements. For example, in an October 1845 article that was carried by many other newspapers, the *Nairnshire Mirror* eulogised Hudson as 'a most potent and distinguished individual', adding that although some had suggested he had reached his eminent position due to 'chance and good luck' and 'lucky speculation', others had said his success was down to his genius in all matters related to railways. It continued:

> If honest enterprise is speculation, George Hudson is a speculator, and so are the Barings and our other merchant princes. But if by the epithet speculator is meant a rash theorist, who embarks on a sea of speculation without rudder or compass, placing his dependence on the chapter of accidents, reckless as to consequences, and rushing with all the desperate energy and infatuation of a gambler into the vortex of danger, then George Hudson is most unquestionably not a speculator.

Concluding its article, the paper said that if Hudson's career had been that of a speculator then:

> it has been one that has been beneficial to his country and rebounds to his credit, and many to whom statues have been raised in our cathedrals have less deserved the perpetuation of their name. In his own neighbourhood, for which he has done so

much, Mr. Hudson is universally esteemed and respected. He is kind and affable to all who approach him; and he has earned for himself a title of even greater distinction than that of 'The Railway King', for he is 'the friend of the poor.'

Following his success in delivering results for his shareholders, Hudson was often approached to manage other railways, so he could do the same for them. He resisted these approaches, preferring to promote the railways and routes he had directly helped to establish. However, there was to be one exception and one that he would come to regret. He was approached on more than one occasion to take on the chairmanship of the Eastern Counties Railway (ECR), which opened its first line between a temporary station in East London and Romford in June 1839. Other lines followed but they mostly conveyed agricultural traffic in what was then a sparsely populated part of the country. The railway had been badly managed from its inception and had struggled to make a profit sufficient to pay a dividend of more than 1 or 2 per cent.

By 1845 the ECR's directors (and shareholders) were getting increasingly desperate to improve their railway's profitability and they decided to approach Hudson to ask him if he would become their chairman. Although Hudson showed some reluctance in taking up the ECR's offer, it has been suggested that he may have encouraged the approach because he had mentioned the potential for extending the ECR's London to Cambridge line (then under construction) further north, particularly as at this time there were plans afoot for the newly created Great Northern Railway (GNR) to build a direct route from London to York via Peterborough, Grantham and Doncaster. It seems Hudson was finally persuaded when the ECR's directors offered him carte blanche control over their railway. Such an offer was one that Hudson could not refuse. He more or less ran his other interests as his own fiefdoms and being allowed to do the same with the ECR is likely to have appealed to him.

Hudson was elected chairman in October 1845 and just two months later, in December and before the company's half yearly accounts had been finalised, he recommended the annual dividend be raised from 2 per cent to 6 per cent. This was a risky move as even he must have been aware that such a dividend could not be sustained with the level of profit being made by the company. However, he was determined to show his new shareholders that he could make a difference to the company. The shareholders were ecstatic, but it was a decision that would come to haunt Hudson as, whatever he tried to do to increase the company's traffic, the revenue was never sufficient to sustain such a high level of dividend. Later it came to light that Hudson had massaged the company's accounts to support the payment of the increased dividend. Instead of paying the higher dividend out of increased profits (there weren't any), he authorised the payment to be made out of the company's capital account.

Francis noted such a move was utterly 'indefensible' and was shocking to the public when they found out. Hudson claimed that the exceptionable circumstances of the ECR required an exceptional response but, as Francis says, such a reason was insufficient. To make matters worse, no one expected the company to increase its dividend, so there was no reason to have done so. Hudson must have felt that he had to increase the dividend in order to justify his appointment as Chairman. Francis described Hudson's decision as a 'most unwise experiment' and one that impeached his commercial judgment and proved that the power bestowed on him had been too great. Were he to have his time over again, Francis said Hudson would be unlikely to repeat the same mistake. Hudson's behaviour at the ECR was certainly a turning point in his railway career. He could not, however, be accused of not trying to do his best for the company. Between October 1845 and his resignation as chairman in early 1849, the ECR increased its route mileage from 141 to 324 miles, including the lines between Ely and Peterborough, Cambridge to St. Ives and between Maldon and Braintree.

Hudson's policy of pursuing only worthwhile and profitable schemes was noted in an article published in the *Pictorial Times* in July 1847 which noted that he became much sought after by many other railway proprietors so they too could enjoy the advantage of his co-operation, if not his presidency. Writing before Hudson's decisions at the ECR came fully to light, the *Pictorial Times* lauded Hudson for not being persuaded into lending his support for schemes that were either impractical or of 'doubtful utility' further commenting that he did not allow his reputation to be tarnished by associating himself with hopeless schemes. Hudson, the paper went on, always limited his ambition to the improvement or extension of lines with which he had long been connected.

Undaunted by the failure to preserve the Corn Laws, Hudson, who by now was reaching the peak of his power and influence, allowed his name to go forward for election as York's Lord Mayor for a third time. At the annual Council meeting of November 1846, fellow councillor William Richardson put forward the proposal for his appointment. In recommending Hudson, Richardson said it was unnecessary for him to go into great length about the man who had done so much for the city and who could do a great deal more. Concluding his effusive introduction, Richardson said he would only be doing half his duty if he did not also 'allude to the better half of that worthy alderman', whose courtesy and hospitality they had previously experienced and who he was certain the city would be pleased to have presiding as the Lady Mayoress. Alderman Sir William Clark said in support of the motion that Hudson was well and eminently known in York and across the country, if not the world for his achievements. He had made York 'the Queen of railway towns.' With such an introduction it was no surprise his election was supported unanimously by the Council and it was not long before he was seeking election again, this time at the 1847 general election in Sunderland.

Having been elected just two years earlier and having kept many of the promises he made to the Sunderland electorate in 1845, including the construction of a new dock, for which an Act of Parliament was obtained in 1846, Hudson was virtually assured to be re-elected as one of Sunderland's two MPs. The real battle in Sunderland would be between David Barclay and William Wilkinson for the town's second MP. So confident was Hudson, he did not attend the canvass which took place in the days leading up to the election. However, he did visit the constituency at the end of July to address his supporters. Introducing him to the meeting, his agent Christopher Bramwell said that every year, every month, increased the love and esteem that Hudson's constituents felt for him. Acknowledging Bramwell's remarks, Hudson expressed his gratitude for the handsome, friendly and enthusiastic reception he had received in the town. In a long and rather rambling speech he detailed his first two years in the Commons. He said some – but none who were present – might dispute the course of action he had taken, but he had always acted honestly and to the best of his judgment. On the Corn Laws (which had been repealed in May 1846), he said repeal had not provided the poor cheap bread, nor had it benefitted farmers and although he did not consider the new system would provide security of supply, if proved wrong he would admit his error. He apologised for not attending the canvass and explained this was due to him being detained in York during the summer assizes (he was currently Lord Mayor and as such also Chief Magistrate). He said he was sure his supporters would make allowances for him when they considered the amount of business he had on his hands, particularly those duties he owed to those who had entrusted a large amount of capital to his care (his railway shareholders). If returned to parliament, Hudson assured his audience they would find no pledges unredeemed, no promise broken, no principles forsaken and no conduct to forfeit their confidence and regard. He was loudly cheered at the end of his speech.

At the election, held in early August, he comfortably came top of the poll with 879 votes. David Barclay polled 642 and was re-elected, whilst William Wilkinson came third with 568 votes. After the election, several newspapers noted that over forty MPs in the new parliament would have railway interests. Apart from Hudson, amongst those mentioned were Robert Hildyard (Whitehaven), a leading railway barrister; John

Cobbold (Ipswich), chairman of the Ipswich and Bury St Edmunds Railway and a director of the Eastern Union Railway; George Carr Glyn (Kendal), chairman of the London and North Western (LNW); David Waddington (Maldon, Essex), deputy chairman of the Eastern Counties and the Leeds and Bradford and a director of the Midland; Robert Stephenson (Whitby), engineer to the LNW, the South Eastern, the West London, the Leeds and Bradford etc; Joseph Locke (Honiton), a railway engineer; and William Cubitt (Andover), railway contractor and director of West London Railway.

Hudson's contributions in the Commons often came late at night, most likely because he had spent the evening 'convivially' with friends at the Carlton Club or elsewhere in London's smartest restaurants. It was inevitable, therefore, that sometimes he would turn up to the House a little worse for wear. *The Satirist; or, the Censor of the Times* was a satirical newspaper that often poked fun at people and events of the time and Hudson would often come within its sights. One such occasion was a debate in June 1848 on the future of the Navigation Laws. During the debate he picked an argument with the Radical MP Richard Cobden which had nothing to do with the debate. Joseph Hume, MP for Montrose, stepped in to rebuke Hudson for coming to the House 'well primed' and for addressing his comments to an individual MP rather than through the Speaker. *The Satirist* reported that:

> The House of Commons was enlivened from its usual dullness on Friday night by Mr. Hudson returning after dinner in a state of anti-sobriety, and half-unbuttoned white waistcoatism. The debate being on the Navigation Laws, the worthy gentleman thought proper to talk about his navigators, and to rail at Mr. Cobden as a man leagued against him. Mr. Hume blamed the Honorable Member for coming down to the House well primed with, he would not say, "champagne," and accused him of indulging likewise too much in personality, instead of simply addressing the Speaker.

It seems, however, Mr. Hudson was innocent of the last breach of custom, as, according to his own admission, he had all along been speaking to the chair; but we suppose, owing to the unsettled state of his system, he could not keep his eyes fixed in the right direction. He apologised for sporting his super-white vest on the ground that he had intended taking his family to another party, and wound up with a good rub at Mr. Hume by declaring, however personal he might be, he should never think of accusing the Member for Montrose [Hume] of receiving an invitation himself, or giving a dinner to a friend. All this was funny although petty enough, but later in the evening, Mr. Hudson and Mr. Cobden fell foul of each other, and their squabble degenerated into a complete row. During the whole of this disgraceful scene not a word fell from the Speaker, an old gentleman paid several thousand annually to preserve order in the House. Would it not be an improvement and a vast saving to the country for a policeman to take his place for the future, and thus, in the event of a worthy being obstreperous after dinner, he could forthwith be shown his proper station?

Hudson laid the foundation stone for the new south dock at Sunderland on 4 February 1848. The *Yorkshire Herald* reported that the occasion had been celebrated with 'extraordinary rejoicings.' Shops and businesses remained closed for the day, church bells rang and all the boats in the harbour were decorated with flags. Hundreds of people had lined the streets of the town. A marching band led a procession through the town to the site of the new dock. The procession included the Mayor of Sunderland (John Scott), George Hudson and the Lord Mayor of York (George Seymour). Hudson placed a time capsule containing the coins of the realm and a plan of the new dock within the cavity of the foundation stone, which was then filled with gutta percha (liquid rubber) and covered with a zinc plate on which was inscribed the date and the names of the dock company directors. The stone was then lowered into position accompanied by what was described as salvos of artillery.

Standing on the foundation stone, Hudson made a long speech extolling the virtues of the new dock. He said he was certain it would prove productive and that it would be a valuable harbour of refuge and thus protect life and property. If the new dock proved as profitable as other undertakings he had been responsible for in other parts of the country, he would give acknowledgment of the debt he owed to the people of Sunderland for the confidence and kindness with which they had treated him on all occasions. Following the ceremony, the directors, led by Hudson, hosted a dinner at the Bridge Hotel where many more words were spoken and toasts raised to Hudson and others who were involved in the project. In the evening a 'very splendid ball' was held at Sunderland's Atheneum Rooms. The *Herald* reported that the workmen involved in the project had not been ignored as, after the guests had departed, they had been provided with a 'good substantial dinner.'

The *Nairnshire Mirror's* claim in October 1845 that, if speculators pursued profits without regard to safety 'then George Hudson is most unquestionably not a Speculator', was not a view held by many of Hudson's critics. They very much regarded him as a speculator and when any accident occurred on a railway under his control, this would often be blamed on his company's pursuance of profit. However, accidents occurred on all railways in the early years and a number inevitably occurred on lines under Hudson's control. Hudson himself was involved in two accidents on the North Midland Railway (NMR) in 1848.

The Times reported an accident on the NMR whereby the four-wheeled carriage in which Hudson was travelling lost its axle and hind wheels due to the train travelling at what was described as 'a rapid rate.' Hudson's coach was dragged along for some distance before the engineman could stop the train. The carriage behind Hudson's and the luggage van were parted from the train and left stranded on the track. The reason for the excessive speed of the train was, according to a correspondent to *The Times*, due to Hudson taking too long to eat his dinner at York and the engine driver having to make up time.

According to this correspondent, who simply signed himself 'A.B.', a similar incident happened a week later when he was travelling on an Edinburgh-bound express. As was usual, the train stopped at Derby to change the engine. During the change over Hudson stepped out of his carriage to speak to a railway official. The engine had been changed but Hudson's conversation went on and eventually a passenger:

> desired the guard to say, with his compliments to Mr Hudson, that when his gossip was over, we should be glad to get on. The time lost had to be made up, so the train proceeded at a terrible pace... until about a mile beyond Chesterfield a violent tossing and pitching began with a dreadful shock [jolt]... the engine driver soon stopped and on scrambling out, the fearful state of things appeared. The train consisted of one second class carriage, three first class carriages and a luggage van behind, in which was the guard. The second class coach, which was immediately behind the engine, and the first class coach were uninjured [still on the rails]. The next carriage, in which Mr Hudson was travelling, had been dragged along the fore wheels, without any hind wheels or rear axle; the back part was nearly knocked to pieces... the third first class carriage was left a quarter of a mile behind...without any wheels or axles at all and behind that, the luggage van was knocked to pieces and turned over twice and yet the guard was almost uninjured.

Amazingly neither Hudson nor any of the other passengers on the train were seriously hurt. In the aftermath of the accident, AB wrote that Hudson 'bustled about with his usual volubility.' But perhaps the most extraordinary outcome of this terrifying event was that within 45 minutes of the accident happening, the passengers and their luggage were put in the two coaches that were still on the rails and they continued their journey to Normanton. A little bit different to how things would be today!

Chapter 9

The Kingdom Unravels

By the end of 1848, Hudson controlled over 1,000 miles of railway, about a quarter of the total mileage in England at the time. Francis commented that these railways were all paying good dividends and that it was this success that 'sanctified the power of Mr Hudson.' Francis noted Hudson's name was associated with shares and profits and that he wielded an influence in England that was unparalleled and unprecedented and that peers had flattered the dispenser of scrip and that peeresses had fawned on the allotter of premiums. Francis further noted that at Hudson's London residence, 1 Albert Gate, ducal crests were often seen on the carriages at his door, whilst rich foreigners had sought his society and government ministers and bishops had 'bent in homage' and that the ermine of the Judge had lost its dignity and the uniform of the officer its pride. However, the clouds were gathering.

In the summer of 1848, a pamphlet was published entitled *The Bubble of the Age, or The Fallacies of Railway Investment; Railway Accounts and Railway Dividends*. This document alleged that dividends in Hudson's railway companies had been paid out of capital rather than revenue. This assertion led some investors to take a closer look at his activities.

The first sign of trouble came at the Midland Railway's half yearly meeting on 15 February 1849. Hudson and his fellow director, John Ellis were accused of keeping the fees charged for the transport of coal deliberately low (both had interests in coal mining) and there were also complaints that the Midland was paying too much to use other companies' lines. One particular critic, Houghton Brackner, a Liverpool ship owner, then complained bitterly about Hudson's negotiations with the Great Northern Railway (GNR), which was on the verge of opening a direct line between London and York. Hudson had, in fact, fought long and hard against the GNR proposal as he was well aware their more direct route would out-compete the Midland's route to the north via Rugby. Eventually, to avoid the GNR opening their own station in York, he came to an agreement whereby the GNR could use the YNM station.

At this time, shareholders had the power to set up a committee of inquiry if they considered the directors of their company had made mistakes or were considered to have made errors of judgment in managing the business. Many in the MR, like Brackner, felt that Hudson had sold them out and they demanded a committee of inquiry to look into the board's activities, particularly Hudson's conflicting involvement with the MR and the YNM and YNB railways.

Hudson, and his deputy chairman John Ellis, argued that the proposal for an inquiry was, in effect, a censure of the board and, with Hudson threatening to resign, the idea of a committee was dropped. However, subsequent events at the ECR, YNB and YNM caused a rethink amongst the directors and shareholders of the Midland. At an extraordinary general meeting held on 19 April, the MR made the decision to set up an inquiry. Hudson must have feared that this would happen as, two days before the meeting, he wrote a letter tendering his resignation as chairman, ostensibly on the grounds that he recognised the conflict of interest posed because the GNR would be a direct competitor to the Midland for London to York traffic.

In the event, the Midland committee of inquiry found little of concern with Hudson's management of the company, apart from some minor questions about how depreciation should be accounted for, a problem which many railway companies had at the time, stemming from having so many depreciating assets such as locomotives and rolling stock. R.S. Lambert questioned whether this was a genuine acquittal of Hudson, or if it was because of the difficulty of isolating Hudson's actions from those of his fellow directors. The reality was probably that it was more due to the fact that Hudson had already resigned and the company's desire to protect its reputation and its share price.

Meanwhile, the half-yearly meeting of the YNM held on 20 February 1849 passed off without much trouble for Hudson, despite the fact that the dividend to be paid out had been reduced from 8 per cent to 6 per cent for the first half year (which was down from 10 per cent paid in 1847). However, Hudson had no idea what was awaiting him at the half yearly YNB meeting that followed immediately after the YNM meeting.

Robert Prance, a London based shareholder in the YNB said he had noticed what he considered some odd dealing in the shares of the GNER, which was then in the process of being taken over by the YNB. He referred to the latest accounts of the company which showed that 3,790 shares in the GNER had been bought by the company for £21 between October 1846 and December 1848. At the time of the purchase, the market price per share was £16 10s. Having stated the facts, Prance asked Hudson who were the fortunate sellers? Hudson blustered saying he did not have the books with him, but he did admit he had sold 2,800 shares. Recognising the way the conversation was going, Hudson knew that he needed to fend off any thoughts of a committee of inquiry. Still blustering, he said that, if he had erred in this case, he had been right in many others. He had never thought about the transaction but, if he had made an error, he was ready to refund the profit he had made. In previous years such an assurance would have been enough to satisfy the shareholders, but Prance was not to be deterred. He was determined that the shareholders of the YNB should set up a committee of inquiry to look into the transaction and uncover precisely what had happened. It was the start of what would prove to be Hudson's downfall, as his mistakes and business dealings came under the spotlight.

Reporting the events of the meeting, the *Yorkshire Gazette* suggested that if the shares were bought by the YNB for £21, that was actually quite prudent considering their value at the time they were due to be fully paid up (in July 1849) would be £22.10s. The *Gazette* wrote that Prance's premeditated attack on Hudson was met with the latter's usual candour and openness and that Hudson would pass through the ordeal of any inquiry in a highly creditable manner. Hudson, the paper continued, could not have been more reasonable than to have offered, as he did, to buy back the shares if that was what the shareholders wanted. But another commentator at the time noted that if a miscreant had made such an offer in a Court of Law, the magistrate would be certain not to accept it as a palliation of a crime. Nevertheless, the *Gazette* considered the whole affair would be satisfactorily explained before a committee of inquiry and that Hudson would be proved fully entitled to a renewed vote of confidence from the shareholders. It warned that those hostile to Hudson would not be sparing in calling him names or accusing him of the most corrupt methods. Although it was spot-on with this warning, the *Gazette* was very much wide of the mark in predicting that all would be well for Hudson.

The immediate impact of the YNB's decision to set up a committee of inquiry was that Hudson was now under suspicion and, whilst matters against him were to be investigated, he began to be ostracised. For example, he was due to attend a meeting of MPs in London shortly after the YNB meeting, but was advised he was not welcome, not until the issues in question had been satisfactorily resolved. It would seem Hudson knew that he was about to be found out as, to escape attention, he left London for his home at Newby Park in Yorkshire. Hudson had bought Newby Park (not to be confused with Newby Hall) in October 1845 from the Earl de Grey and had bought the neighbouring Baldersby Park Estate in 1844. Together the two properties formed a substantial country estate which had become the Hudson's family home when in Yorkshire.

Hudson's flight to Yorkshire was captured in a cartoon published in *The Puppet-Show*, a satirical magazine of the time similar to *Punch*. The cartoon shows Hudson fleeing Albert Gate for Newby Park. The £14,000 on Hudson's bag of money referred to the cost of 1 Albert Gate which, although shown as 'To Let' in the cartoon, continued to be owned by Hudson until 1854, when it was leased to the French Embassy.

In April 1849, shortly after he left London, Hudson wrote an open letter to YNB shareholders in which he referred to the fact that the committee had said he should have acted as a Trustee for the YNB and that he should only have been paid the sum he originally paid for the shares he bought and that he should have been charged interest on the amount he had benefitted from. Hudson said he had always thought it his duty to watch over and further the interests of the company, adding he did not consider himself a Trustee as such. He never thought himself restrained from entering into personal arrangements, just as if he had been an ordinary shareholder. He said he had never hesitated to take any amount of personal responsibility on behalf of the company and that it was important to bear this in mind when he was charged with having made a profit of the company in the character of a Trustee. This is a very important point to take into account when considering Hudson's behaviour as it helps to explain, in part at least, his behaviour with respect to the GNER shares. Whether right or wrong, he clearly did not see himself as a Trustee as some expected him to be as Chairman of the company. At the time of his actions, the way he behaved was not unlawful (though the law was changed subsequently).

Hudson went on in his letter to say that he took on personally guaranteeing the funds that needed to be raised to extend the railway to Newcastle (he is referring here to his purchase of the Brandling Junction Railway). This risk was his and, with some justification some might think, he was entitled to the advantages that eventually arose to him and the other guaranteeing parties. When the interests of the company required him to transfer his Brandling shares to the company, he did so and, in doing so, he sacrificed a considerable annual income in dividends. Thus, he did not agree with the committee's conclusions, but if they were right then it should be carried out, but not by his repaying the difference with interest, but by cancelling the whole transaction. Such would involve a larger pecuniary sacrifice for him, as the shares were now in a depressed state, but the company would have their money back. He finished his letter by saying he cared nothing for the money, but that he had to pursue a course which he judged to be correct, even if in circumstances of a particularly painful nature, and in circumstances in which he had become involved, without 'the slightest idea on my part that I was doing anything deserving reprehension.'

It could be argued that 'he would say that wouldn't he?' And many have, but it is clear from his own words that he really did not see he had done anything wrong. History shows that despite his protestations, the committee was not going to listen to him. They had made up their minds that he was guilty of fraud and nothing he could say in his defence would sway them from their point of view. It was inevitable therefore that Hudson would eventually be forced to resign his chairmanship of the company, which he did on 4 May 1849.

Four days after his resignation from the YNB came the devastating news that his brother-in-law, Richard Nicholson had been found drowned in the River Ouse near the Scarborough railway bridge in York. Hudson had had a torrid few months at the beginning of 1849, but the loss of Richard was an extreme blow to him and more particularly of course to his wife, Elizabeth. Hudson had known Nicholson for over 35 years, since he first arrived in York aged 13. Nicholson, who was born in 1793, had been closely involved with Hudson's railway ventures since the YNM was first established in the 1830s. The inquest into his death was held the following day, Wednesday, 9 May. Nicholson's valet of seventeen years, John Reynard, told the inquest that in the days before his death, Nicholson had not been his usual self, appearing somewhat restless. Another witness said that on the evening he died he had seen Nicholson on the riverbank near the Scarborough railway bridge and described him as walking in a 'slow and moody' manner. This witness added that Nicholson had his head down and appeared wrapped up in thought which, the witness said, was not Nicholson's normal 'deportment' in public. The inquest heard it was unclear how Nicholson had come to be in the river, for example whether he had been pushed, had fallen in accidentally or, whether he drowned himself wilfully. The Jury's verdict was that he had been 'found drowned; there being no sufficient evidence to show how he got into the water.' However, there is little doubt that Nicholson committed suicide, the ignominy that was befalling Hudson and by association, all his associates had proved to be too much for him. Nicholson's death is likely to have been the final straw in Hudson's decision to resign from his beloved YNM.

A special meeting of London based YNM shareholders was held in London on 17 May to discuss the problems surrounding the YNM and to help prepare for the general meeting to be held in York on 24 May to establish a committee of inquiry to look into the company's affairs. William Crawshay, who held stock valued at £300,000 in the company, was appointed chairman of the meeting. Crawshay told those present that he had recently spoken to Hudson and advised him to resign as Chairman, to which Hudson had readily agreed. Crawshay said Hudson's greatest fault was his predominance over the board of directors, which had happened as a result of his self-will and self-confidence. That was the bane under which he suffered, rather than from any intended misdeeds. He said Hudson now suffered the results of his peccadilloes. After noting the difficulty of reading his handwriting, Crawshay read out Hudson's letter of resignation:

> I have to convey to you my resignation of the office of director, which I have so long had the honour to hold in your company. The position in which I have felt myself to be placed has been so painful to me so as to incapacitate me from the discharge of those active duties which you have a right to expect from whoever may be entrusted with the conduct of your affairs. It becomes me, therefore, to retire from your service. In doing so, I would express my anxious hope that the depression which now exists, aggravated in your case by causes of a temporary character, may pass away, and it may again be my good fortune to witness the renewed prosperity of a line in which I retain so deep an interest.

Crawshay concluded the meeting by describing Hudson as a 'fallen man'; he had fallen from the highest pinnacle of railway glory to the lowest grade and Crawshay said he felt for him from his heart and soul. He would not kick a fallen man in any way, adding that he hoped Hudson would be able to vindicate his character, but it was by no means possible to say he was blameless for everything that had happened to him.

On 28 February 1849, a week after the YNM and YNB half yearly meetings, Hudson was due to attend a half-yearly meeting of the ECR. It would seem he knew the game was up. His time at the ECR had not been the success he had hoped it would be. He had fought long and hard against the Great Northern Railway's rival route to the north of England and lost. In addition, the ECR had terrible problems with punctuality and safety, which he found difficult to resolve. Nor did his cost cutting help and shareholders were beginning to get restless about the Chairman they had eagerly appointed, but who had not delivered the promised higher profits. Having suffered the embarrassment of having a committee of inquiry set up by the YNB to look into his management of that company, he clearly understood he would be in for a tough time in front of the ECR's shareholders. He was not usually fazed when it came to difficult meetings but, following his experience with the YNB a few days earlier and knowing it would be yet another difficult meeting, he decided against attending the meeting. He wrote a letter from Newby Park, dated 25 February, advising David Waddington, the vice chairman of the ECR, that he would not be attending the meeting. Effectively this letter sealed his resignation as chairman of the company. At the meeting Hudson, Waddington and the other directors of the ECR were heavily criticised by the shareholders, who resolved to set up a committee of inquiry to investigate the board's management of the company since Hudson was appointed chairman in 1845.

Following the publication of the committee's findings at the end of April, two separate groups of shareholders submitted petitions to the Commons calling for Hudson, Waddington and a third director, John

Bagshaw, to be expelled from the House. One petition was signed by 60 shareholders, the other by 31. Both petitions were debated in the House on 17 May 1849. In his statement to the House, Hudson said that although he had been unwell recently, he considered it important to attend the House in order to answer the petitions. Reflecting his poor state of health, both physical and mental, Hudson was recorded as speaking with some agitation and occasionally abruptly and hurriedly, making it difficult to hear some of his words. Explaining his position, Hudson recalled that in October 1845, seven-eighths of the ECR's shareholders had asked him to become chairman of their company. At first he had refused, but after some pressure, he had agreed. He had no shares in the company before he became its chairman. His main aim in joining the company had been to improve matters for the shareholders and to effect some arrangement with the then projected London and York railway.

He told the House that he had raised the company's dividend from 3 shillings to 9 shillings per share in his first half-year. One of the petitions had claimed that he did this without any change in the financial status of the company but, Hudson said, when he joined the ECR, the shares rose to the 'highest level they had ever been since' and that there had been ample justification for an increase in the dividend. In the half year ending July 1845, gross income of the railway was £114,000 and in the half year to July 1846, £173,000. He claimed that during the period of his chairmanship the capital value of the company had risen from £5.3million to £10.8million and turnover had increased, from £228,000 in 1845, to £800,000 in 1848. Such increases, he said, brought to the ground the petitioners' claims that money was wasted and extravagantly used.

Hudson criticised the ECR's committee of inquiry for not giving him any information about his alleged misdemeanours and for not giving him a hearing, although he did admit he had received 'three or four' written questions – this statement was not wholly accurate as he had been questioned in person by the committee in April 1849. He said he had been shown some documents, allegedly in his own handwriting, that were purported to prove he had altered the accounts but, he said, the documents were not in his handwriting, and he denied he was responsible for making any alterations to the accounts. He said he had been accused of authorising a charge of £115,000 to be moved from the revenue to the capital account, but he had no hesitation in saying he had done no such thing, adding that the ill-will directed at him by the ECR's committee of inquiry showed they were not entitled to any credit from the House.

Hudson insisted he had done nothing to improperly enhance the value of the ECR's shares and that he had not bought or sold any shares since those he bought when he became chairman. At the end of his statement, Hudson said he was ready to bow to any decision the House might come to, especially as he was ready and anxious to clear his name of any wrongdoing. When he sat down there were loud cheers in his support. Despite his problems, Hudson clearly still had many friends in the House. David Waddington and John Bagshaw also successfully defended themselves and, at the end of the debate, the petitions were ordered to 'lie on the table', effectively meaning that no further action would be taken.

The ECR petition infuriated the people of Sunderland. To show support for their MP, a deputation from the town, led by Mayor Joseph Simpson, visited Hudson at his Newby Park home in May 1849 to present him with a testimonial of their appreciation. In his formal address to Hudson, the Mayor said that he wanted, on behalf of the people of Sunderland, to express their confidence in him and that they abhorred the 'unjust attacks and unmeasured abuse to which you have been recently exposed.' The aspersions that had been cast on his reputation were, Simpson said, the result of disappointed feelings of those who had suffered from the depressed state of the railway share market. He added that he believed there was no intention on Hudson's part to do wrong. The people of Sunderland, he said, wanted to express their gratitude for the extensive benefits to the nation that Hudson had brought about by his 'gigantic undertakings' and his untiring energies.

Replying to Simpson's address, Hudson said it gave him great satisfaction to know that he still had the unshaken confidence of his constituents. Agreeing with Simpson, Hudson said he had no intention to do wrong. On the contrary he only ever considered the general advancement of the great concerns under his care. In his opinion, there was no doubt that the serious economic depression of the times had caused considerable disappointment to many and none more so than himself. He expressed the hope that once the present 'excitement' had passed, the right judging British public would again give him 'indulgent consideration.'

Commenting on Hudson's troubles, the *Elgin Courier* wrote that he may truly say 'misfortunes never come singly' and, as if losing all his railway companies was not bad enough, on 11 July 1849 he lost his final directorship when he felt obliged to tender his resignation as chairman of the York Union Bank.

A staunch defender of Hudson at the time of his troubles in the first few months of 1849 was the York-born artist William Etty. Like Hudson, Etty had himself been a controversial figure in younger days, principally because many of his paintings depicting nudes were considered to be too lifelike. Despite such critics, he was otherwise much acclaimed for his work. He exhibited at the Royal Academy for the first time at the age of 24 in 1811 and in 1828 he was elected a Royal Academician, at the time the highest honour available to an artist. Richard Nicholson was one of Etty's most enthusiastic benefactors, buying more than fifty of his paintings. In 1838 Etty painted Elizabeth Hudson's portrait, which has a story of its own (see Chapter 19).

In a letter addressed 'To My Fellow-Citizens' published in the *York Herald* in April 1849, Etty strongly defended Hudson. He said he had written to the public press on various occasions to advocate measures he thought good for the interests of York. Now he was moved to write about George Hudson who, even if guilty to the extent his worst enemies suggested, was still deserving of charity. 'Here is our brother', he went on, 'fallen under our censure! What did Christ say?

"He that is without fault amongst you, let him cast the first stone!'" Even supposing Hudson might be culpable, Etty said he would still feel safe to risk his 'existence on the honour and honesty of George Hudson.' Etty continued:

> He was made for carrying this mighty change, a powerful engine, changing the current face of society, and none but a man of his power and energy could have done it. But if ever I set eyes on a man — and I have had some experience — whose manly port, physiognomy, and whole bearing, characterized an honest man, a man superior to all meanness, it is George Hudson, a man I am proud to call my friend because I know him to be kind-hearted, generous, and public-spirited to the last degree.
>
> I was only twice in my life in a railway carriage with him, and on one of them Mr. Hudson gave £400 or £500 to a church at Darlington for the railway men without hesitation. Let us not, because a man, a fellow-citizen, differs from us in religion or politics ... regard him, in some degree, as an enemy, in a free country like this.
>
> Let me entreat of you, my fellow-citizens, to think of the great personal exertions he has made for your welfare, as your chief magistrate, of the sacrifices he has made to public duty on so many occasions and charitably to give him that consideration and confidence again I think he so entirely deserves.

In his biography of the artist, published in 1853, Alexander Gilchrist wrote that Etty was not an investor in railways and so had not become a friend of Hudson for a 'sordid purpose' that is, to curry favour for shares. His friendship was based purely on the fact that Hudson had always treated him in a friendly manner. Etty was not the type of person to think ill of another just because all the world did. Nevertheless,

Gilchrist says, people in York, in the midst of the odium then surrounding Hudson, were astonished to see Etty's letter defending him and he was subjected to much criticism. Gilchrist comments that to those who did not know Etty, his comments were inexplicable, whereas those who did know him saw his 'childlike goodness of heart and unworldliness.' He showed courageous good faith to say that he was proud to call Hudson his friend at a moment when Hudson had few friends. He remained a friend of Hudson to the end of his days.

In its leader article of 1 May 1849, *The Times* noted that when Hudson had first come on the scene, railways had been at a very low ebb and had paid little in the way of dividends, and shares were at a discount. In the midst of this gloom *The Times* said that it had become known that there was a man in the north of England who had created order out of the chaos. George Hudson had filled northern England with good dividends and good share premiums and was worshipped with thanks for what he had achieved for all and had been awarded a Testimonial for his efforts.

How times had changed. Now Hudson was taking the blame for the collapse of the railway bubble and the losses many suffered through declining share prices and dividends. His critics took little account of the prevailing economic crisis, except to blame that on the folly of the Railway Mania and no account had been taken of the fact that none of the principal railway companies went out of business as a result of the crash. Many observers had forecast the bubble would burst at some point, so it should not have been a big surprise when it finally did. It is somewhat ironic that Hudson should have taken the blame when the person to have suffered the most as a result of his fall from power was Hudson himself.

In an article entitled 'The Horrid Hudson', which was originally published in the *Spectator* magazine and then syndicated to newspapers across the country, the correspondent wrote it was remarkable that, in all his manoeuvres, Hudson had never lacked an accomplice. There was always someone to sign a cheque without asking any questions; to make a fictitious registration; or accept a judicious allotment of shares.

These accomplices acted with their eyes shut. The correspondent said it was very difficult to think that these people did not know what they were doing, thus their culpability matched Hudson's; there was general acquiescence amongst those who now accused him and whose virtuous indignation only dawned when there were no more profits. They and the shareholders had made Hudson what he was.

Reporting on the second report of the YNB committee of Inquiry in July 1849, the *Leeds Intelligencer* agreed with the *Spectator,* commenting that, from the 'astonishing facts' the committee had found, there was 'great disgrace upon many more persons than him [Hudson] who has hitherto been considered the chief offender.' The *Intelligencer* implicated a number of other directors as being complicit in Hudson's unlawful deals, including Richard Nicholson, James Richardson, Thomas Backhouse, George Dodsworth and Robert Davies, although, in their defence, the *Intelligencer* wrote that they had benefitted far less than Hudson. The paper said the enormity of the charges against Hudson had shown that:

> the character of this man, once so high, is utterly blasted. Yet for how much of this has not the grasping, tortuous and gambling spirit of Railway policy to answer? One can now better comprehend the secret of those bold engagements, those extensions, and leasings and guaranteeings, and huge purchases, and various collateral undertakings, which, while they astonished by their vastness, were regarded, with implicit and unreasoning confidence, as master-strokes of enterprise and daring success. These were the transactions which chiefly afforded opportunities and temporary concealment for the private booty now detected.

Following the exposure of his misdemeanours in the spring and summer of 1849, it would not have been a surprise to Hudson to learn that many of his colleagues on York Council would seek to end his political association with York. Bearing in mind the discredit that attached to him as a result of his fall from grace, many on the council hoped that Hudson would do the decent thing and resign his Aldermanic office. But, if he did not, they were ready to have him expelled.

A prerequisite for qualifying for the office of Alderman was that the person had to be resident in York, but Hudson had sold his house in Monkgate during 1847 and was now, whilst in Yorkshire at least, living permanently only at his Newby Park home. Whether he knew that not having a permanent residence in York would affect his position as an Alderman is not known. When he needed to stay in York after he sold his Monkgate house, he would take up residence in a flat at York railway station. Nevertheless, it seems odd and out of character, for him to have sold his York residence when he still had business interests in the city. As the 'Railway King', Hudson may have considered himself immune from any rules about residency. Whatever he thought, he was about to find out that his non-residency would cost him his role as an Alderman. At the annual Council meeting in November 1849, it was agreed that because he had not been resident in the city for the past six months, his office was now considered void and his office declared vacant.

If being stripped of his Aldermanic office was not humiliation enough, Tory Alderman Matterson put forward a motion that his portrait, in which Hudson was depicted in the City's full mayoral robes and regalia, be removed from York Mansion House. The Lord Mayor elect (George Seymour) and others, possibly fearing that Matterson meant that the portrait should be destroyed, considered that to preserve the dignity of the City Council, such a proposal should be ignored at least for the present. Matterson persisted and his proposal went to a vote of the whole Council. Eleven members concurred with Matterson's proposal, whilst 13 voted against. Nine members of the Council abstained from the vote. Amongst those who abstained were William Gray, the former Lord Mayor Sir John Simpson, George Seymour and most notably of all George Leeman, Hudson's long time and most vociferous foe. It needs to be borne in mind that the vote was more about the principle than the person. Nevertheless, the abstention of Leeman would have been quite unexpected. The *York Herald* commented it could not but 'admire the delicacy and forbearance of the present Lord Mayor and Mr Leeman and others' in abstaining from the question. It singled out Leeman in particular, saying he was an opponent of Hudson in the Council and was his successor as chairman of the YNB company. Any other course of action from Leeman would, the paper wrote, have been anything but dignified or gentlemanly. The paper noted that the portrait would be removed at some point but in a different manner, without any appearance of bitterness.

Inevitably cartoons, humorous songs, stories and jokes began to appear in the press about Hudson and his predicament. For example, the following joke from *The Puppet-Show*: 'The Queen has lately held an Investiture of the Most Honourable Order of the Bath. We are perfectly surprised that Mr Hudson was not one of the highly favoured, as his conscience must require a most extraordinary washing.'

The nineteenth-century social philosopher and satirist, Thomas Carlyle was no fan of Hudson. He was also unimpressed by the public rush into railway shares during the Railway Mania. In July 1850, with reference to a suggestion that the testimonial raised for Hudson in 1845 should have been used to raise a statue in his honour, Carlyle wrote a polemic called 'Hudson's Statue', in which he mockingly wrote that Hudson was by far the most authentic king that had been elected by the people. Carlyle took the opportunity to savagely criticise those who had taken part in the Mania for railway shares. Being deliberately ironic, Carlyle wrote it was a matter of regret that the statue was not built, as the incarnation of the 'English Vishnu' could not now be molten. Had it been, Carlyle wrote, the country's new 'religion' could have been represented by a locomotive 'garnished with scrip-rolls' and erected next to the Wellington Arch at Hyde Park Corner in London. He chided Hudson's supporters by saying they should go ahead with the statue, so that all could see the pinnacle of the English world. He said Hudson's worth to mankind in the matter of railways would prove to be 'trifling' and that as 'much as we love railways ... no town will stand where it did', which would be a most 'unexpected and indeed most disastrous result.' Carlyle said business would be lost to other towns, which was completely the opposite of what happened in reality, as towns and cities that joined the network were able to send their goods and manufactures far and wide around the country and abroad.

The railways, according to Carlyle, had spread too quickly. He said Hudson, who he described as a great 'swollen gambler', had driven the railway revolution too fast and that had the railways been built over fifty-five years rather than five, scrip-holders who were now coinless would have had more of a chance of keeping their money. He also questioned Hudson's worth to railways and concluded that it would turn out 'to be extremely inconsiderable.' He could not have been more wrong!

A cartoon of the time showed Hudson's effigy being moved to Madam Tussaud's Chamber of Horrors, whilst another reflected on the fate that befell those who were taken in by the mad rush into railway shares during the Railway Mania.

It was widely rumoured that Hudson's waxwork was melted down after his fall from grace, but this was not the case. It was taken down and put in to storage and following his death in 1871, it was put back on display.

But not everyone was unsympathetic to Hudson. In March 1849, shortly after Hudson's errors first came to light, the *Carlisle Patriot* carried an article in which it said that under the maxim of English Law, a man remained innocent until he was proved guilty but, the paper emphasised 'not in this case.' It suggested that Hudson had hosts of enemies, some from the motives of self-interest, some from envy, some from jealousy and a still greater number from motives altogether political. As a result, the *Patriot* concluded, Hudson had first been found guilty and then tried. The paper also took aim at its rival newspaper the *Carlisle Journal* which, following Hudson's offer to repay his companies any sums he may have gained at their expense, quipped there was not a pickpocket who, on threat of imprisonment, would not offer to repay their ill-gotten gains. The *Patriot* responded, 'How extremely virtuous all this is we need not say', adding that the moral philosophers would be charmed by it and the haters of railway gambling would be in ecstasies. The paper went on to list some prominent citizens of Carlisle who had themselves indulged in railway gambling, such as James Steel, the owner of the *Carlisle Journal*, who had 'no less than' £1,500 invested in railway shares; Robert Bendle, a solicitor, who had £10,000 invested; Thomas Coullard, a well-known naturalist, £12,360; and George Dixon, the Mayor of Carlisle at the time, £2,500. The *Patriot* said they had not expected to find James Steel, who had so indignantly denounced Hudson for railway gambling, was himself up to his neck in the thing he so severely condemned. 'All men are liars' the Psalmist says, but 'certain it is that some men are hypocrites.'

In July 1849, under the heading 'George Hudson and His Censors', *John Bull* magazine published an article strongly criticising the behaviour of the press for its treatment of Hudson:

> 'Shed blood enough old Renault!' exclaims Pierre, in Venice Preserved, to a hoary headed conspirator, to whom victory is nothing without wholesale slaughter, and in whose eyes justice herself looks vulgar and commonplace unless crimsoned with gore. 'When you have an enemy in chancery' reasoned old Renault, 'there is nothing like giving him a bellyful', so think of some of our contemporaries with the Member for Sunderland at their mercy. It is not often that you can kick a man with perfect satisfaction to everybody, except the individual immediately concerned in the performance, and it is therefore a pity not to make the most of a rare opportunity. It is tolerably certain that the writers against Mr. Hudson, at the present period of that unfortunate gentleman's career, are safe from contradiction.

They are fighting in a field in which they have not only the choice of position, and the sympathy of every bystander, but their opponent disarmed, and tied hand and foot before them. Under such circumstances, to strike once is to answer all the purposes of the meeting; to strike not at all is chivalrous; but to strike again and again, till the victim not only loses the breath of life but the form of humanity itself, is the rankest cowardice.'

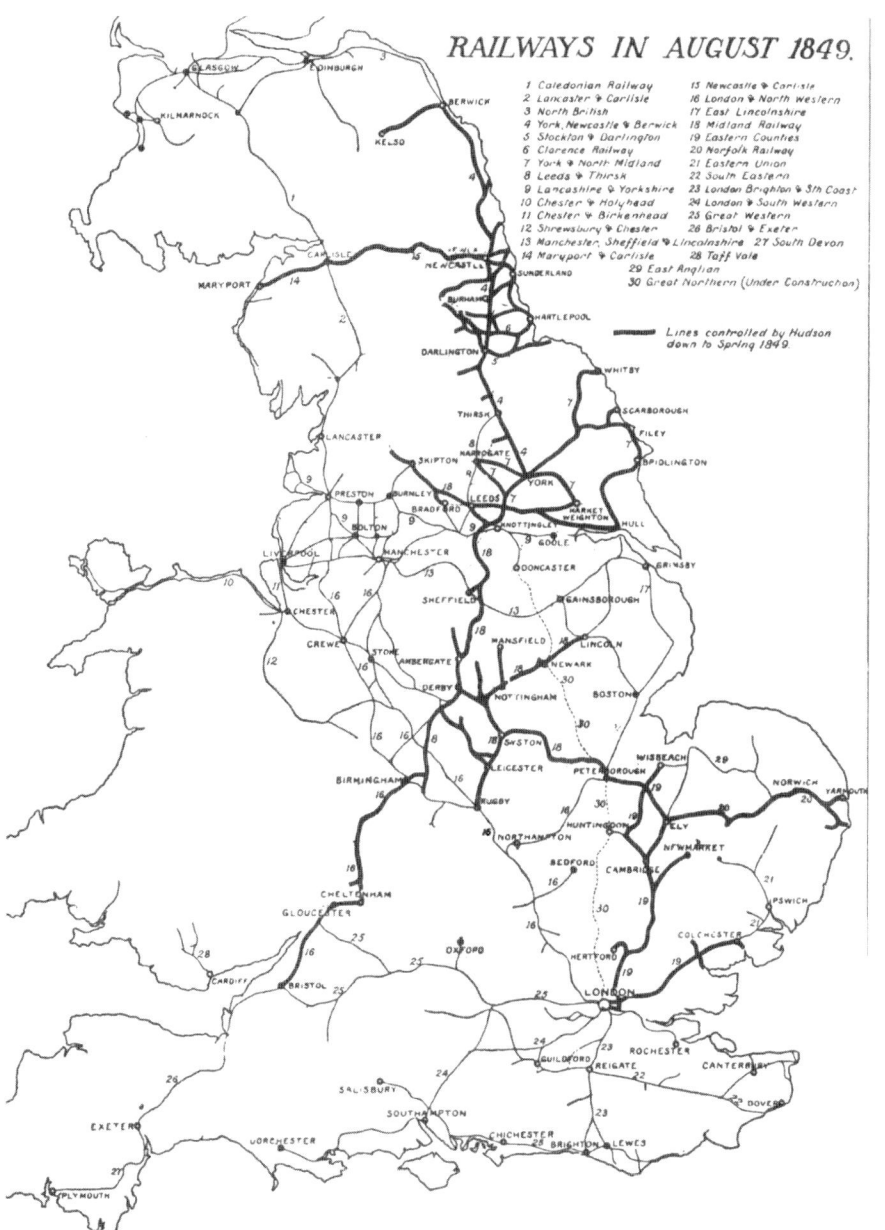

Map showing lines under George Hudson's control in Spring 1849.

Portrait of George Hudson by Thomas McLean, November 1845. (Author's collection)

Hudson's drapery shop in College Street, York, depicted in April 1849. (Illustrated London News)

Silhouette and water colour portrait of George and Elizabeth Hudson and their four children, William, George, John and Ann at York Mansion House in 1838. Artist unknown. (National Portrait Gallery, London)

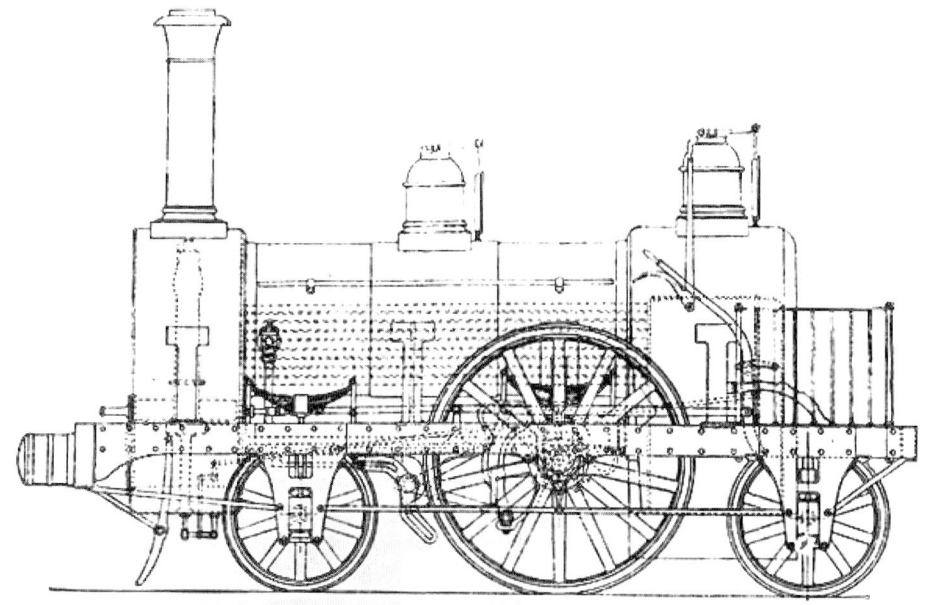

York and North Midland 4-coupled express locomotive No 185, built by Robert Stephenson & Co of Newcastle in 1848. (Author's collection)

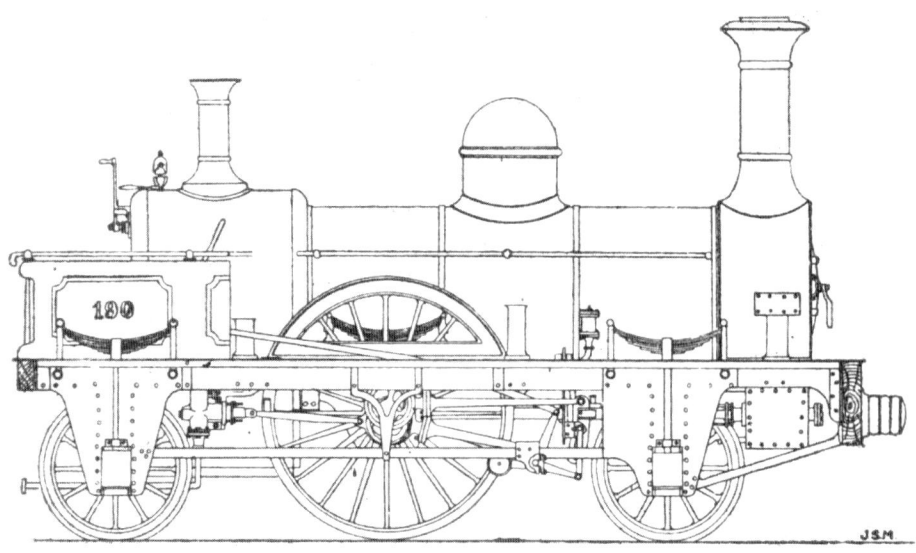

York, Newcastle and Berwick locomotive No 190, built by Robert Stephenson & Co of Newcastle in 1849. (Author's collection)

Marble bust of Hudson, sculpted in 1847 by Matthew Noble, on display at the National Railway Museum, York. (Author's collection)

A contemporary cartoonist's comical design of a statue that could have been funded by Hudson's testimonial. (Author's collection)

Handbill announcing a Hudson campaign meeting in Sunderland, July 1845. (David Hudson Smith collection)

Hudson welcomes Queen Victoria aboard the Royal Train at Cambridge following Prince Albert's installation as Chancellor of Cambridge University in July 1847. (Illustrated London News)

Hudson portrayed at a committee meeting of the House of Commons, July 1847. (The Pictorial Times)

The Hudsons' Newby Park home in the 1930s. (David Hudson Smith collection)

Poster advertising a Hudson election meeting in Sunderland, August 1847. (David Hudson Smith collection)

Hudson laying the foundation stone of the new dock at Sunderland, February 1848. (Illustrated London News)

1 Albert Gate, the Hudsons' London home 1845-1854. (Martin Addison, Creative Commons, wikimedia.org)

The drawing room at Albert Gate in 1902, showing the ornate foliate decoration on the wall panels and ceiling. The room likely little changed since the Hudsons' occupied the house. (Historic England)

The Ballroom at Albert Gate, with its classically influenced decorations, in 1902. Like the drawing room, it had probably changed little from the time the Hudsons' lived there. (Historic England)

THE LAST ROYAL FLIGHT;
OR, GOOD-BYE TO THE RAILWAY KING.

The Last Royal Flight – Cartoon published in 1849 by *The Puppet-Show*, a satirical magazine similar to *Punch*. (David Hudson Smith collection)

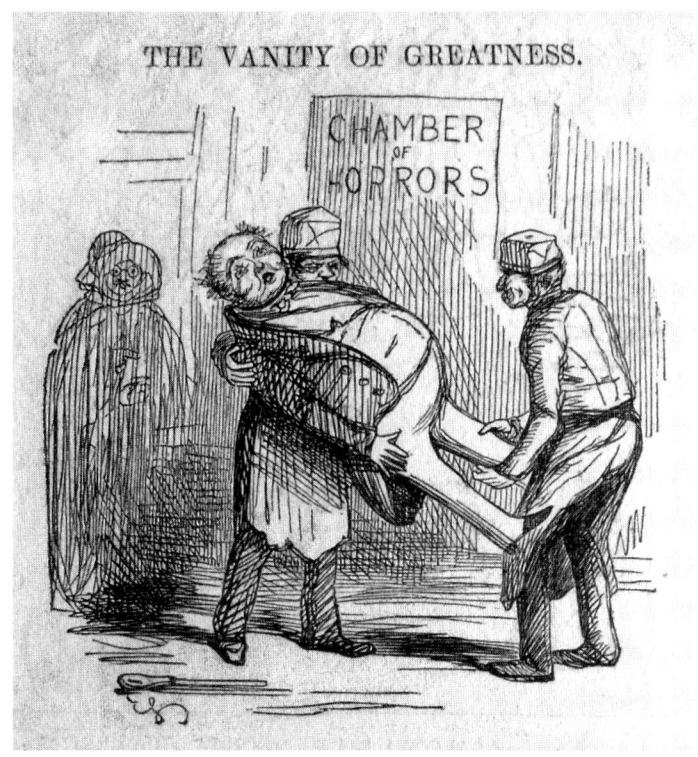

Cartoon showing Hudson's effigy being moved to Madame Tussaud's Chamber of Horrors in 1849. (Author's collection)

Investors sliding into the pit of ruin. (Author's collection)

REPORT OF THE EVIDENCE

OF

GEORGE HUDSON, ESQ., M.P.

ON THE TRIAL OF THE CAUSE OF

RICHARDSON *versus* WODSON,

York Summer Assizes, 1850.

EDITED BY A BARRISTER.

SECOND EDITION.

LONDON:
JOHN HEARNE, 81, STRAND.

Price Sixpence.

Cover of John Hearne's pamphlet summarising the Richardson v Wodson libel trial. (Author's collection)

No. 18.—SUNDERLAND.—"The Railway King."

Hudson was said to look ten years older than his real age. This caricature of him appeared in the satirical *Diogenes* magazine when he was in his mid-fifties. (David Hudson Smith collection)

Hudson's last resting place at Scrayingham church in 2022. (Author's collection)

Chapter 10

Hudson's Explanation

It should not, perhaps, have been surprising that with the enormous burden of work which he set himself, Hudson lost focus when conducting some of the arrangements necessary to ensure the success and profitability of his railway companies. For much of 1849, he remained at his home Newby Park in North Yorkshire, no doubt ruminating on his predicament and thinking about his future. He spent much of his time formulating a long letter in which he would put his side of the story concerning the actions he took during his time as chairman of the YNB. The letter was published in January 1850 and was carried by many of the newspapers of the day. Inevitably there was criticism that he had taken too long to write the letter and that it was deficient in admitting that he was at fault for the problems that had arisen at the YNB.

Introducing his letter, Hudson wrote that whilst the questions between him and the company were pending a decision by a legal tribunal, he had no alternative but to wait before the questions could be calmly and impartially discussed. However, now the YNB had decided not to take legal proceedings against him, he wanted to take the opportunity to answer some of the imputations made against him, particularly with regard to the Brandling Junction Railway shares; the Newcastle and Berwick shares; his shareholding in the Sunderland Dock company; and the iron rails.

Referring first to the Brandling Junction Railway, Hudson said the shares had been given to him at a meeting of the company held on 4 February 1845 and that no one at the meeting opposed this proposition. Having acquired them, he had given some to people who had given valuable assistance to the company. He never imagined that four years later the company's shareholders' decision to allocate these shares to him would be questioned in the way it had been.

So far as his shares in the Newcastle and Berwick Railway (N&B) were concerned, Hudson said these did not exceed the number he had subscribed for before the company received its Act of Parliament. Having subscribed for them, he considered himself obligated to take them up and never imagined there would be any doubt or question about his acquisition. Had he not taken them, he said he could imagine the committee of inquiry recommending he be compelled to take them up rather than, as now, calling on him to account for the proceeds. He said he did not want to say any more about the powerful opposition he encountered to get the N&B Act through parliament, or the personal sacrifices he made, but it was widely recognised that he had worked very hard to get the Act passed. As a result he considered he was justly entitled to the shares for which he had contracted, a right he said that was now being denied him.

On the Sunderland Dock company, Hudson said he had subscribed for 2,500 shares on a personal basis. It was evident to him that the YNB would benefit hugely from the new dock and that the company should assist in speeding up their completion. He discussed the matter with two directors at the time and it was agreed that the company would buy 2,345 additional shares. He admitted these shares had been registered in his name and those of the other two directors, but there was no prospect of direct benefit. He admitted he and the other two directors had exceeded their legal authority, because they had not sought parliamentary approval as was required at the time, nevertheless he and the other two directors had acted in the best interests of the company. Now, he said, the company was refusing to recognise these shares and holding him accountable for them. He added that the company had accepted the purchase of shares in the West Durham Railway bought by him in a similar manner but, as it was advantageous to the company to have these shares, they accepted them. Hudson further admitted that legally speaking the responsibility of buying the Sunderland Dock shares might rest with him, but every shareholder 'must feel that I have been guilty of no dishonourable act.'

Hudson then turned to the issue of the iron rails. He recounted that in October 1844, when the price of iron was low, he thought a speculation in rails would likely be successful, so he made a contract for a large quantity from Thompson and Forman of London (T&F). He offered others a share in the speculation, but they considered the risk of loss too high to take part and the speculation remained his own. The price of iron subsequently rose, and he considered he was entitled to the enhanced worth of his own iron. In March 1845, tenders were invited to supply iron rails to the YNB. T&F was amongst the tenderers and they won the tender. They supplied not only rails from their own stock but also some which they had sold to Hudson and which they still held on his behalf. Hudson said this transaction was complained of by the committee, but he considered it entirely legal; he had received the market rate for the iron, the same price that T&F received. If he had not supplied one ton of iron then the whole order would have been supplied by T&F at the same price, which the YNB would have paid. Hudson said he did not benefit by the transaction, as he could have procured iron from other companies at the same price. He said some might say it was illegal for him to sell iron to a company of which he was a director, but he did not believe such a transaction was invalid for, even though the law had recently been changed to prevent such an occurrence from happening in the future, in his case the transaction occurred before the law changed and thus the new provisions of the law did not apply to his transaction.

Addressing the fact that he had agreed and paid a sum of money to the company, Hudson said he was strongly opposed to giving in to the company's demands and had taken legal advice and been advised that no legal claim could be made against him by the company. However, he was also advised that if he were to pursue his case through the courts this would likely result in years of litigation and be the cause of enormous expense and endless annoyance and anxiety. Thus, he had decided to agree to the arrangements proposed for the Brandling Junction shares and to take on the entire responsibility for the Sunderland Dock shares.

Hudson said he would not make any comment on the keeping of the company's accounts as 'no two men' could agree what should be allocated to the capital and to the revenue accounts; every item allocated would require examination. He did, however, provide an explanation for the perceived errors in the YNB's accounts. It was, he said, reported that in 1848, £107,371 was charged against capital rather than revenue and that traffic had been over reported by £14,353. Under the former sum, £17,959 occurs under 'Interest on Debentures.' This was the only sum since the formation of the railway to have been carried to the debit of the capital account. £59,812 arose from the directors not having charged some interest which was due but not paid and some tradesmen's bills which had not been seen by the directors at the time the accounts were prepared.

A balance of £29,601 also needed to be accounted for, much of that sum was in respect of charging to capital the cost of repairing engines and stock of the Brandling Junction Railway which had been inherited by the company in a bad state of repair. There were, Hudson admitted, some errors in the accounts which the committee should put right. For example, a sum of £62,452 was shown as due for the stock of the Hartlepool Dock and Railway. This had been paid previously and was an error of no slight magnitude, but one which he said had its origins in a mistake. Of the over-reported traffic, £3,797 arose from an over-estimate of receipts for carrying mail. The balance of £10,755 was an over-estimate of traffic. Hudson said this was due to including fractional weeks at the year-end which would have righted itself in the following year's accounts in which case he would have avoided any censure.

Hudson then addressed the accusation that the company's accounts had been swollen with a view to increasing the share price and increasing the rate of dividend, both for his own gain. A charge of unquestionable importance, as Hudson put it, but he said, fortunately for him, one that rested on no solid foundation. Actual earnings of the company were £1,621,569, a sum which he said made the over-reported traffic of £14,553 utterly insignificant, to say nothing of the dividend being more than covered by the undivided profits of £59,777. In addition, the accounts had not been credited with the large sum due for interest on arrears of share calls, even though the accounts had been debited for the dividends declared, a circumstance which was unlikely if it had been intended to publish inflated accounts.

Hudson noted there had been a decline in the value of all railway shares, but in all but one case the falls had been much larger than in the YNB. He commented that one of the causes for the decline in share values was the creation of competing lines of railway and the premature establishment of branch lines. He was against both, but his advice was unheeded. He added that, in approving many new railways, parliament had been carried away with the outcry for competition, shortened distances and cheaper fares. As a result, he and other railway promoters had been obliged to adopt the same 'objectionable system' in self-defence, not having the power to resist. It was of note, he said, that the committee had not found it possible to condemn such lines. In respect of competing lines and unprofitable branch lines, Hudson could be said to have been 120 years before his time. The infamous Beeching Report of 1963 similarly attacked the operation of competing lines and loss-making branch lines. Had Hudson's policies been adopted by parliament at the time, Beeching may not have had so much work to do!

Concluding his letter, Hudson admitted that some of his transactions were to be regretted, but it was some consolation to him to reflect that the company had in no instance sustained pecuniary loss. He also made the very valid point that the company's shareholders should have considered these transactions taking into account the excited period in which they occurred – the years of Railway Mania – and the multiplicity of concerns that he was superintending and directing, and of the brief opportunities he had to think and reflect and the impossibility of him giving sufficient attention to the public and private matters that claimed his attention. Hudson said he was convinced of the soundness of the company, and that he would continue to take a great interest in it, with the anxious hope for its future prosperity. He finished his letter by saying 'I disclaim all animosity even towards those who have shown me the least consideration.'

Despite the time and effort Hudson had put in to his letter, the press of the day was not satisfied with his explanations or his reasoning. He was still viewed with disdain. It would seem that whatever he said would have no influence on how he was perceived by the press. They had set out to destroy him, not just for his alleged misdemeanours but because they considered he represented all that was wrong with a public which had sought to profit from the Railway Mania. The *Sunderland Herald*, for example, commented that in his letter Hudson had omitted a number of facts, including that the committee of inquiry had found that the shares in the N&B he held had realised £145,704 for him. So far as the Brandling Junction shares were concerned, there was no actual resolution passed to effect Hudson's allocation, although the paper did admit that, had there been a formal resolution, then it would likely have been approved. But even though the paper accepted Hudson's explanation as satisfactory, it asked if the 'weight of dishonesty which lies upon his shoulders is sensibly diminished?' Answering its own question, the paper said, no – 'we humbly opine that it is as heavy as ever.'

Of the Sunderland Dock shares, the *Herald* noted that Hudson had admitted these were not taken by him and his other directors with legal sanction, but that he would have legalised the purchase had it not been for an accident [unspecified] and this was an error on his part. The paper said Hudson bought the shares on behalf of the company, but there was no record of them being on the company's books and the payment for the shares was made from company funds, which was kept out of the accounts until two years after the payment were made. On the iron rails, the *Herald* said Hudson had admitted the facts, but he seemed unable to understand the impropriety, the illegality, of what he had done. The *Herald* made no attempt to tell its readers of Hudson's explanation that he did not see anything wrong in what he did or that the law changed after Hudson had struck his deals.

The *Herald* said it was the 'very sublime of coolness' that Hudson wrote it was some consolation to him that, while some transactions were to be regretted, the company had sustained no pecuniary loss. The paper blamed Hudson's dishonesty of management for the depreciation in the company's share price and claimed that many hard-working people who invested their money in his 'crooked accounts' and 'fictitious dividends' were ruined. The paper completely ignored the fact that the public invested in railways other than Hudson's and that they too lost money when the bubble burst. As for claiming that Hudson authorised 'fictitious' dividends, although the basis on which they were calculated might have been questionable, the fact remains that they were actually paid out. In this sense they were genuine dividends. No one complained at the time, and no one lost out, though they may have been gullible in thinking that the situation could last. The dividends may have been high in relation to earnings and profits, but greedy investors were happy to receive them while they lasted. Perhaps investors should have known better; there had been previous investment bubbles that had ended in tears (the much smaller railway bubbles of the 1820s and 1830s for example). It is said that if something is too good to be true, then it usually is, and this was the case with railway share prices and dividends during the Railway Mania.

The *Herald* wrote of the 'misery of widows and orphans made beggars by their trust in the falsehoods of this man and his imitators.' Whilst it is true that those investors who were unfortunate enough to have invested when the market reached its peak would have lost money, they would not have lost everything provided they had invested their money sensibly. None of Hudson's companies actually went out of business as a result of the bubble bursting and they were still paying out dividends, even if at a much lower rate than during the heady days of the Mania.

The paper's reference to Hudson's imitators is an interesting observation. Who were these imitators and what penalties did they suffer as a result of the bubble bursting? Certainly none on the scale of Hudson.

Concluding its article, the *Herald* underlined its opinion of Hudson as the nation's bête noir so far as the collapse of the Railway Mania was concerned. Hudson, it said, remained the 'most degraded' figure of the nineteenth century – 'a golden calf hurled off his pedestal into the mire.' But, one might ask, who threw him off? And the answer would be newspapers of the time such as the *Herald*. In one final blast, the *Herald* stated that Sunderland was disgraced by its 'association with this man' as one of their two MPs. However, the *Herald* proved itself to be completely out of step with Sunderland's electors, as they would send Hudson to parliament as their MP in the next two elections!

In addition to its own observations, the *Sunderland Herald* included a copy of a *Times* editorial on Hudson's letter, which was no less condemnatory of his actions. *The Times* wrote that, if Hudson's 'miserable palliations' were compared step by step with the committee's reports, it would be seen he did not deny its conclusions; he had agreed he may have acted illegally over the purchase of the Dock shares and that he bought the iron at a low price and sold it to the YNB at a profit which, if not illegal, was morally wrong. With some indignation, the correspondent said that Hudson had declined the opportunity of going to a tribunal or a court of law but his letter, essentially his admissions, convicted him of the charges against him. The writer did not mention that Hudson had said he had sought legal opinion and was advised he had not done anything unlawful. Then, almost contradicting his own opinion, the writer admits that the YNB decided not to take Hudson to court, as it did not wish to make the situation worse, nor did it want to negatively impact its share price with further bad publicity.

The *Sunderland Herald* also included a piece that appeared in the *Daily News*, a newspaper founded in 1846 by Charles Dickens (no friend of Hudson) as a radical alternative to the *Morning Chronicle*. Hudson, being an ally of arch Conservatives such as Lord George Bentinck and Benjamin Disraeli, was bound to receive extreme criticism from such a publication. The *Daily News* exclaimed:

... this reckless, coarse, insensible and bad man must not be allowed to escape from the consequences of his misconduct, which has ruined hundreds and injured thousands and has damaged the national character itself, by bullying audacity ... if amidst the wreck and devastation of other peoples' fortunes, he cannot recognise or won't feel the immorality of his acts, he ought to be taught in a manner palpable and patent, even to his dull senses, that the country feels for the disgrace he has inflicted on it.

The *Daily News* went on to call for Hudson to be expelled from the Commons – 'If Sunderland can endure such a representative, parliament ought not to tolerate such a member.' The paper commented that although directors of other railway companies had been found wanting and had erred in their judgment (Hope Johnston of the Caledonian Railway and William Chaplin of the London and South Western Railway were mentioned), none had been caught *in flagrante delicto* as Hudson had. This is a very interesting admission as it clearly infers that Hudson was not the only railway director to have had dubious standards. The paper reported that the only reason Hudson had agreed to pay £100,000 back to the YNB was to avoid Chancery proceedings and possibly paying back more. The paper commented that 'Chancery is, no doubt, a dismal place for honest men; but it is the very paradise of rogues.' If that was the case then surely, if Hudson was such a rogue, he would have preferred to have ended up in Chancery? 'No' the *News* said, it was because he did not want to pay more than the £100,000.

The *Newcastle Guardian* was a little more sanguine, saying Hudson's letter was a mild harmless document that resembled what might be called in a Scottish Court, after someone has been found guilty, 'exculpating evidence.' However, the paper said, Hudson's letter was not evidence. The facts and figures were against him therefore his letter did not need to be discussed in any detail, except to say that it did not alter their view of Hudson's behaviour 'one jot', he was still as guilty as ever. The paper said Hudson's letter did not disprove a single charge against him and he could not be whitewashed by himself or his friends. His disgrace must adhere to him so long as morality and honesty influence society.

One of the major criticisms levelled at Hudson was his desire to pay out high dividends to shareholders. However, even Hudson recognised that the high dividend levels of the mid-1840s could not be sustained for ever. In the final years of his time as chairman, dividends of his companies went down. From his reputation it might be assumed that Hudson's railway companies were the only ones paying high dividends to shareholders. Although the YNM dividend remained high, a number of other railway companies also paid out high dividends during the years of the Railway Mania, as the following Table shows:

Year-end dividend payments of England's leading railways:

	1844	1845	1846	1847	1848
LNWR	*	*	10	8	7
GWR	8	8	8	7	6
Midland	6	7.5	7	7	5
L&Y	8	8	7	7	5
YNM	10	10	10	10	6
YNB	8	9	9	9	6
LSWR	8	8.5	8.5	8	5
SER	4.5	5	6	6	5
LBSCR	-	-	7	4	2.5
ECR	2.5	6	6.5	4	-**

Source: *The Railway Mania and its aftermath* by Henry Grote Lewin (published 1936)

* Lewin noted that the constituent companies of the LNWR (i.e. the Liverpool & Manchester; the London and Birmingham Railway; and the Grand Junction Railway) all regularly paid 10 per cent dividends in the years prior to 1846.

** although the ECR declared an interim dividend of 4 per cent in 1848, it did not declare a year-end dividend.

Although his railway career had come to an end and his reputation in York had been shattered, Hudson remained a popular figure in Whitby, Sunderland and Newcastle. In Whitby, his development of grand houses and a luxury hotel had brought prosperity to the town; in Sunderland he had played a major role in the construction of the town's new docks and was still a popular MP; in Newcastle he remained popular for pushing for the construction of the high-level bridge over the River Tyne, thus ensuring the railway went through the town rather than around it.

Chapter 11

Hudson's Last Hurrah

1849 had truly proved to be Hudson's *annus horribilis*. In an attempt to break the monotony of gloom and regain some sense of normality, if not self-respect, Hudson decided to return to London and immerse himself once more in the business of the Commons. On 15 April 1850 he took part in a debate on new Stamp Duty legislation and later the same month, he spoke in favour of settling a question concerning the duty imposed on timber imported for use in shipbuilding. In June, during the second reading of a proposed 'Burgess List' Bill (which sought reform for listing eligible electors at local elections), he said he had received a petition from his Sunderland constituency entreating him to vote against the Bill.

On 19 June 1850, the day before the opening of Sunderland's new dock, Hudson was invited to an evening reception at Joseph Wright's house in Fawcett Street, Sunderland. At this reception he was presented with an address from the Committee of Seamen of Sunderland. Printed on satin, the address thanked Hudson for his kindness to the seamen of Sunderland and for his support in parliament in connection with the Merchant Seamen's Fund Bill and the Merchant Service Bill. It thanked him also for his support in supporting the legal preference for the use of British built and outfitted ships manned by British seamen as opposed to foreign ships manned by low paid seamen. The address acknowledged his support for the new dock which, without his enterprise and endeavour, would never have been built. The new dock would be appreciated by all in the town and neighbourhood of Sunderland. They thanked him too for his 'munificent donations' to private and public charities and noted that he had greatly contributed to the promotion of trade in the town and to providing employment to thousands of people. The address wished him and his 'very amiable lady and family' health and happiness for the future.

Hudson was greatly touched by the gesture. He thanked the Committee for their address and assured them of his full support for defending their rights. He would also assist in continuing to help with carrying out social improvements in the town. He noted particularly that the Committee in their address had referred to Mrs Hudson. He said she would be deeply appreciative of their kindness and the honour of remembering her in their address.

On the morning of 20 June, a large procession was assembled in Sunderland High Street to march to the Ferry Boat landing. The Dock Master led the procession with the Union flag, accompanied by the band of the 33rd Regiment of Foot, which had a barracks in Sunderland. They were followed by the River Commissioners, the Mayor (William Ord), shipowners, coal owners, and various others including the directors of the YNB and directors of the Dock Company. All boarded boats to the new dock accompanied by a huge array of other craft, including the oldest lifeboat in England.

This being a Hudson event, there was a huge banquet provided by the directors of the Dock Company. Food and wine were in abundance. When Hudson entered the warehouse where the banquet was to be held, he was met by an outburst of cheering, a compliment said to have been repeated throughout the proceedings. Hudson made a long speech summarising the efforts that had gone into the building of the new dock. He said it was the equal of any dock in the country and he hoped it would mark the beginning of a new era for Sunderland and proposed the toast 'Success to the Sunderland Docks!'

Joseph Wright responded to Hudson's speech. He said the new dock would prove to be one of Hudson's greatest achievements, along with the high-level railway bridge over the Tyne in Newcastle, another monument that would ensure his name would never be forgotten. Wright then proposed a toast to Hudson. Somewhat surprisingly there were, the *Newcastle Journal* recorded, some 'discordant voices' but these were soon drowned out by enthusiastic cheering and applause. A round of hearty cheering was also given for Mrs Hudson.

Hudson felt obliged to say a few more words for the toast and the reception he had received. He said that whenever he went to Sunderland, he was always met with kindness even from political opponents. He would always have nearest his heart the benefit and welfare of Sunderland, which of course was met by more hearty cheers. Following the ceremony, when all the major guests had departed, some 400 or 500 labourers who had worked on the new dock were allowed into the warehouse to be treated to 'substantial viands', or, we might say, the leftovers. In the evening there was a Grand Ball attended by 450 guests, including Mrs Hudson and their daughter Ann, which went on for 'several hours with unflagging spirit.' The evening was rounded off with a display of fireworks.

For Hudson this would have been a very special day, reminding him of many similarly happy days when opening railways or presiding over proceedings at York Mansion House. One can be sure that he made the most of an event which would eventually prove to be the last such gathering he would preside over. Even though expanded and altered over the intervening years, the dock today is still known as the 'Hudson Dock.'

Just four weeks after the joyous opening of the new dock, Hudson was brought back down to earth when he was called as a witness in a libel case brought by his close friend and associate, James Richardson, against *The Yorkshireman* newspaper.

Chapter 12

James Richardson v Thomas Wodson

On 9 February 1850, *The Yorkshireman* newspaper published an article about the failings of the York Union Bank and commented that there appeared to be:

> ... a charter for mismanagement, artifice and defalcations in every joint stock company over which George Hudson and James Richardson have had control ... no man should be trusted in a responsible situation who was normally associated with Mr Hudson; that man is not only corrupt himself but corrupted everyone around him.

James Richardson was the official solicitor of the York Union Bank (of which Hudson was chairman) and a director of the YNB and YNM railway companies. Whilst Hudson was always sanguine about the comments made about him in the press, Richardson was deeply affronted by *The Yorkshireman*'s suggestion that he had been corrupted by Hudson. As one of York's leading solicitors, he had his reputation to protect and he decided to sue the newspaper for a libel. Thomas Wodson, as the owner of *The Yorkshireman*, was the principal defendant, hence this trial is referred to as *Richardson v Wodson*. The trial has gained some notoriety as it proved to be the only time that Hudson was cross examined under oath about his activities in a court of law.

Following the trial, which took place in York on 18 July 1850, *The Farmers Friend and Freeman's Journal,* and a number of other newspapers carried an article in which they explained that although Thomas Wodson was the registered publisher of *The Yorkshireman*, he was so in name only. The *Journal* described him as a quiet inoffensive sort of person who had good-naturedly allowed his name to be gazetted as publisher of *The Yorkshireman*. Although Wodson was named as the defendant in the case, the *Journal* said the real malignity of the libellous articles, for which *The Yorkshireman* had become 'lamentably notorious', was down to 'satanic influences behind the scenes.'

Other newspapers and periodicals published not dissimilar articles, including *The Railway Record and Joint Stock Companies Reporter*, which commented that, from what they had read and heard about the case, they were sure that Hudson had been too hastily condemned. The paper added that the harsh criticisms of Hudson had taken on a different aspect when the more sympathetic barrister (Mr Martin – Richardson's lead barrister) had sought answers to questions that were put with a view to finding explanations of Hudson's behaviours, rather than those urged by the acrimony of his accusers. Having read his evidence, the *Reporter* said there was no doubt that Hudson had been treated unfairly. It also criticised the report of the trial in *The Yorkshireman* – 'the principal engine working against Mr Hudson' – which had cut his evidence down to just 17 lines and that this had not been rectified in the newspaper's subsequent pamphlet on the trial. The *Reporter* could not understand 'a man's notion of honesty who, whilst accusing someone of dishonesty, carefully reports all that tells against a man and carefully withholds all that may be held in his favour.' The *Reporter* noted that several newspapers both in London and the provinces had taken up Hudson's case and that they were determined to give him the fullest opportunity of 'righting himself.' The paper concluded by saying that now the initial shock of Hudson's fall had passed, it hoped the truth, whichever way the inquiries went, would prevail.

The Yorkshireman's pamphlet summarising the trial, referred to by *The Railway Record and Joint Stock Companies Reporter*, was, of course, none too complimentary about Hudson, forcing the *Yorkshire Gazette* to write:

The most casual examination of it [the pamphlet] will show that in the really important part of the whole trial, viz the evidence of Mr Hudson, it is mutilated, garbled, abridged – not giving a full and fair report of Mr Hudson's testimony or oath, as it was, in common decency, not to say common honesty and common fairness, bound to give, but clipping his answers and condemning his explanations.

The *Gazette* commented that the distortion of Hudson's evidence showed the level of malevolence and prejudice *The Yorkshireman* held against Hudson and its sinister motive of keeping up misconceptions about his conduct.

In November 1850, the *Yorkshire Gazette* reported an article about the trial that had appeared in a London based newspaper called *The Sun*. In this article, *The Sun* had described Wodson's barrister, Charles Wilkins, as one of the best *nisi prius* advocates in the country and that during the trial he had attempted to elicit anything and everything from Hudson that might impugn his reputation and throw suspicion on the purity of his motives. But, *The Sun* reported, Hudson had acted calmly and collectedly to the storm of invective, ready to answer any question that was put to him. The *Yorkshire Gazette* agreed, saying that in response to some severe questioning, Hudson had answered with frankness and had provided reasonable explanations in his answers, which had struck those present as powerfully in his favour. The paper added that Hudson had been 'compelled to incriminate himself and supply facts out of his own mouth for his own condemnation' and that public feeling in York had been heated by the vehement diatribes of *The Yorkshireman*.

But, the *Gazette* said, even Hudson's 'most envenomed' opponents were forced to admit that he had achieved considerable public good and had promoted public work that would last for generations. The eyes of Europe would have seen a large portion of the British public turn and 'assail with indiscriminatory obloquy, the person they lauded to the skies as long as railways were making large profits.'

The Sun had shown, the *Gazette* said, the injustice of putting upon Hudson the responsibility of the wide-spread ruin and multitudinous evils which had arisen as a result of reckless speculation in railway shares. In fact, the *Gazette* went on, Hudson 'invariably cautioned parliament and the public against such speculation' pointing out that ruin would inevitably follow. Hudson had also warned the public against investing in some of the wilder schemes that were being proposed, particularly during the years of the Railway Mania. The *Gazette* said he could not be held responsible for men's own rashness, recklessness, cupidity, insatiable avarice, selfishness, folly, miscalculation and disregard of good faith – they bought shares on their own heads. Such a statement was spot on; it was all very well for *The Yorkshireman* to spin its story to show Hudson was completely responsible for the ills of the Mania, but it was far from the truth. The editor of the *Gazette* later reflected that public opinion had done Hudson a great injustice, but public opinion, if it was unjust, was always so from the lack of information. No one would ever appeal as Hudson had done, to Englishmen for 'fair play' and be so 'disappointed in their response.'

In response to *The Yorkshireman*'s treatment of Hudson, another pamphlet was published recording Hudson's evidence in full. This was most likely at the instigation of the *Yorkshire Gazette*, or at least with that newspaper's full support. In his introduction to the pamphlet, the publisher (John Hearne of London) recorded that *The Yorkshireman*'s pamphlet had devoted only a few lines to Hudson's evidence compared to a third of a column in *The Times* and half a column in each of the *Yorkshire Herald* and the *Yorkshire Gazette*. This briefness, Hearne wrote, made it all the more important to publish Hudson's evidence in its entirety. Being the only occasion that Hudson was questioned in a court of law about his activities, Hearne's pamphlet is an extremely important contribution to Hudson's story, as it provides an opportunity to hear Hudson's account of events.

The full title of this pamphlet was *Report of the Evidence of George Hudson MP on the Trial of the case Richardson v Wodson, York Summer Assizes 1850. Edited by a barrister.* The barrister in question was William Digby Seymour of 2 Inner Temple, London (of the northern circuit). Seymour based his record on reports of the trial and was revised and corrected by him taking account of notes made at the trial. He wrote that the aim of the pamphlet was to do 'justice to a deeply-injured individual' and to enable a wider public to form their own opinion of what occurred from unquestionable facts established in a court of law, rather than rely on uncertain rumour. Hudson's friends, Seymour added, were anxious that a full and accurate report of his remarkable evidence should be recorded to be read by 'fair and candid men.'

In the pamphlet Seymour explained that the aim of cross-examining Hudson was to establish by his own admissions the charges that had been made against him and to connect these to Richardson. Hudson was called to be a witness at short notice, and with little time for preparation, to answer questions in detail and to explain the minutest details of transactions which were subject to much public comment 'and obloquy.' Hudson would have expected, Seymour said, that he would be subjected to a 'most rigid and searching cross-examination.'

Defending Counsel Charles Wilkins QC cross-examined Hudson with consummate skill and ingenuity, eliciting every point which would make Hudson's conduct 'censurable or throw suspicion on the purity of his motives.' It was manifest, Seymour said, that Hudson's answers to those questions, and the manner in which he delivered them, under the ordeal of a cross-examination on oath in court, gave a marked and powerful impression in his favour, even amongst those with the strongest prejudices against him.

Wilkins began by asking Hudson about his involvement with the York Union Bank. Hudson confirmed that he was a director of the Bank from its instigation, becoming its chairman in 1841 until 1849. Asked about the practice of the board of directors in running the Bank, Hudson said decisions were made jointly with the directors but, after further questioning, he did admit to making some advances without consultation for smaller amounts (less than £50) but not for larger amounts.

Hudson was questioned about Bartholomew Wilkinson, the manager of the Bank from its inception in 1833 until his resignation in June 1849. Hudson said he was not aware that Wilkinson had been speculating 'thousands' on railway shares. He did, however, admit that Wilkinson had bought shares on his behalf because he (Hudson) did not want every transaction of his to be published to the world. In addition, if he ever sold shares, he would first transfer them to a third party, so he would not be shown as the seller, which Hudson said was absolutely necessary in his position – Hudson was very aware that his share dealings could affect the price of a share and always strove not to publicise his share dealings. At this point Hudson's lawyer, Mr Martin, interjected and asked what this line of questioning had to do with the case being heard. The presiding Judge William Wightman agreed and asked Wilkins whether Hudson's conduct with the Bank had any relevance to the case before the court. Wilkins said he felt that it was relevant but was told by Wightman to confine his questions to the libel case.

Hudson stated he was chairman of the YNB at its formation in 1844 until May 1849. He was then questioned about a contract to buy iron rails from Thompson & Forman (T&F). Hudson told the court he had entered a contract for 20,000 tons of rails in October 1844 and that this contract was completed (signed for) in January 1845. He said the number of rails finally contracted for was reduced to 10,000 tons. He agreed a price of £6 10s per ton for the original request of 20,000 tons. He, along with Mr Richardson and at least one other director were at a YNB board meeting on 30 January 1845, where it was agreed to advertise for 20,000 tons of iron. An advert was placed in the *Railway Times*, signed by Hudson.

A meeting was held on 5 March 1845 to look at the tenders received. Hudson was asked if T&F had sent in a tender to supply 14,000 tons at £14 per ton? No, Hudson said, the T&F tender was for £12 10s. He added that another company, Guests, had tendered at £12 and Hill & Co at £13. Tenders for smaller amounts of rails were received at £11 17s 6d and all of these were accepted.

Hudson said T&F's tender was accepted after Mr Thompson agreed to reduce the price to £12 per ton. Hudson was then asked if any of the 10,000 tons for which he had bargained at £6 10s were supplied to the YNB at £12? Hudson said he could not say exactly. When T&F sold to the YNB it was agreed between 'T&F and me' (Hudson) that on 7,000 tons they supplied to the YNB, he would receive the difference between £6 10s and £12, that is £38,000 in total. Hudson said he had agreed to this arrangement despite having been offered £50,000 by another party for the rails.

The questioning then turned to Hudson's arrangements with landowners. The Construction Ledger of the YNB included the following entries for land purchased by the YNB:

Lord Tankerville £4,000
Duke of Northumberland £10,000
Earl Grey £5,000
Sir Matthew Ridley £3,000
Earl Carlisle £7,000
Lady Mary Stanley £2,000
A total of £31,000 at 30 December 1845.

A cheque for £4,000 payable to Lord Tankerville by the YNB was shown to the Court. It was signed by Hudson, Robert Davies (a director) and John Close (secretary of the YNB). Hudson admitted that this cheque had never been paid to Lord Tankerville. Instead, it had been paid to his own account on the same date. Hudson said he was in the habit at the time of paying out large sums on behalf of the YNB (advancing upwards of £100,000 he said) and he held this money for the purpose of paying the landowner.

Another cheque was produced for the £10,000 payable to the Duke of Northumberland. This cheque was also paid to Hudson's account on the same basis as above. This money was paid to the Duke in May 1849. Hudson said the reason he personally paid the money was because he had managed the purchase of land himself and considered himself responsible for paying the purchase money to the Duke. It was revealed in Court that Hudson had dealt similarly in many other cases, being paid company cheques to pass on to landowners where he had personally negotiated the purchase of land. Cheques for the other amounts listed above were produced to Court and Hudson described what had happened to the funds involved: he had paid £6,000 to Earl Grey; he had received the extra £1,000 from the YNB sometime afterwards; he had repaid to the YNB the £2,000 due to Lady Stanley. He expressed a doubt that this money had yet been paid to Lady Stanley; he repaid Sir Matthew Ridley's £3,000 to the YNB in May 1849; the £7,000 due to Lord Carlisle had not been paid. This sum had been repaid to the YNB in May 1849. He had also repaid Lord Tankerville's £4,000 to the YNB. In addition to these sums, he had paid the YNB 5 per cent interest.

Hudson said it was usual for him to buy land on behalf of the company and to be reimbursed at a later date. He paid interest on the money he received in advance and was paid interest on sums he had personally paid out before being reimbursed. He said it was quite absurd to lay any imputation on him in relation to these cheques.

It would seem that, because Hudson at this time (after 1845, at the very height of his activity during the Railway Mania period) was under so much pressure to complete and pursue deals, he often made and received payments into his own account, as though it was a company business account. This inevitably led to a lot of juggling of funds, the figures for which were clear in his head if not on paper. While he was still in charge of the companies concerned, this practice worked well for him and indeed the company. But, as soon as he lost control, other directors, quite rightly, needed to know where the money was and where it had gone. They needed the deals to be shown written down.

Later in the hearing, Hudson told the Court that he had no doubt that he told every landowner that he was ready to settle with them and pay them at any time. This begs two questions. Firstly, why did Hudson not just make the payments and secondly, why did the landowners not demand payment at some point? The answer to the first question is probably that Hudson was happy to keep the money in his account, even though he would eventually feel obliged to pay interest on the sums involved to the YNB. The second question was one only the landowners could have answered.

The questioning then moved to cheques found in the Construction Ledger as at 31 December 1847, payable as follows:

Rush & Lawton £30,000
Hattersley & Nowell (1). £2,500
Hattersley & Nowell (2). £2,500
Mackay & Co. £5,000

Hudson was asked when the cheque to Rush & Lawton (R&L) was paid. He said the sum was 'virtually' paid to the company at the time (December 1847) but in practice the first £25,000 was not placed in their account until January 1849. He explained that at the end of 1847 (a time of economic recession) R&L were overdrawn at the Bank by £50,000 and Hudson was the firm's surety to the Bank. When he received the cheque for £30,000, he brought the matter before the YNB board. He decided to hold the £30,000 cheque as further security. It was put to Hudson that anyone would think that the payment of £30,000 to R&L was made on 31 December 1847.

Hudson replied simply, 'No doubt.' He went on to explain that R&L received £25,000 in January 1849 and £5,000 in May 1849. He maintained that the action he took was the best course for all parties. If he had not taken this action, work on the railway would have stopped and the Bank would have stopped its advances. Hudson said nobody lost a penny in the transaction and he personally did not benefit at all.

In fact, he had paid 5 per cent interest (totalling £1,802.13s) to the company for the money held by him.

It was a similar story with the cheques payable to Mackay & Co and to Hattersley & Norwell (H&N). The latter were overdrawn at the Bank and Hudson was their surety (as he was for R&L). When he paid the sums due to H&N, Hudson paid interest on the sum to the YNB. Mackay & Co cheques were placed in his account and he paid them to the company in January and February 1849.

It is evident that Hudson used railway company money in his own account much as a bank would. At first glance (and maybe a second one), this is a fraudulent practice because in effect he is using other people's money to fund his own lifestyle. However, the clear difference is that he knew that he held this money only on account and that it would have to be paid out eventually to the railway companies' creditors. If Hudson was truly a fraudster, he would not have paid the money out and he certainly would not have paid anything back to the railway company, let alone pay interest on top.

Hudson was asked if his personal bank account was overdrawn when the cheques referred to above were paid into his account. Hudson replied that at the time he had a balance of nearly £80,000. He was then asked if he was overdrawn at any time between 1845 and 1849. Hudson did not think so. When pressed on the question, he said he may have been and if so, it would have been on account of the railway company. In one instance he recalled, in 1844 or 1845, he had advanced £130,000 for a railway company, but he did not think this advance caused him to be overdrawn.

Questioning then turned to his involvement with the Brandling Junction Railway, which he acquired in June 1844. Hudson said that, at a meeting held on 16 August 1844, it was agreed that he would transfer the Brandling Junction Railway to the Newcastle & Darlington Junction Railway (NDJ) on the same terms as he had purchased it, plus 500 new shares in the NDJ were to be allotted to him. Hudson and Richardson had become directors of the NDJ in 1842. The purchase was finalised at a meeting of the NDJ on 4 February 1845, when it was also agreed that 22,000 new shares should be created to raise the capital required; 20,000 shares were to be offered to existing shareholders at one new share for each share they held in the N&D. The remaining 2,000 shares were at the disposal of the directors. These shares were allotted as follows: 100 to Richardson, 100 to Robert Davies, deputy chairman of the company, 50 to Mr Close, secretary of the NDJ, and 25 each to Mr Harrison, Robert Stephenson and Mr Wood. Hudson received 1600 shares.

Hudson admitted the shares went to £21 premium. Wilkins said this made his allocation worth £40,000. Hudson said the figure was in fact £37,600. Wilkins asked Hudson if he really thought the shareholders had gifted these shares to him. Hudson replied that he firmly believed they did. He said he handed over to the company the £6,000 or £7,000 profit the line had made during his brief ownership.

Hudson was asked if he had sold 400 Hull & Selby shares to the YNM for £100 each in February 1848. Hudson said he thought the price was £98. It was put to him that the market price was actually £90. Hudson denied this was the case; he had sold some further shares in the Hull &Selby at £100 'the other day.' It was put to him that he had received £4,000 over the market price for these shares. 'Certainly not', Hudson said, he had sold them at the market price, and they were worth more after he sold them. Hudson said the directors of the company had objected to the transaction because they were of the opinion directors (including the Chairman) could not sell shares to their own company, so he took them back. He confirmed he had paid the company the amount he was paid. Wilkins put it to Hudson that the directors' objection was more because he had charged the company more than the market price. Hudson refuted the allegation. He said he had never heard of such a charge being made. He admitted he made a profit of £3,000 on a transaction valued at £40,000. So, Wilkins surmised, the fact he was a director was not the only grounds for the directors' objection? Hudson admitted as much but added that, in an instance where there had been a similar transaction that had benefitted the company by £35,000, it was not questioned by the directors.

In 1846, the YNM created 50,000 new shares (Hudson said it was more than that) to fund new railways in the East and West Ridings of Yorkshire. Existing shareholders could buy shares at the rate of one per existing share. Hudson had 1,000 existing shares and was asked by Wilkins why he was allowed to take up 2,000 shares. Hudson said he was allowed 1,600 or 1,700 shares, not 2,000. In mitigation for the extra shares, he said that, as the largest landowner along the proposed lines (particularly in the East Riding), he was entitled to a further allocation. He said the shareholders had been informed of his allocation and no objections had been raised.

Wilkins asked Hudson if he had made any payments in respect of the claims made against him. Hudson replied, he had paid £35,000 to the YNB but, if he had been left to his own judgment, he would not have paid this sum. His legal advisers had told him that he had a perfect defence for not paying the money, but his persecutors took advantage of 'private and domestic events.' He said had it not been for 'circumstances distressing to persons nearly connected with me I would never have compromised.' Hudson was adamant that he did not owe this money to the YNB – 'I shall regret it as long as I live.'

Hudson was then cross-examined by Richardson's QC, Mr Martin. Hudson told Martin that he still held £100,000 of shares in the YNB. He said if he was still managing the company, he would be capable of realising large profits through dividends for shareholders. He was asked if this would be paying dividends out of capital. Hudson denied ever paying dividends out of capital and he was ready to be asked about any balance sheet that had been given to shareholders. Hudson said if he had been dealing dishonestly, he would not have kept his shares to the extent he did when he left his companies.

Asked what shares he still had in the companies he had managed, Hudson said he had 12,000 shares in the ECR that he had bought for £24,000, which he had sold 'the other day' for £6,000. He also held

£18,000 in the Midland Railway, £26,000 in the YNM and £40,000 or £50,000 in the YNB (which was at variance to the figure he gave earlier – see above).

Mr Martin then questioned Hudson about the iron rails. Hudson said that he had agreed to buy 20,000 tons of iron rail from Thompson and Foreman at £6 10s per ton. A dispute arose when the price of iron went up and as a result, he agreed to take only 10,000 tons. In response to questioning by Mr Martin, Hudson said he contracted for the rails on his own account, 'the railway company was not in existence when I entered into it.' Prompted by a further question from Mr Martin, Hudson told the Court that, before Thompson and Foreman's tender was accepted by the company, William Crawshay, ironmaster at the Cyfarthfa Ironworks in Merthyr Tydfil, had offered him £50,000 for his bargain. He was asked if the rails had been supplied to the company at a fair price, 'Most certainly', he said, explaining that T&F had offered rails to the company at £12 10s per ton, but he had beaten the price down to £12. He confirmed that the market price for iron had almost doubled since his original bargain.

Martin then asked Hudson about the Brandling Junction Railway. Hudson said he paid £550,000 for the company out of his own pocket and that he owned the company for a short while before he transferred it and the accrued profits to the NDJ. He was to receive 500 shares and pay for them at par. The other directors who received shares from this allocation were also bound to pay for them at par. The only way to profit from the shares was if they were to rise to a premium in the market (which they did). It was unanimously agreed at the meeting where this arrangement was made that the recipients of these shares could benefit from any rise in their value. Hudson said it was specifically agreed he could benefit in 'consideration of the good services I had rendered.'

Asked about his sale of Hull and Selby shares to the YNM, Hudson replied that he bought them for 'a pound or two' less than he sold them, but from that small profit there were brokerage and other expenses. With the East and West Riding company shares, he 'most certainly' considered any profit from their sale would be for his benefit. In response to a question as to whether the YNM had been ruinous to its shareholders, Hudson said the original shareholders who had continued to hold their shares had, with the dividends declared, nearly covered the cost of their investment.

Hudson added that he bought and sold shares in the names of other parties because it was necessary, and right, that he should not affect the value of railway shares by buying or selling shares in his own name. The ECR was a case in point – their share price increased dramatically when it was announced Hudson would take over the company. He was asked for his opinion of James Richardson. Not unexpectedly, he said Richardson had always acted in the most honourable way.

He was then re-examined by Charles Wilkins. In answer to a question about the holdings he held in February 1849, Hudson listed £45,000 in the Newcastle and Darlington, £12,000 in the Eastern Counties, £26,000 in the YNM, £18,000 in the Midland Railway as well as smaller amounts in other railways. Wilkins then asked him to put a figure on the largest amount he had ever held in railway shares. Hudson did not think this was a fair question and that it was unreasonable to expect him to answer. Wilkins pressed him to answer and after doing some calculations on a piece of a paper, Hudson told the court 'between £200,000 and £300,000.'

Wilkins asked Hudson if he had ever paid dividends out of capital. Hudson insisted that he had never done so. 'And that you swear?' Wilkins asked. 'I do, most solemnly', Hudson replied.

Drawing Hudson's time in the witness box to a close, Wilkins referred to the fact that the YNB had issued a claim against him and asked if he had paid any part of the claim. Hudson said he had paid a large portion and that he thought he had no more than another £5,000 to pay, 'certainly not more than £10,000.' Hudson added that, although he had agreed to pay the sum requested, he protested that he was neither morally nor legally bound to do so; he had been advised by 'most eminent counsel' that he was not liable but, he said, 'they [the

YNB] had the meanness to sue me for that which they had given me in the most public manner.'

At the conclusion of his summing up, Judge William Wightman asked the jury to consider three questions. Was there a libel? Did Hudson induce and corrupt Richardson to take the shares? Had there been mismanagement, artifice and defalcation in the railway companies over which Hudson and Richardson had control?

The jury reached their conclusions after one hour and twelve minutes deliberation. The foreman told the judge that the jury did not consider the article to be libellous, but another juror interjected to say their decision was based on 'certain qualifying circumstances.' The foreman then handed a piece of paper to Wightman on which was written, 'We look at the circumstances of the plaintiff [Richardson] receiving the [Brandling Junction] shares with great suspicion.' This was an unusual step for a jury to take. Ordinarily they would give their verdict and the judge would proceed from there. Reading the note, the judge said, 'This will not do.' He put it to the court that if this was the jury's opinion, then there was mismanagement, artifice and defalcation and that, with respect to the second question, he did not understand the jury saying the plaintiff received the shares with great suspicion; if anything, it meant that he had received them corruptly.

Mr Price, a member of the defence team, attempted to clarify the issue. He said, what the jury meant was, the shares were received 'under circumstances of suspicion.' Wightman retorted 'That is nothing, that is finding for the plaintiff' and then, turning to the foreman, he said, 'I think that is the meaning of your note. That he [Richardson] did not take the shares corruptly but under suspicious circumstances.' The foreman agreed, saying that was their opinion, because there was no evidence to show there was corruption, but plenty of suspicion.

Accepting this explanation, Judge Wightman laid out the verdicts in the case; the article was not a libel on the plaintiff; the plaintiff had not been corrupted to take the shares; there had been mismanagement, artifice and defalcations in the railway companies over which Hudson and Richardson had control.

After the trial *The Farmers Friend and Freeman's Journal* commented that Wodson and *The Yorkshireman* had had 'a very narrow escape', their triumph in the case being solely due to the splendid talents of their barrister, Charles Wilkins. The *Journal* expressed its hope that *The Yorkshireman* would turn from the evil and libellous tenor of its ways, 'before it is too late.'

Reflecting a different view on the trial outcome, the *Hull Advertiser and Exchange Gazette* wrote that *The Yorkshireman* had 'rendered a great service to the country' by its spirited denunciation of George Hudson and his co-directors. The paper remarked, if other newspapers had done similarly then 'thousands of ruined families in these islands would now be in a state of comfort and affluence.' The problem for Hudson and particularly his legacy is that many people believed such hyperbole at the time and have continued to do so down the years.

The *Hull Advertiser and Exchange Gazette* also wrote that it was to his everlasting disgrace that Hudson was still MP for Sunderland. Such a remark shows how out of touch the newspaper was with reality. Sunderland took a much calmer view of Hudson's railway proclivities. He had after all helped to put the town firmly on the map with the construction of its new dock.

But maybe the newspapers should have waited before crowing about *The Yorkshireman*'s apparent success. Richardson was, understandably, not happy with the verdicts reached and a hearing to consider if he could have leave to appeal was held at the Queen's Bench in London on 7 November 1850. Richardson was represented by Mr W.H. Watson QC. The presiding judges were Lords Campbell, Coleridge, Erle and Wightman, the latter was the judge in the original trial in York. At the hearing Watson told the court that *The Yorkshireman* article, was clearly a libel as it cast aspersions on his client's character and conduct. Lord Campbell, one of the presiding judges, noted that the comments were also a libel on Mr Hudson 'but I am not his Counsel.' Watson agreed, adding that Hudson's explanations on the points put to him at the original hearing were most satisfactorily answered.

At the time of the trial in July 1850, Watson said it would have been impossible to have found anyone in York, let alone anywhere else in England, who had not been injured by investing in railways. It was not a surprise, therefore, that the jury in the case should conclude that the article was not a libel. Watson also expressed concern that the second verdict (relating to the corruption issue) had not been made clear enough. Judge Wightman, who was the presiding judge in July 1850, said he thought the verdict had been entered on behalf of Richardson.

After much discussion amongst the judges, Lord Campbell agreed there could be an appeal for the verdict of libel and that a verdict should be entered for Richardson on the issue of corruption and being corrupted by Hudson.

Richardson's appeal was heard at the Queen's Bench on 7 February 1851. Judge Wightman was again amongst the judges sitting. The others were Justices Patteson and Erle. The hearing included an application to recover compensation in damages from *The Yorkshireman* (the defendant) for a libel. The judges ruled that when a libel consisted of a number of sentences, it was not for the Court to separate them but to consider them as a whole. With this in mind, as the jury had in effect found that the part of the passage referring to corruption was a libel, the defendant could not claim the plea was divisible, in other words they could not claim a verdict for a portion of the passage. Thus, as the jury had concluded that the article was a libel for the comments concerning Richardson's alleged corruptness, the verdict should stand for the plaintiff. In effect, *The Yorkshireman* had committed a libel. The newspaper was ordered to pay the full and substantial costs of the case.

A week after the appeal hearing, the *Yorkshire Gazette* added some clarity to the decision reached by the Queen's Bench. The judges had, it wrote, expressed a clear opinion that the verdict in the case must be entered generally for Richardson and not divided as it was at the trial in July 1850. The Judges decided that the part of the plea in the original case, which was in favour of *The Yorkshireman,* was an immaterial issue and could not be allowed to destroy the effect of finding a libel for the plaintiff. The defendant ought to have made two distinct pleas, instead of pleading one general justification. The Judges considered it would be unfair to allow the defendant the advantage of having a verdict entered in his favour merely because of an immaterial issue, which ought not to have been put on the record, when the material and libellous charge was distinctly negatived by the jury. That is the reason why the judges ruled that entering the verdict for the plaintiff must be made absolute. The *Gazette* hoped that in future the proprietors of *The Yorkshireman* would not allow themselves to be dragged through the dirt, and their journal to be prostituted to the purposes of malicious slander.

Hudson's appearance as a witness in Richardson's libel case was the only time he appeared in a court of law to answer questions about his railway business. Prior to the Regulation of Railways Act 1868, no precise form of accounts was required of railway companies and, although the keeping of accounts was required under the Companies Consolidation Act of 1845, the form in which the accounts were prepared was left to the companies to decide. There was, for example, no explicit requirement for the division of capital and revenue expenditure. This lack of regulation allowed Hudson and, it must be said other railway companies, to take advantage of the confusion when preparing their accounts. In short, Hudson had not committed an offence under the law as it stood at the time. This was confirmed by two Opinions of Counsel obtained by the YNM in November 1849, when they advised that the company had no remedy at law against Hudson, although they could pursue him in the Rolls Court.

Counsel further advised that it would be best in the first instance for the company to pursue relief for those transactions that concerned Hudson alone rather than attempt to disentangle those transactions that involved other directors. This further advice is interesting because it suggests Hudson's fellow directors also had questions to answer as a result of them benefitting from some of the financial decisions he made.

It also confirms there was a deliberate policy of pursuing only Hudson, despite the fact there were others who should have shared some of the blame for the decisions he made. These other directors could and possibly should have exerted more influence in order to restrain Hudson, however difficult that became whilst his aura as 'Railway King' grew. Had they done so, Hudson might not have found himself so much in the mire when his kingdom collapsed.

In October 1850, a rumour was reported in the *Railway Record and Joint Stock Companies Report* that Hudson had been approached to help retrieve the affairs 'of a certain railway company', whose dividends had nearly disappeared since Hudson had relinquished his position on the Board. There is no clue as to which company the article was referring to, but most likely it was the Eastern Counties Railway, which was still in a parlous state. However, it was said that Hudson would only have been interested in doing so, provided there was some form of apology for the 'unqualified abuse and slander' that had been 'heaped on him by former friends and dealt with as if proved.' The idea that Hudson could return to improve the financial position of an ailing company was probably no more than wishful thinking, either on that company's behalf or that of the writer.

Instead, at least in the aftermath of Richardson's libel trial, he immersed himself once again in the work of the Commons, where he still had friends and where he still had respect. In August 1850, he spoke against a clause, in a proposed Customs Bill, for widening the powers of the Board of Customs. He said the people of Sunderland had just built a large new dock, but they were prevented from using it by the Treasury (because of customs duties). This was likely to have been complete hyperbole from Hudson, but whatever the facts of the case, he was once again on-side as the clause that he was referring to (which had been opposed by other MPs), was withdrawn. Then he was not recorded by Hansard as having contributed to the House again until the budget debate held on 4 April 1851, when he again referred to the duty on imported timber duty and asked for it to be reduced. He likened the level of duty to a 30 per cent bonus for foreign shipbuilders. The President of the Board of Trade (Henry Labouchere) disagreed with Hudson's claim. He said that during the previous year many larger and more advanced ships had been built in Sunderland than in any previous year. Hudson agreed but highlighted that the shipbuilders had not made a profit. He knew this because, having been in the shipbuilding industry for two years himself, he too had made no profit. It was, he said, 'impossible for a shipbuilder, any more than a farmer, at once to retire from his business.' During a debate on the Smithfield Market Removal Bill on 9 April 1851, Hudson, along with a number of other MPs, suggested that demanding the removal of the livestock market from Smithfield (in central London) to a place outside the city, was tantamount to a vote of no confidence in the Corporation of the City of London. He believed it would be the first time a corporation had been deprived of managing its own market. He suggested that the improvements to Smithfield then being proposed by the Corporation would be very effective in improving the site for the local community. The Bill eventually received the Royal assent in 1852 and the livestock market moved from Smithfield to Islington, then north of London rather than as we think of it today in North London.

With the dark cloud of an impending Chancery case being brought by the YNM still hanging over him, Hudson knew that if it was found that he did indeed owe the company the vast sums they claimed, he would not be able to pay and that, as a debtor, he could then find himself incarcerated in a debtor's prison. However, so long as he remained an MP he would be exempt from imprisonment as a debtor. It was imperative, therefore, that he was re-elected at the 1852 general election. It comes as no surprise therefore that, before the election on 7 July, he contributed no less than nine times to Commons business, including debates on timber import duties, the Budget and a draft Corrupt Practices at Elections Bill.

As the general election approached it was said that, as a result of his work in connection with the construction of the new dock, his return as an MP was assured, but Hudson did not take anything for granted. He visited Sunderland numerous times before the election to canvass for support. He had been a staunch supporter of the Corn Laws before they were repealed in June 1846 but, in a speech to his supporters on 20 April, he said 'it would be madness to talk of a reimposition of the corn duties.' He also spoke in favour of an extension to the franchise which could happen 'without any disadvantage', but disappointingly, he did not elaborate on how this would be achieved. In the event, he probably need not have been too concerned about his prospects for re-election. Sunderland returned two MP's and the real electoral battle took place between the Liberal candidate, Henry Fenwick and the Radical candidate, William Seymour. Thus, as expected, at the poll on 7 July, Hudson secured 866 votes, against 814 for Seymour and 654 for Henry Fenwick.

Although reinvigorated by his election success, according to Hansard Hudson did not attend the House again until December 1852, when he contributed to six debates including on the Budget, the cost of the Duke of Wellington's funeral and on a proposal to establish a Select Committee to consider the principles to be adopted by the House for considering the amalgamation of railways and for railway legislation. In the railways debate, Joseph Henry (MP for Oxfordshire) had said that no railway should be allowed to close to the public as a result of an amalgamation. In response, Hudson, who had long been opposed to government intervention in the running of the railways, said he hoped that parliament would not force railways to complete schemes that would result in financial loss.

Chapter 13

In Chancery

In July 1849, Hudson appeared in the Court of Chancery, not for his own debts but for a debt owed to him by a Lloyds of London surveyor, a Mr Brunton. In October 1845 he had loaned Brunton £1,030 which had not yet been repaid. Hudson won his case and in addition Brunton was ordered to pay 5 per cent interest for the period of the loan as well as 'damages' of £54 10s. It is not known if Brunton actually paid his debt but, whatever happened, that case would prove to be comparatively minor compared to the one that the York and North Midland Railway (YNM) would eventually pursue against Hudson.

Following his fall from power, the YNM had suggested to Hudson that he pay a sum of £50,000 additional to the sums he had already paid the company to clear all his liabilities with the company. Although Hudson understood that he might owe some more money to the company, he did not think it was anywhere near £50,000. So, when the company demanded a payment in September 1849, it was little surprise that no payment was forthcoming from Hudson. Realising that Hudson was not going to accede to their demand, in November the YNM sought legal opinion from three leading counsel of the time, Charles Swanston, Joseph Godson and Arthur Hobhouse, for advice on the best course of action. Counsels' Opinion was that 'under the circumstances of the case [the company had] no remedy at law' but, they said, a Bill of Equity could be filed on which relief could be procured in all transactions.' This meant that although the company could not take Hudson to Court for his misdemeanours, (because he had not broken the law as it stood at the time), the company could apply to the Court of Chancery (also known as the Rolls Court) for repayment of monies they considered he had misappropriated.

With this advice in mind, in January 1850 the YNM again approached Hudson for payment of the debts they said they were owed. Once again there was no response from Hudson, so the YNM considered they had no choice but to present their claim to the Rolls Court. The suit was filed on 13 February 1850 and Hudson was given until 30 March to answer. Inevitably, he missed the deadline and was in default of the Court from 9 April. At a short hearing in the Rolls Court on 8 May, Hudson's lawyer, a Mr Toller, sought an extension of two months in the time allowed for Hudson to answer the suit. Toller said the request was not being made to delay the suit but to allow Hudson to fully answer the YNM case. The presiding judge Lord Langdale asked for affidavits in support of the application, to be submitted in time for a fuller hearing on 22 May. At the 22 May hearing, Toller repeated that the extension of two months was required to enable his client to answer complicated questions, particularly concerning some disputed share transactions. The YNM's lawyers opposed the request but Lord Langdale agreed to a further three weeks for Toller to submit affidavits in support of his application to extend the period for reply.

Understandably, Hudson was keen to avoid a hearing in the Rolls Court because he knew that such a case could take a long time to resolve. In the summer of 1850, he agreed to pay a sum of £40,000 to the company in respect of the sums they were demanding from him. But the company wanted more. At the half-yearly meeting of the YNM held in York in August 1850, a shareholder asked the new chairman of the YNM, Harry S. Thompson, why the directors would not accept the £40,000 as a full and final payment from Hudson and thereby save the company the time and expense of taking him to Court. Thompson sternly advised the questioner that, as long as the directors of the company had the confidence of the shareholders to manage the business of the company on their behalf, they should be allowed to pursue the matter as they thought fit. In the case of Hudson he said, it was about restitution not arbitration and he was strongly of the opinion that Hudson owed more to the company than he had already paid and he, Thompson, would not agree to take less. A proposal was then put to the meeting that legal opinion should be sought about the case for proceeding further against Hudson and other directors and servants of the company. This motion was defeated almost unanimously by the meeting as Thompson and the YNM shareholders were determined to pursue Hudson.

Like Leeman, Thompson was a Whig and therefore a political enemy of Hudson. However, unlike Leeman, Thompson had no underlying respect for Hudson, his dislike verging on hatred. This was most likely strengthened in 1845 when Hudson bought the Newby Park estate. Thompson was born at Newby Park in 1809, when the estate was owned by his parents, Richard and Elizabeth Thompson. There can be little doubt that he was deeply affronted that Hudson, whom he considered a country bumpkin, should have been in a position to buy the house and estate once owned by his ancestors.

In contrast to their attitude towards Hudson, Thompson and his fellow directors agreed compromise arrangements with two other former directors of the company, who it was considered had misappropriated company funds. It was agreed that James Richardson and Robert Davies need only repay half of the premiums on shares it was considered they had misappropriated. Respectively, these amounts were £1,250 and £1,000.

Meanwhile, Hudson was also being pursued by the YNB, which was now under the chairmanship of George Leeman. The YNB demanded that Hudson pay £50,000 in respect of sums the company said he had misappropriated. In November 1849 he paid £40,000, with a further £10,000 to follow. Still outstanding so far as the YNB was concerned was a sum in respect of shares in the Sunderland Dock company, which they alleged Hudson had purchased with company funds.

It is evident that much, if not most, of Hudson's fortune lay in his property and shareholdings rather than in cash for, in November 1849, he sold his Londesborough, Octon Grange and Hutton Cranswick estates, to enable him to make the payment to the YNB. It is likely that despite his initial prevarication, he knew that at some point he would also have to pay a similar amount to the YNM.

Harry Thompson kept his promise to YNM shareholders at the half yearly meeting in August 1850, that he would pursue Hudson for the restitution of further sums he considered Hudson owed the YNM. Although the case is usually referred to as being brought by the York and North Midland Railway (YNM), Thompson worked closely with George Leeman, who was chairman of the YNB, to jointly present the two company's claims to the Rolls Court. After months of preparation, the YNM and YNB presented two suits to the Rolls Court in January 1853. The first suit was heard on 17 January in front of the Master of the Rolls Sir John Romilly. The Court heard that the object of the suit was to obtain from Hudson the value of shares misappropriated by him in the East and West Riding Extension Railway, and the Hull and Selby Railway. As can be imagined, 'voluminous evidence' was presented to the Court.

The Solicitor General Sir Richard Bethell set out the YNM's case. He began by explaining that the East and West Riding Extension Railway (E&WR) had been formed in January 1846 to construct two lines, one from York to Beverley and the other from York to Leeds via Tadcaster and Aberford. Fifty thousand shares at £25 each were issued to fund construction. Existing YNM shareholders were entitled to buy one share of the E&WR for each £50 share they held in the YNM. Under this arrangement, 37,950 shares were allocated to YNM shareholders, leaving 12,050 still to be allocated. Hudson claimed the shareholders of the YNM had agreed these shares could be allocated as the directors thought fit. In practice, this meant Hudson and he soon proceeded to allocate the shares to various people, including those who had undertaken services for the benefit of the company, for example Members of Parliament and some of his close associates. It was alleged he had also placed a number of shares in the names of others and when he ordered that these shares be sold, he paid the profits into his own bank account. There was a similar issue with 100 shares in the Hull and Selby Railway, for which the company was seeking £1,000, the amount Hudson is said to have profited by misappropriating them.

The total amount being sought from Hudson by the YNM and YNB is not entirely clear. Bethell said they were seeking repayment of the profit Hudson had made on the E&WR shares which it was alleged Hudson had misappropriated. In total this was £14,677. The company was also seeking repayment of the original value of the shares which it said Hudson had not paid for. During the summing up of the prosecution's case, Mr Roundell Palmer QC, a member of the company's legal team, mentioned that Hudson's debt to the company was 'a sum a little short of £40,000.'

Sir Fitzroy Kelly QC, who was MP for East Suffolk and a former Solicitor General, opened the case for Hudson's defence. Kelly stated that the charges made against his client were 'contrary to law, inconsistent with equity and in direct violation of good faith' and that the YNM at present possessed all they were entitled to in law. Now, Kelly continued, the YNM was coming to Hudson to claim what belonged to him solely, over which they had no claim. Kelly argued that the shareholders had a right to give the shares in question to Hudson and asked whether it was now to be said that a man who had done so much for their company should not benefit from these shares? Kelly denied the right of the YNM to come forward and call Hudson to account for actions which he had undertaken for the benefit of the company.

John Rolt QC, a member of Hudson's legal team, further explained that, on average, thirty-three shares were allotted for each acre of land purchased. Hudson owned 69 acres and so on this basis was entitled to between 2,000 and 3,000 shares. He was entitled to a further 500 shares in connection with his subscription of £10,000 to the Whitby Building Society which he had helped to set up. Further, Hudson had already paid £16,000 (in July 1848) to the company for the profit on 2,300 shares he had been allocated, leaving 4,991 unallocated shares on the books of the company. Rolt said that Hudson had bought, for the benefit of the company the Londesborough estate for £500,000 and on the sale of this estate he had lost £21,000. Bearing in mind this loss was sustained for the benefit of the company, Hudson was entitled to the protection of the Court. He added that Hudson had never denied the allocation of several hundred shares to landowners and others who could assist in promoting the aims of the YNM. These shares were issued with discretion and, even now, Hudson refused to name names.

Sir Richard Bethell was astounded at the case being made for Hudson. 'What in fact is the nature of the defence?' he demanded. He asked what Hudson's answer was to the charges laid against him and whether he showed any regret or remorse for his actions. Answering his own questions, Bethell exclaimed 'No!' Hudson had the effrontery to come to Court to express wonder at his own morality. About the shares given to landowners, including Hudson himself, Bethell suggested that Hudson had simply taken advantage of the shareholders' resolution to take shares for his own benefit adding that the delinquency and iniquity of Hudson was not only taking shares, but corrupting those around him to collude with him (a reference to Richard Nicholson and James Richardson). Bethell hoped the Court would bring Hudson to justice and compel him 'to disgorge the immense amount of property he had so improperly' appropriated to himself.

A second suit, heard on 20 January, also in front of Sir John Romilly, concerned a small sum the YNM contended Hudson owed the company in respect of 2,000 shares in the North British Railway. These shares had been bought by Hudson on behalf of the YNM in February 1844. He had sold them in 1846 and 1847 but had not credited the company. In March 1849, shortly after he resigned as Chairman of the company, Hudson paid the company £60,251 in respect of these shares. The company were now claiming 5 per cent interest on this money while it resided in his bank account, believed to be just short of £2,000. The company also requested a lien on Hudson's properties to prevent him from mortgaging them. In his defence, Hudson's lawyers told the court that Hudson had variously over the years in question, paid the sums now claimed and that he considered he was owed £1,600 by the company. Mr Toller QC, for Hudson, complained that this suit had been brought against Hudson unnecessarily, saying it 'originated in vindictive feelings' against his client. Romilly decreed that an account should be made of the transactions and that credit be given to Hudson for the sums he had paid to the company. He dismissed the claim for the lien and ordered that the costs for applying for one be placed against the company.

Romilly delivered his judgment on the first suit on 11 February. In a long summing up of the case, he said he was of the opinion that the chairman of a railway company was a trustee for the shareholders. It was incomprehensible that the shareholders should have given their chairman such an absolute allotment of shares which could have enabled him to pocket £100,000. In this case, Hudson was not only a trustee, but also the owner of land that the railway needed to purchase to build its line – a landowner who needed to be 'bought-off.' It was inappropriate therefore for him to agree the price to be paid for land as he had a vested interest. Romilly stated that no director should gain any personal advantage from the position in which they had been placed. Moreover, Hudson was not entitled to help himself to further remuneration. Romilly was referring to the 12,050 shares that were issued in respect of the East and West Riding Railway which Hudson had said shareholders had agreed could be allotted by the directors of the company as they thought fit.

There was some confusion of the exact number of shares Hudson was alleged to have misappropriated. Following the hearing, a newspaper report suggested Hudson had to account for all 12,050 E&WR shares. Hudson's solicitors wrote to *The Times* newspaper, to explain that of the 12,050 shares, 1,800 were not in dispute, whilst Hudson had paid the company £16,000 in respect of 2,300 shares and 4,991 shares were unsold. This left only 2,959 shares in dispute, many of which, the solicitors said, had been sold at a discount.

Romilly accepted Hudson had paid £16,000 to the company in respect of 2,300 shares. Referring to 1,105 shares that had been given to those who had helped the company, Romilly said it was apparent Members of Parliament might refuse a monetary bribe but showed no scruples towards accepting shares at the issue price which were capable of being sold for a profit. He did not think this behaviour was necessary to get a bill through parliament. It certainly would not be sanctioned by the court.

Romilly said Hudson's claim that, as he was not properly paid for his work on behalf of the railway company he was entitled to some benefits, was irrelevant. He added Hudson would have known when he took up the role of Chairman, the only payment he could expect would be the £1 a week honorarium that was ordinarily paid to persons in his position. As a trustee for the shareholders, Romilly said Hudson was liable for the shares he had disposed of and must account to the YNM for the shares that he allotted to himself, including all profits and premiums. Any losses could not be offset. Romilly also directed that Hudson would be charged 5 per cent interest for the period for which he held these shares and, as he had resisted liability to account, he was to pay the costs incurred in the suit and for the hearing.

Hudson was not going to give up his struggle with the YNM lying down. Shortly after the hearing, he sought counsel's opinion on his case and was advised the judgment could not stand. He appealed the Rolls Court verdict but, in a decision made on 9 July 1853, the Appeal Judges, unsurprisingly perhaps, upheld Romilly's judgment.

A few days later the YNM presented a third suit to the Rolls Court against Hudson. When the case was heard in court on 20 July, Sir John Romilly commented that he was shocked at seeing a third suit between the two parties saying that he would have thought all the matters between them could have been settled in one suit. Prosecuting Counsel, Sir Richard Bethell, agreed with Romilly that it was shocking that there should be a third suit, but there were still nine claims outstanding that the company wanted resolved. This suit concerned the profits and money obtained by the defendant from the YNM partly by means of untrue representation and partly by means of improper appropriation.

The first claim related to the iron rails. Bethell said his clients had paid a premium of £9,000 for the rails and though Hudson had paid this sum to the company in May 1849, interest was being sought for the period between when the company was first charged this amount in June 1846 and the date Hudson made his payment. Interest was also claimed on a sum of £10,558 which was drawn from the company's bank account in April 1846, but not paid to Thompson and Forman until December 1846.

The next claim concerned an amount of interest the YNM had to pay in respect of a loan they took out from the Bank of England for the purchase of the Whitby and Pickering Railway (W&P) in July 1845. Hudson negotiated the purchase agreement with the W&P in September 1844. This included a provision that the purchase money of £80,000 would be paid by the YNM within one month of the takeover receiving parliamentary approval. This was given on 30 June 1845, meaning the YNM would have to make their payment by 31 July. In readiness for the purchase, Hudson had arranged for a loan from the Bank of England to be paid to him; £50,000 was paid into his own bank account on 31 May. The balance of £30,000, the prosecution said, had been traced to the Duke of Devonshire's solicitors account and was used to help fund Hudson's purchase of Baldersby Park, near Thirsk. However, Hudson had purchased this estate in 1844, so it is more likely the money was used to help facilitate his purchase of the 12,000 acre Londesborough Estate, which he was in the process of buying at the time, again from the Duke of Devonshire, for £475,000. When he did eventually pay the £80,000 over to the YNM, he did so in two tranches, strongly suggesting he might have used the money for his own purposes. He paid the first tranche of £11,150 in July 1845 and the balance in September the same year. Whilst Hudson had the money in his account, the YNM was being charged interest at 5 per cent by the Bank of England as well as interest on the same amount that they had to borrow from Hudson's York Union Bank to effect the purchase of the W&P. The company was seeking £1,370 in overpaid interest.

There were various other claims, £300 in respect of debentures of £300,000 which Hudson held in his account for a short period, £360 interest for share calls that Hudson did not pay on time, and £70 for dividends on shares in the Hull and Selby that were allegedly sold to a fictitious buyer but were appropriated by Hudson. The YNM also claimed £90, the difference between a debenture of £4,000 that Hudson had sold for £3,910. The company once again applied for a lien on Hudson's properties.

Hudson's legal team, Rolt and Toller, argued that Hudson's purchase of 2,513 tons of iron rail was on his own account and therefore he had a right to charge the company the going rate when he sold it to them. Furthermore, when Hudson bought the rails in October 1844, there was no existing order by the company or its predecessors for rail, nor was he an agent for the company. Had he been able to do so he would have been at liberty to sell the rail to a third party. Rolt argued there was no law to prevent a railway director from selling any goods to their company. He noted that the Companies Clauses Act simply said that if a director was involved with a contract, he could not act within the contract. Hudson's agreement with the company was not a clandestine one, it was open and avowed. When the agreement was made, the directors of the YNB did not object to it, in fact, they had joked about Hudson's profit.

With respect to the claim by the company for interest on the sum of £9,000 that Hudson had paid to the company in May 1849, Rolt contended that, as the company had not mentioned any charge for interest at the time the payment was made and because they had accepted Hudson's payment, they had foregone any claim for interest.

Rolt had put forward some strong arguments and in his summing up Romilly was not wholly unsympathetic. So far as the iron rails transaction was concerned, Romilly said that when Hudson bought the rails there was no doubt he did so as a trustee on behalf of the company and therefore there was no justification for him charging the company £12 a ton when he had paid only £6 10s a ton. With respect to the claims on the Bank of England loan and the interest on the debenture amount, the Master of the Rolls found in favour of the company, although he did add that hardly any blame could be imputed to the defendant. Hudson also had to account for the interest on his delayed share calls. However, he rejected the company's claim for £90, being the difference between a debenture of £4,000 that Hudson had sold for £3,910 as well as the claim for £70 for dividends paid on some Hull & Selby Railway shares that were sold to a nominee and allegedly appropriated by Hudson. The company had once more applied for a lien on Hudson's properties, but this too was dismissed by Romilly. He reserved judgment on the question of interest on the £9,000 that Hudson had paid in respect of the iron rails, but the following Monday, 25 July, he announced that although interest at 5 per cent could have been charged on this amount, the company had received Hudson's cheque without making a claim for interest and therefore the payment must be regarded as a settled account. As such he dismissed the company's claim.

A week later, on 1 August, Romilly issued a decree ordering Hudson to pay a total of £54,590 (equivalent to almost £5million in 2023) to the YNM by 11 January 1854. Hudson immediately appealed the judgment. The basis of his appeal, which was heard by the Appeal Judges on 2 August, was that the sum ordered to be paid was subject to 'exceptions' (i.e., subject to reductions for items which Hudson might subsequently be found not liable). The Appeal was presided over by Lord Justice Bruce. Hudson was represented by John Rolt QC and Mr Toller and the YNM by Mr Roundel Palmer and Mr Hobhouse. Bruce asked Rolt why Hudson was in such a hurry to appeal, bearing in mind payment was not required until 11 January 1854? Rolt said his client's concern was that the YNM would move to register the amount as a debt, but it was his client's contention that the amount would prove not to be payable as he believed that, when 'exceptions' to the amount are taken into account, the amount payable would prove to be very small.

Bruce said it was quite startling for Rolt to suggest that a sum as large as £54,590 could be reduced to almost nothing but, after some further discussion and with the agreement of the YNM's lawyers present, it was agreed Hudson would be required to pay an initial sum of £20,000 by 11 January 1854 with the balance to be paid as directed at a future hearing in the Rolls Court.

Almost immediately Hudson's legal team applied to the Rolls Court to put forward their case for the 'exceptions.' The request for such a hearing, which was held on 2 and 3 December 1853, was very unusual. During discussion prior to the case being heard, the Master of the Rolls made it clear that, in his mind, once a case such as this had been decided, it could not be re-opened. This was not a good start for Hudson, but fortunately Romilly relented on the basis that this was the first time that the question of 'exceptions' had arisen and that it also allowed the opportunity to address any doubts in the case. Rolt then set out the 'exceptions' for the Court to consider. The first related to 300 of 12,050 East and West Yorkshire shares, which had been valued at £8,400 in the Court decree. Rolt said that, as Hudson had sold these in 1849 for £4,575, the lower figure should be taken into account, rather than their value at the date they were issued to him. The second exception was for 100 shares, value £2,337, which Rolt claimed were part of 1,800 shares in the East and West Riding Railway the company had agreed not to call into account. The third was for 200 shares, value £2,931, which had been allotted to Mr Close but which the YNM contended had been held in trust for Hudson, despite the fact that no evidence of the arrangement had been provided. In addition, for a sum of £768 held similarly, but charged against Hudson. Rolt then referred to 1,105 shares, value £6,300, which had been distributed by Hudson to various third parties for the company's benefit, and to £3,120 paid on behalf of the company to defray the costs of obtaining an Act of Parliament for the new Lendal bridge in York. There were also a number of smaller amounts not mentioned in Court. In total, the exceptions amounted to just over £21,000.

Rolt had presented a comprehensive list of exceptions, some more justified than others. Unfortunately for Hudson, Romilly thought differently and disallowed all of them. As a result, Hudson still owed the company £54,590. Taking account of the decision of the Appeal Judges on 2 August, Romilly confirmed that a first payment of £20,000 was to be paid into Court by 11 January 1854 with the residue due by 25 March 1854.

Following this unsuccessful appeal, an article appeared in the *Newcastle Guardian and Tyne Mercury* reflecting on Hudson and his case at the Rolls Court. The writer said that Hudson's chief barrister, John Rolt, had used all his trickery, mystification, evasion and procrastination, but he had been worn down by his 'persevering hunters' and any further appeal Hudson might contemplate would likely fail and he would have to pay and satisfy his creditors, his victims. Referring to shares that were distributed to various landowners and Members of Parliament, the writer said Hudson should be called on to name those involved. If he did, Hudson would prove his complicity in acts of bribery and shame and if he did not, he would show his capacity for 'falsehood and calumny.' Hudson, the correspondent said, would suffer for 'the sins of others' but, as he had shared in the profits, it was only right that he took a proportionate part of the penalty. The correspondent then turned his attention to the electors of Sunderland who, he said, had not accepted Hudson's candidature for his merits, but rather for his money, for his dock shares and his railway bargains. The electors, he wrote, should be heartily ashamed but at the same time they should be lauded for remaining faithful to Hudson when so many others who had shared his hospitality and fattened themselves on his bounty, forsook him as soon as his irregularities came to light. Many in Sunderland refused to believe anything bad about Hudson, but even allowing for friendships and personal services, the correspondent said it would be impossible for him to continue to enjoy this respect and that a recent rumour he would resign would soon come to pass.

The correspondent also referred to Charles Dickens' recently published novel *Bleak House*, which at the centre of its story had an interminable case in the Court of Chancery, Jarndyce v Jarndyce. The article describes how in Dickens' work, there was a seemingly endless round of questions between lawyers and nothing was ever decided, but recent reforms had led to such old practices being changed. Hudson's case was conclusive proof of the benefits of the reforms – a Chancery suit could now be concluded in the lifetime of the suitors. Little was the writer aware that such optimism would prove to be misplaced in this case!

Although Hudson had been told by the Rolls Court to make his first payment by 11 January 1854, come February 1854, he had failed to make a payment. However, rather than being an outright refusal by Hudson to comply with the Court's direction, the reason was that he was now in the midst of negotiating an out of Court settlement with the YNM. At the company's half yearly meeting held on 17 February 1854, the directors announced to shareholders that, in January 1854, they had reached an agreement with Hudson whereby he would pay a slightly lower overall sum of £50,000 plus £1,000 towards the company's legal costs (which totalled £2,000). The directors explained that they could have demanded more as per the Rolls Court decision, but they sought a compromise with Hudson bearing in mind his 'still unexhausted power of appeal.'

The revised sum would be abated by £3,120 in respect of Hudson's claim for costs against the proposed Lendal Bridge in York, which the committee of inquiry had said should be credited to Hudson whenever a settlement with him was reached. Also, a further £631 would be deducted in respect of copyhold fees due to Hudson when he was Lord of the Manor of Weighton whilst the owner of the Londesborough Estate. Together with other adjustments, the revised amount agreed with Hudson was £46,249.

The directors noted that, in addition to further payments made by Hudson, this agreement would make a total of £72,696, which compared favourably to the total they had originally claimed at the Rolls Court (£71,462). In detail, the arrangement was that a mortgage would be placed on Hudson's Newby Park property for £21,000, to be repaid by 25 March 1854, by which time the house was to be sold. The balance would be secured by a first mortgage on Hudson's Whitby properties, on which he would pay 4 per cent interest but which he could pay-off in three equal annual instalments. The directors expressed their opinion that this revised arrangement would be received by shareholders as a satisfactory settlement of what was a tedious and difficult question.

The compromise agreement between Hudson and the company was replaced by a new deed dated 21 October 1854. This provided that £33,000 from the sale proceeds of Hudson's Newby Park estate would be passed directly to the newly created NER and the remaining £13,249 (plus legal costs of £1,000) would be secured by a mortgage on Hudson's Whitby property, as this was now the only property he owned. This mortgage would be discharged by Hudson making two equal payments in October 1855 and October 1856. The deed also provided that, if he defaulted on these payments, the NER could claim the full sum of £54,590 from Hudson.

It is not known what Hudson's true financial position was at this time. He had disposed of all his properties, but he and Elizabeth had to live somewhere. Whilst in the north of England attending his Sunderland constituency it is likely he had lodgings in Whitby. He still owned property there, despite it being mortgaged to what was by now the North Eastern Railway company (NER). In London he may have lodged with friends, although he is recorded as living at 10 Half Moon Street in London's West End at some point; whether this was with Elizabeth is uncertain, but unlikely. Wherever he or Elizabeth lived, he would have needed money to pay for his lodgings and his upkeep.

Chapter 14

Hudson Goes Missing

Despite all of his problems with the NER, Hudson continued to represent his Sunderland electors in the Commons, particularly on matters relating to shipping. In 1853, he contributed to eight debates. These included one supporting the duty on imported glass, whilst the others were all to do with shipping. During a debate about a new Pilotage Bill on 4 April 1853, Hudson and his fellow MP from Sunderland, William Seymour, had a disagreement about whether the measure would be acceptable to the shipping interests of Sunderland. Early in the debate, Hudson had said that, although some amendments might be needed to the draft measure, he and the shipowners of Sunderland, thought it would be very beneficial to the shipping interest. Seymour expressed surprise that Hudson thought the measure would be satisfactory to his constituents, as he considered they would in fact be a great burden to Sunderland's shipping interest. In response, Hudson clarified that he had pointed out his objections to the Bill and provided these were addressed, he was sure his constituents would be satisfied with the measure. This exchange is of interest because, at a by-election in January 1855, a major reason for Seymour not getting re-elected was because it was said he did not adequately represent the mercantile interests of Sunderland. The by-election had been brought about because, towards the end of 1854, Seymour had resigned his seat on account of being appointed Recorder of Newcastle. Quite why he thought he had to resign is unclear, particularly as he put himself forward for re-election. He might have expected to have been returned unopposed. However, there were many in Sunderland who were unhappy with his representation of the shipping interest in the Commons, and it was decided to find a candidate to stand against him. The candidate chosen was Henry Fenwick, who Seymour had defeated in July 1852. After what was described as 'a very violent contest', it was Fenwick who topped the poll, with 956 votes against 646 for Seymour.

Hudson's most important contribution to the House in 1854 came when he felt obliged to respond to Thomas Duncombe, the Whig MP for Finsbury in London who, during a debate on 7 February about the alleged corruption of MPs in Ireland, had accused Hudson of, in effect, bribing MPs. Supporting a motion calling for the Privileges Committee to investigate the claim, Duncombe said the inquiry should not be confined to Ireland but should include the 'Honourable Member for Sunderland.' Duncombe referred specifically to a statement made by Hudson under oath at the Court of Chancery during a hearing of the case of YNM v Hudson. Duncombe said that according to a report in *The Times* newspaper, Hudson had admitted that £6,300 had been paid by him in the shape of shares to certain people of influence 'connected to the landed interest and parliament for the purpose of securing their good offices' in connection with railway business and that Hudson had claimed these payments as a set-off against his indebtedness to the YNM.

Duncombe said Hudson had refused to tell the public Court who the recipients were, but that he would tell the Master of the Rolls in private, 'of course his Honour refused to have anything to do with so dirty a transaction.' Duncombe said that 'such a distribution was exceedingly improper, and as little creditable to the parties receiving as to the defendant who bestowed [them].' He added that, if the Privileges Committee was going to inquire into the case of two MPs from Ireland, then it was utterly impossible for the government to ignore the Master of the Rolls' comments. Hudson must be held responsible for what he did, but the matter was not so much about Hudson as about those in and outside parliament who received the shares. Duncombe said 'This is serious, indeed, and can hardly, I think, even in an age so apathetic as to wrong and so tolerant of public delinquencies, be allowed to pass without investigation.'

Hudson was not in the House to hear Duncombe's allegation. He was in Sunderland attending to constituency business. When he heard what had been said about him, he was fuming and he broke off his engagements in Sunderland and rushed back to the capital so he could immediately make a statement in the House to answer the allegations made against him. His statement, made on 8 February, became known as his 'Vindication speech' and in it Hudson gave an impassioned response to Duncombe's accusations.

Hudson told the House that he had always understood that if an MP was going to disparage another MP, it was usual to give that MP notice of such intention. He had received no such notice and for that reason at least, he had good grounds for making a complaint. Hudson said that, when reporting on his chancery case, *The Times* newspaper had made charges that were either totally untrue or, if not untrue, had been given a very different construction to the actual truth. Hudson said he would not have complained had Duncombe also read a letter from his solicitor to *The Times* repudiating the charges they had made and which quoted from the affidavit he had made in the case. Hudson said he had never made or intended to make, either privately or publicly:

> any charge or imputations against any Member of this House. It is utterly impossible, during my long intercourse with this House and with society, for any gentleman, be he whom he may or where he may, to charge me with having said, directly or indirectly, that I ever tampered with any Member of this House, directly or indirectly. Therefore, I say the charge is as false and malicious as it is unjust and untrue.

Hudson also told the House that he had been advised that he had a good right of appeal, and contended that it was by legal construction that he had been placed in the position he now found himself:

It is admitted, even by my opponents, that a large sum of the money which I am obliged to refund to that company never reached, nor could by any possibility have reached my hands. Therefore, I say my position has been one of misfortune; I have been morally right, but legally wrong.

He invited his accusers, if they thought right:

to take me from my cradle and follow me to this day, and if they can fix upon me any charge of dishonourable conduct, or of anything which would dis-entitle me to the confidence of my friends, I will instantly bid adieu to this House and to my public position. But until I am convinced that I have done anything not only legally but morally wrong, I shall abide, amidst the vituperations of the press, or of any other individual who may choose to attack my character or position.

Hudson said he could have pursued his accusers in Court, but had abstained from doing so. He said he knew what it was like to be popular and to enjoy the smiles and confidence of the world, but he:

had a bitter reverse to bear. I hope I bear it with the fortitude with which a man who is conscious of his innocence should bear it. I may perhaps leave to posterity, and may in after life refer with pride and satisfaction to works which I have either projected or promoted – works of utility, which will bear my name.

He invited Duncombe to pursue the course he wished, to set up a committee of inquiry, as he was 'ready to unravel and unfold everything.' He referred then to the time he was questioned during the Richardson v Wodson libel case in 1850:

I have stood the brunt before a jury of my countrymen, and when attacked by all that the intelligence and the ability of counsel could bring to bear against me, I have left Court, after two or three hours' examination, with the smiles and congratulations of my friends, and the discomfiture of my enemies. I have been subjected to vituperations. There is scarcely a work which I projected, in the plenitude of my power, which has not been condemned at the moment, and with regard to which all sorts of charges have not been brought against me of being actuated by motives of anything but those of a public character. But I have already lived to see nearly every one of those works carried out, and if they have not been, it is the fault of those who censured me and visited me with pecuniary loss.

When at the height of his powers Hudson said he had many opportunities to enrich himself and if making money had been his sole object, he could have accepted any number of shares:

I have sat at boards when shares have been distributed and have been offered to me, and, on public grounds, I have declined them, and they have been taken by my colleagues. If money had been my sole object – I do not mean to say that the attainment of wealth is not a fair and right ambition – but if that had been my sole object, I say that means were placed in my power of such a gigantic nature that I might have revelled in it to any amount. But my colleagues will do me the justice to say that I rejected it on many occasions.

Hudson finished his statement by saying that he could say many things about other people but he only sought to vindicate himself, not to impugn others. He said he thought that Duncombe, having left the sting, would have been in the House to hear his statement but, should Duncombe move for a committee to investigate him, Hudson said he was ready to meet that challenge and to abide by any decision of the House.

After his 'vindication' speech, as it became known, Hudson made just four further contributions during 1854 and then, after he had taken part in a debate on the tolls charged on ships passing Ramsgate Harbour on 15 May 1855, he was not seen in the House again until 11 May 1857, when he appeared in a debate about a Select Committee being set up to look into the operation of Bank Acts in England, Ireland and Scotland.

The reason for his absences from the House and from Sunderland during this time is explained by the fact that he was spending a lot of time in Spain, exploring the possibilities of cooperating with railway contractor George Mould in developing Spain's railway system. Mould had been awarded the Order of Charles III by Queen Isabella II of Spain in February 1855, for his work on Spain's early railways, including the line between Santander and Madrid. Hudson clearly sensed a business opportunity. However, when it was announced that there would be a general election in April 1857, he was clearly spooked. He was in Paris at the time, and it was from there that he wrote a letter to the electors of Sunderland, pleading for them to support him at the election. In his letter, dated 7 March 1857, he explained he had been 'unavoidably' detained on business in Spain and that he had been severely ill for three months. He admitted his private interests should not stand in the way of his public duties but, as the undertaking in Spain involved his fortune, he trusted the electors would understand. He added that as he had now been 'happily relieved of this absorbing claim' on his time, he was again free to devote all his time and effort to their service. Presumably that phrase meant that he had not found the opportunities he had hoped for in Spain, as he never subsequently pursued any business opportunities there.

The fact that he had gone missing was, of course, not lost on the people of Sunderland. In February 1857, Henry Fenwick, Sunderland's other MP, complained to the *Sunderland Daily News* that he was having to represent the town on his own because Hudson had gone missing. The paper decried Hudson as the 'once all potent iron monarch whose authority is despised and his sway despoiled.' However, the correspondent did acknowledge that Hudson had contributed to the development of the vast resources of the country and that the new south dock in Sunderland was an imperishable monument to him, but it was now time for him to resign and allow the town's representation to be in the hands of someone else. In March 1857, a month before the general election was due, the *Northern Daily Press* commented that Sunderland was growing weary of Hudson. Although the town would always be grateful for his work on the new dock, the paper said that even his most ardent allies might now consider that his account with Sunderland had been squared. It went on to say that possible replacements for Hudson were being considered, including the London banker Richard Hoare who would be a safe pair of hands for Sunderland's mercantile interests. Hudson, however, had different ideas and, so it would seem, did many electors in Sunderland.

Not long after his letter of 7 March was received in Sunderland, Christopher Bramwell chaired a meeting of Hudson's supporters in Sunderland to rally support. The meeting sympathised with the reasons Hudson gave for not attending the House and, taking account of all that he had done for the town, agreed he was still eminently qualified to continue to represent the town as one of its MPs. The meeting resolved to make every effort to secure his return at the election. A correspondent writing at the same time in the *Newcastle Guardian and Tyne Mercury* was not so convinced of Hudson's fitness to continue as an MP. The writer said it was dangerous for Hudson to rely on public gratitude at the election. Whilst acknowledging he had improved the Durham to Sunderland railway and Sunderland Docks, the money to do so came from public companies which Hudson was bound to protect but which he did not. The writer could not believe Hudson would dare to show his face again in Sunderland but, of course, he did!

There were rumours he might resign before the election, but this was always very unlikely. As long as he remained an MP, Hudson was exempt from any threat to place him in a debtor's prison for his indebtedness to the NER. As if to underline this point, on the day of nominations for the election, an attempt was made to arrest him for his debts, but Hudson claimed exemption on account of him being a candidate for election and the threatened writ was dropped. The prospect of imprisonment was very real and shows there was no chance of him resigning. The only way Hudson would cease to be an MP would be if he was not re-elected.

Hudson arrived in Sunderland at the end of March to begin his canvass. Bearing in mind the rumours being spread about him and not least the fact that he had been absent from the Commons for almost two years, Hudson was cautious about the reception he would receive. He need not have worried, when he arrived in the town he was met with the 'utmost enthusiasm.' As for Hudson himself, he was reported by the *Newcastle Journal* as looking very hearty and well and that the meeting room where he would make a speech to his supporters was 'crowded to suffocation', with many of his supporters stranded outside because there was no room inside. Despite the criticism he had received in the press over the previous few weeks, when he entered the meeting room, Hudson was met with 'hearty and deafening applause' such that he had not received for a long time. The *Newcastle Journal* added that:

> Mr. Hudson addressed the meeting in a speech full of that energy and ability which invariably characterize him, and never did he appear to greater advantage than he did on this occasion, when rising Phoenix-like from those difficulties which would have overwhelmed others similarly placed. With dexterous skill, the hon. gentleman referred for a moment to the past, and glancing rapidly at the future, proceeded to explain his views on the several subjects of interest upon which the electors were presumed to take an interest, and the consummate address with which Mr. Hudson alluded to the Bank Charter, Church Rates, Income Tax, and other matters, drew forth loud and repeated plaudits from the large assemblage of electors.

That Hudson would be re-elected was never in doubt. The main battle in the election was between the two Whig candidates, Henry Fenwick and Ralph Walters. As expected, Henry Fenwick topped the poll (with 1,123 votes), Hudson was second (with 1,081 votes), and Ralph Walters third (with 863 votes).

Returning to parliament was not, however, as straightforward as Hudson might have hoped. Shortly after the election, a petition was submitted to the Commons calling for him to be expelled, on the basis that he was not qualified to stand as an MP. Quite who submitted the petition and on what grounds they thought him unqualified was unclear, though one newspaper suggested it could have been a property qualification. The defeated candidate, Ralph Walters, denied all knowledge. There was a rumour that someone in Newcastle was owed £1,000 by Hudson and that it could have been him. Understandably, his supporters in Sunderland were very upset with the petition, considering it a cowardly act against a man who had done so much for their town, but who had fallen on hard times. In the event the petition was abandoned and was not heard by the Commons.

After the election Hudson took part in numerous debates in the Commons, including pressing the government for the repeal of passing tolls for shipping. In this, he succeeded in persuading the government to introduce a Bill, but they gave him no assurance when this would be. He also took part in a long debate about a new Probate and Letters of Administration Bill in July, but then he went 'missing' again. The *Essex Standard* reported in September 1857 that Hudson intended to go again to Spain, where he was about to carry out a 'vast railway project.' His Hansard record confirms his absence, as he did not make any contributions in the House between 20 July and 9 December 1857. He might well have been in Spain at this time. In his Will, which was dated February 1858, he mentioned bequeathing to his two surviving sons, William and George, his 'interest in the Spanish Railway in the course of construction by me in conjunction with George Mould.' He was clearly planning something, but quite what is not known. Maybe the plans did not come to fruition or maybe he later sold any interests he might have had. All that is certain, is that he is not recorded as having had any involvement in Spanish railways.

He returned to the House in December 1857, contributing to a debate on a Bank Issues Indemnity Bill, which sought to indemnify the Bank of England in respect of their bank notes. In the debate, Hudson recalled that in the course of his chequered life no one had dealt more with money than he had – no man had greater command of it and he now had the satisfaction of seeing there was no railway on which he had spent money that was not 'productive to the shareholders and beneficial to the public.' He said, the economic crisis of 1847, when the Mania bubble burst, was blamed on the railways and he remembered being asked by the then prime minister Robert Peel where the money for the railways had come from. Hudson told Peel that it had come from the pockets of industrious men who, if they had not invested in English railways, would have invested in foreign securities. The money invested therefore remained in the British economy, with landowners, with iron masters and with others in the country. The crisis of 1847 was not caused so much by the railways, but by money supporting British investment abroad. He concluded his speech by expressing the hope that the government would introduce a Bill to abolish the rule that limited the issue of notes to the amount of gold bullion held by the Bank.

In 1858 Hudson appeared in the House just four times, and then only contributing in a very minor way to debates concerned with procedural matters. During one of these debates, there was a discussion about the cost of repairs to the British Embassy building in Paris. During the debate it was mentioned that the French 'only paid £1,000-£1,500 per annum' for their Embassy in London. Hudson was quick to point out that the French paid considerably more than that for what was his former London home!

The repeal of timber duties had been a topic of interest to Hudson throughout much of his time as an MP. Timber was extensively used in shipbuilding and the duty on imported timber was an issue for his constituency. In a debate in early March 1859, Hudson showed he had left behind any support he may have had for import protection when he made a short speech about the import duty on timber being a blot on the 'statute book in an age of free trade.' Timber, he said, was almost the only raw material to be subject to an import duty. Its removal would not only help manufacturers but make it cheaper for use in 'the building of houses and cottages for humbler orders of people.'

On 31 March 1859, at the end of what was quite a busy month for him in the House, Hudson made what would prove to be his last speech as an MP. In a debate about the extension of the franchise in county boroughs, he expressed a number of doubts about the value of the Bill and referred back to the Reform Act of 1832, saying that when that Bill was enacted, the popular feeling was that every servant maid and man believed they could cease work and never know any more trouble or sorrow, misery or grief, whilst others thought it would ensure future prosperity and peace for the country. In other words, the Reform Act had received credit for far more good than it had really done. Whatever doubts he may have had, Hudson said he would vote in favour of the Bill going to Committee. In practice, however, what became known as the Second Great Reform Act would not be passed until 1867.

Following the general election of 1857, Lord Palmerston had become prime minister, but splits in the Whig coalition that supported Palmerston led to Lord Derby forming a minority Conservative government in February 1858. Derby managed to remain in control for over a year, but eventually his government proved unsustainable, and another general election had to be called in June 1859. The national political tide had been turning for some while in favour of the Liberals who, by now, had united its factions behind Lord Palmerston.

Hudson's task to be re-elected for a fifth time would prove to be formidable. With the political tide turning against the Tories and in favour of the Liberals, Henry Fenwick proved early on to be the favourite to top the poll in Sunderland. Added to this was the fact that the Liberals were determined to win the second seat in Sunderland.

They asked William Lindsay, a prominent shipowner, to directly oppose Hudson. Some of the local press were delighted, the *Durham Chronicle* enthused that at last the shipowners and shipbuilders of Sunderland had a candidate in Lindsay who, as an MP previously for Tynemouth and North Shields, had brought sound, practical knowledge to the House, particularly in campaigning for the 'abolition of passing tolls, dues and duties.' And what had Hudson done? 'Nothing!' the paper exclaimed. Since his fall, the paper added, Hudson had been cold-shouldered by every member of the House and was only partially listened to because he represented such an important constituency. As for his knowledge of shipping or shipbuilding, he was 'a Tom Thumb' compared to Lindsay. The *Chronicle* completely ignored the fact that over the past fourteen years, Hudson did have the respect of many members of the House and had been involved in numerous debates on matters concerned with the shipping interests of his constituency, not least his steadfast and vociferous opposition to passing tolls and duties.

In contrast to the *Chronicle*'s sentiments on Hudson, the *Newcastle Journal* considered that in normal circumstances there was no chance Hudson would be defeated. It railed against the 'mischievous' Liberals for selecting a candidate (Lindsay) of no benefit to the community but just so they had access to his money in the election campaign. It described Lindsay as a 'political charlatan and imposter' who had failed previously as an MP and who in the past had unsuccessfully applied to be a candidate in Monmouth and in Dartmouth. The paper said in past elections Hudson had helped Fenwick overcome Radical candidates, but here was Fenwick now in league with a candidate whose sole purpose was to oust Hudson, who had represented Sunderland for fourteen years and had done so to the great advantage of the town.

The poll opened at 8.00am on Saturday, 30 April. By 9.00am, It was said that Hudson knew it was not going to be his day. At this point he had polled just 166 votes as opposed to 322 for Fenwick and 307 for Lindsay. Around 1.00pm, rumours began to circulate that Hudson would retire from the contest and his decision was confirmed when some of his team withdrew from the voting booths. Despite the air of defeatism that must have surrounded his support, votes continued to be cast for him. The final poll was as follows: Fenwick – 1,527, elected; Lindsay – 1,292, elected; Hudson – 790, not elected.

In the event, Hudson's total number of votes was not as bad as he might have anticipated and he may have earned a few more had he not decided to withdraw from the contest early. He is said to have made a 'plucky' speech at the close of the poll, telling the crowd of some 15,000 people that he would forever cherish a warm and grateful recollection of their good town.

Hudson may not have been a great parliamentarian but, apart from those periods when he went missing from the House, it is evident that many of his contributions were made with the best interests of his electors in mind. These contributions are recorded in Hansard. There is no record of the work he may have carried out in the lobbies of the House, where much parliamentary business would have been conducted.

Hudson's political career was over, but what next for the now former MP?

Chapter 15

Exile

Following his electoral defeat, Hudson lost his immunity to imprisonment in a debtors' prison. To avoid such a fate, he had no choice but to escape to the continent. He is believed to have gone to Paris in the first instance, but very little is known about his time in exile. Lambert wrote that Hudson was 'miserably poor' and that there was good reason for imagining that he often 'went hungry to bed.' This description appears to be backed up by a story Lambert recorded about Charles Dickens seeing Hudson at Boulogne in the spring of 1863 and describing him as looking 'shabby' and 'desolate.' However, Peacock wrote that Alexander Shand, in his book *Old Time Travels*, gave a different picture saying that, when in Paris, Hudson often stayed in the affluent and middle-class Hotel Meurice in the Rue de Rivoli.

The true state of Hudson's wealth following his fall from power and the sale of his properties and the payment of monies owed to his various creditors is unclear. During the 1850s, he is known to have bought consols (government bonds) and shares in the Australasian Pacific Mail Steam Packet Company and he may have invested in Spanish railways. In addition, he would have been receiving dividends from any shares he continued to hold in various English railway companies and, of course, the Sunderland Dock company, though the value of these shares declined somewhat during the 1860s. At the beginning of his exile, he may have been able to live in some comfort, but as the decade wore on and the value of his investments declined, his standard of living will have declined proportionately.

In December 1864, Hudson returned to England briefly to attend the funeral of his brother Charles. During this visit, whilst he was visiting Whitby, it was suggested that he should put himself forward as the Conservative candidate for the upcoming general election. He was told his chances of success were good, as he was still well respected for what he had achieved for the town; not only the development of his West Cliff property but the improvement of the railway to Pickering which, under his management, had been extended to Malton, thereby putting Whitby on the national railway map. A further incentive, if he needed one, was that the sitting MP was none other than Harry Thompson, the chairman of the NER and his nemesis in chancery.

Hudson most likely first visited Whitby following his inheritance of land and property from his uncle Matthew Bottrill in 1827. He is believed to have taken his family on holiday there during the 1830s. On one such occasion, in the summer of 1834, he famously met the 'father of the railways' George Stephenson, who was in the town inspecting progress on the construction of the Whitby &Pickering Railway (W&P). In September 1844, Hudson persuaded his YNM company to take over the W&P, which at the time was little more than a single line wagonway operated with horse power. His drive and determination brought steam locomotion and a double track railway to the old line and a connection to the YNM's York to Scarborough railway. When he fell from power, an investigation into his management of the YNM revealed that the W&P had been something of a vanity project for Hudson, as the cost of rebuilding the railway was shown to have outweighed the prospective return in fares and goods receipts. But the people of Whitby were not concerned with that, they were just happy that at last their town had been connected to the growing national railway network.

Hudson bought land on the West Cliff above the town and built Palladian style terraces including a Royal Crescent, intended to match that of Bath, and the impressive Royal Hotel. Unfortunately, following his fall from grace, the Royal Crescent could not be completed, hence there is only half a crescent today. There is little doubt that Hudson's railway and the improvements he made in the town led to its increasing popularity in the mid-nineteenth century as a health and holiday resort. Numerous well-known writers visited the town including Elizabeth Gaskell, Alfred Tennyson, Lewis Carroll and even one of Hudson's most famed detractors, Charles Dickens.

In 1845 there had been talk that Hudson might stand for election in Whitby. In the event, of course, he stood in Sunderland, whilst Robert Stephenson took the Whitby seat. Hudson remained MP for Sunderland until 1859, but he often visited old friends in Whitby and, although not known for certain, it is very likely he stayed in the town when he was in the north east because he still owned property there.

In June 1857 Hudson was invited to a public dinner in his honour at Whitby. The invitation was signed by 100 tradesmen of the town, who were keen to honour Hudson for the great public service he had rendered to the port and to the town. Surprisingly, for someone who always enjoyed such events, Hudson turned the invitation down. It is unclear why he did so, but it could have had something to do with him recently being re-elected as MP for Sunderland. Having been accused of 'going missing' during his previous few months as that town's MP, maybe he felt it would be inappropriate to attend an event in the town for which it had long been speculated that he could stand as a prospective MP.

In his letter turning down the request, Hudson remarked that it was a source of deep gratification to him to find his exertions on behalf of the town were appreciated and remembered. He said the last two months had afforded him unmixed pleasure. The people of Sunderland had returned him to parliament and now Whitby had acknowledged him for his efforts to improve their 'beautiful town.' The people of Whitby and Sunderland were 'faithful amongst the faithless.' He thanked Whitby for its 'fresh act of kindness and affection' which he said he received with much pride and gratitude that no words could adequately express.

It comes as no surprise therefore to learn that Hudson readily accepted the invitation to stand at the general election in 1865. Not only would he have a chance of representing a town he loved, if elected he would be able to return to England without the dreaded threat of the debtors' prison hanging over him.

He arrived at the town's railway station on 8 June 1865 to begin his campaign and was followed to the Angel Inn in the centre of Whitby by a large cheering crowd. In the evening he gave a speech at St Hilda's Hall in which he mentioned that, although he did not know John Francis, he was aware that Francis had defended his reputation in his book *A History of the English Railway*. However, he said, it was unlikely that those who had come to hear him that evening cared much about his reputation, particularly, as he reminded them, he had invested £100,000 in the town (building and expanding his West Cliff estate), which was the means by which visitors to the town had spent £750,000. Reflecting on his railway career, Hudson denied altering the accounts of the Eastern Counties Railway in 1849 and said that malice was heaped on him with regard to the Midland Railway, yet the amalgamations he oversaw were generally acknowledged as being a wise move. And what was more, the share price rose from £50 to £190. He explained various other aspects of his railway career and referred to the Opinion of Counsel at the time of the investigation into the affairs of the YNM in November 1849, which advised 'that the company [the YNM] under the circumstances of the case [had] no remedy at law.' In other words, he had not committed any crime for which he could be prosecuted. To a chorus of cheers, Hudson concluded his speech by saying that in all matters he had acted honestly, uprightly and fairly. Following his rousing speech, Hudson seemed all set for a return to parliament.

His opponent, Harry Thompson, had held an election rally at the same venue the day before, on 7 June. Unsurprisingly, George Leeman was in attendance to support Thompson. The meeting was a raucous affair, with many of Hudson's supporters heckling and trying to disrupt the meeting. Concern was expressed by one of Thompson's supporters that Hudson might be able to buy out his mortgage on his Whitby properties, which Leeman denied and in reply to another who suggested Hudson had successfully knocked £70,000 off the NER claim, Leeman, shouted over the noisy crowd, 'Bosh! The whole thing is a fabrication, wishful thinking.' Leeman said at the meeting he thought it most unjust for people to say that Thompson had been hard on Hudson. Mr Thompson, Leeman continued, was a man of too high a character to make a false statement or take sixpence out of the pocket of Mr Hudson. Leeman concluded his remarks by expressing the hope that Thompson would be elected for a second term as Whitby's MP.

Thompson was unpopular in Whitby and Hudson's arrival in the town, and the reception he had received, made it quite clear to Thompson's supporters that they were likely to lose the election. Thompson and Leeman would have dreaded the prospect of Hudson once again being an MP and perhaps restoring some of his lost reputation. The pair were nothing if not ruthless when it came to Hudson. They had already shown this in their pursuit of him through the chancery court. How could they stop him from beating Thompson at the election? Hudson would soon find out.

Early on Sunday, 9 July, Hudson was roused from his bed and arrested for three debts and taken to York debtors' prison. Of the three debts, the first was for £23,989 owed to a Mr Sandeman of Sanderson and Sandeman, a firm of iron rail suppliers, the second was for £79 owed to Thomas Ashby and a third was for an unspecified amount owed to Jane and Robert Smith. It was a remarkable coincidence that, although he had been in the town for three weeks and could have been arrested at any time, it was left until three days before the election, that he was bound to win, before the authorities acted. Thompson and Leeman, of course, denied any knowledge or involvement.

Following his arrest, Hudson asked his long-time friend James Foster (the owner of the *Yorkshire Gazette*) to go to Whitby to withdraw his candidature for the election. At a meeting of Hudson's party held at St Hilda's Hall, Foster explained that Hudson's arrest was for an old judgment dating back to 1859. He said the writ could have been served earlier, making it less obvious that the object of the exercise was to prevent him from standing in the election. But, Foster said, this would be to no avail as Harry Thompson would still lose to Hudson's replacement, Charles Bagnall. And so it proved. Bagnall, a local ironmaster who at the time owned an ironworks at Grosmont near Whitby, won by securing 305 votes against 282 for Thompson.

Maybe winning the election was not as important to Thompson, or Leeman, as ensuring that Hudson was not elected, by fair means or foul. The NER, of course, denied they had anything to do with Hudson's arrest. In an open letter to the *Yorkshire Gazette* dated 27 July, the NER's solicitors Newton, Robinson and Brown (Newtons), denied that the NER, Thompson or his fellow directors had any involvement in Hudson's arrest.

In their letter, Newtons wrote that, as the NER case against Hudson had not yet been through the Court of Chancery, his arrest could not have been the responsibility of the NER because his debt had not yet been formally agreed by the court. To 'prove' his arrest had nothing to do with the NER or its directors, Newtons attached to their letter one they had received from Sandeman's solicitors, Wilde, Rees, Humphrey and Wilde of Whitby (Wildes), dated 14 July 1865, in which the latter said they were 'greatly surprised to find that the arrest of Mr Hudson ... issued in this cause by us ... should be attributed to political motives. This assertion is utterly destitute of foundation.' The letter went on to explain that the writ for Hudson's arrest was put in place on behalf of Mr Sandeman three days before the election because, if Hudson had been elected without paying the debt he owed, 'Mr Sandeman's remedy would have been lost or at the least put in abeyance' for however long Hudson remained a Member of Parliament. Wildes concluded their letter by saying they knew 'nothing of politics in Whitby', a statement which stretches credulity, bearing in mind the two very high-profile candidates standing in their town and begs the question, were they put up to issuing the writ by Thompson and/or Leeman?

Hudson's solicitors, Elmslie, Forsyth and Sedgwick (Elmslie), published a response to the NER's letter of denial. Elmslie wrote that numerous and important questions involved in the litigation between

Hudson and the NER had 'not been finally determined' and that the NER's claims about the amount owed to them by Hudson were at variance with their own conclusions on the matter. Pending the decision of the Court of Chancery, Elmslie wrote that the conclusions of the NER's solicitors should not be accepted without large deductions, particularly the enforcement of financial penalties on Hudson in respect of non-performance by him in matters beyond his control. Elmslie commented that it was 'the misfortune of Mr. Hudson to have found united in the person of Mr. Thompson a political adversary and an electoral competitor and, as chairman of the North Eastern Railway, the representative of claims against him susceptible alike of liberal adjustment or of unlimited, stringent and harsh enforcement.'

Elmslie pointed out that Hudson had been very popular on his return to Whitby and his election would have been inevitable had it not been 'averted by some bold coup.' Hudson, Elmslie said, had been arrested for a claim that even Mr Sandeman's solicitors had said was practically worthless because the NER claim had priority for repayment. The result was that the people of Whitby instinctively considered that Thompson and the NER were behind Hudson's arrest. Elmslie said it would be 'unbecoming' of them to question the NER solicitors' denial, but the electors of Whitby themselves could be 'excused in yielding to some scepticism in a matter involving so directly their rights, interests, and feelings.'

The public were deeply suspicious of the role of Thompson and the NER in Hudson's arrest at such a critical time and they wanted their say. The letters columns of the day were flooded with readers' views on the circumstances of Hudson's arrest. The *Newcastle Journal* reported some of these. It quoted a writer saying that George Leeman was behind the arrest, another, who described themselves as 'A Conservative' said such an accusation was nonsense as Leeman was Hudson's 'friend in adversity and trouble.' That correspondent was very unlikely to have been 'a Conservative.' In response to that letter another 'Conservative' wrote 'save me from such a friend!' and went on to comment that Thompson, Leeman and the directors of the NER were the indirect cause of Hudson's imprisonment. Another writer said the NER could easily have settled their debt with Hudson, allowing him to settle with other claimants and for him to become a free man. But the NER refused to do so, seeking rather to harass 'an honest man with ruinous chancery proceedings' and crush someone who had done so much for the railways and for the town of Whitby.

To underline the fruitlessness of Sandeman's claim, it was reported in mid-September that another of his [Sandeman's] solicitors (Mr Rees of London), had sought an adjournment of the case, on account of Hudson's circumstances being 'very bad.' Hudson also sought to adjourn the hearing, saying it would be better to settle amicably out of court. However, the Registrar of the court said he doubted he had the power to postpone an adjudication of bankruptcy, especially as there were creditors other than Mr Sandeman. Hudson then agreed, with the help and support of his friend George Elliot MP, a wealthy colliery owner from Gateshead, to pay off the debt of £79 to Thomas Ashby and the small debt to Jane and Robert Smith. Having paid off these debts, the Registrar was moved to allow Hudson's request for an adjournment of the Sandeman case for at least a month. Hudson was released from York prison in mid-October 1865, whereupon he immediately resumed his exile in France.

Not long after he had forced him into exile again, Harry Thompson was back on Hudson's case and preparing for another hearing in the Rolls Court. With this new court hearing in the offing, in early June 1866, Hudson made the mistake of returning to England to discuss issues concerning his Whitby property with his legal advisers at the chambers of the Rolls Court. Following the meeting, on 5 June, he made his way to the Carlton club in Pall Mall London. It is unclear if he went into the club, but he was arrested on the street opposite and taken to Whitecross Street debtors' prison. He had been arrested on behalf of a mortgage creditor, a Mr Bartlett, who was alleged to have had a mortgage of £13,000 outstanding. Hudson remained in the prison until 29 June, when an application was made to have him released. His lawyer, Mr Cohen, cited that as Hudson was in the process of meeting his legal advisers, he was allowed time to go to the meeting and to return home. On this technicality the court decided that Hudson should be released, though it would take no action concerning his arrest. Once again Hudson had had a fortunate escape from the dreaded debtors' prison and, as before, he immediately sailed for Calais.

Thompson's new hearing was heard by Lord Romilly (who had been elevated to the peerage in October 1865) on 10 July. Hudson's compromise agreement with the NER in 1854 had allowed him to pay £33,000 to the company from the sale of his Newby Park home and to pay the outstanding £13,249, plus £1,000 for legal costs, in two instalments, in October 1855 and October 1856. The agreement also contained a penalty clause that should he default on any part of the payment, Hudson would be required to pay the company £54,590. Although Hudson had paid the £33,000 from the sale of Newby Park, he had defaulted on the balance. As a result, Thompson was now determined to pursue Hudson for the original full debt of £54,590 and he and the NER approached the Rolls Court to enforce the penalty clause. Romilly decreed that as the sum of £54,590 was in the form of a penalty and not a debt, the company could not recover more than the outstanding debt of £14,249 plus interest. At the hearing the NER, who had taken over mortgages to the value of £75,000 on Hudson's Whitby property, also claimed £15,000 from Hudson for the cost of making improvements to the property. Romilly held that, as the NER were not trustees of the Whitby property, they were merely mortgagors, they had no authority to approve or make improvements to the property. Their claim for this £15,000 for against Hudson was dismissed. At a further hearing on 26 July, Romilly confirmed his judgment that the NER could not claim more than £14,249 from Hudson.

Following the hearing, a contributor to the *Christchurch Times* commented that he was glad of the outcome:

I was not one of those who fell down and worshipped the railway king in the days of his prosperity, neither was I one of those who cast stones at him when he tumbled from the giddy height he had attained. At one moment the petted darling of both the commercial and aristocratic worlds, at the next the object of their scorn, and in both instances treated unreasonably, Mr. Hudson has borne his reverse of fortune in manly silence for years, and deserves the piece of good fortune which has at last come to him.

But Thompson was not to be deterred and he decided that the NER should launch an appeal against Lord Romilly's verdicts. The appeal was heard by the Lord Chancellor, Lord Chelmsford, and Lord Justice Turner on 27 January 1867 but the two judges came to different conclusions over the case with Lord Chelmsford agreeing with Romilly's verdict and Lord Turner dissenting. As a result the verdict was left as decided by Lord Romilly. The *Leeds Times* suggested that if this state of affairs remained, then Hudson would soon be 'rehabilitated.'

Still in exile in France, Hudson showed no intention, whether he was able to or not, of making any further payments to the NER. It seems incredulous therefore that Thompson should decide to continue his pursuit and lodge an appeal at the House of Lords, but he was determined that Hudson should be brought to his knees.

The appeal was heard on 4 March 1869 before Lords Hatherley (now the Lord Chancellor following a change of government), Westbury, Chelmsford (again) and Colombay. The question before the judges was whether 'through the force of certain agreements made between the [NER] and [Hudson], the latter was relieved from paying the full debt of £54,590 due by him to the company.' The Lords heard a detailed summary of the case. They disagreed with the Master of the Rolls' conclusion that the covenant in the October 1854 deed, which required Hudson to pay £54,590 (if he did not pay the then outstanding amount of £14,249) was a penalty not a debt. Their Lordships regarded the

£54,590 a debt rather than a penalty as the sum had been part of a mutual agreement between the parties. As Hudson had failed to pay the agreed outstanding amount of £14,249, their Lordships overturned the previous judgments, to conclude that Hudson was now liable to pay the full amount of £54,590 as per the agreement of October 1854. The effect of this judgment was that Hudson's outstanding debt to the NER increased from £14,249 to £21,590. If Hudson had thus far steadfastly refused to pay the lower amount, there was no chance he would pay this new higher figure, whether he had the resources to or not. And he probably did not. Thompson must have known this, in which case he will have appealed to the House of Lords only in hope of having the last word over Hudson, never mind the cost in legal fees to the NER.

Chapter 16

The King Returns

Following his imprisonment at York after his failed attempt to get elected at the 1865 election in Whitby, rumours began to circulate that Hudson was very short of money. These rumours were confirmed by an anonymous letter to the *London Evening Standard* in August 1865, calling for a subscription to be set up to support Hudson during his declining years. The correspondent wrote that many fortunes were made by people of all classes as a result of Hudson's railway acumen:

> Did not archbishop, duke, marquis, earl, M.P., and everyone else who could obtain an introduction to him, avail himself of his aid and influence? And in return he who commenced life behind the counter was, during his short summer of success, the honored guest of our leading families in court and country. Well, the tide turned. The Railway King was dethroned. As he was sinking some of his friends commenced a subscription on his behalf, and it proved a miserable failure. To the shame of human nature, those who had pocketed their thousands through him refused him a pittance to avert his fate. Those who had basked in his favour in his hour of prosperity turned their backs upon him in his day of adversity. And he fell, and for many years past has, I believe, been banished from his home and country. But it is never too late to mend. If the failure of a merchant prince in our great city be deemed venial, let us not eternally ostracise the Railway King, if the *amor nummi* [love of money], with the sore temptations of his position, did indeed prove too strong for him. Let a subscription

be at once raised to relieve him from his embarrassments. Let those who benefited through him (or their descendants, if they have passed away) be the first to swell the amount. It is a debt, and should be repaid with interest. Its success will wipe out a foul blot upon society in our money-getting age.

The writer ended his letter saying he did not personally know Hudson, but he was one who had suffered rather than gained though him. He signed his letter 'A purchaser of York and North Midland £50 shares at £103.'

However, it was not until April 1869 that serious steps were taken to address concerns that Hudson was now living in France 'utterly destitute' and thought given to raising a public subscription for him. The former Railway King was as much 'sinned against as sinning', the *Luton Times* said. The paper mentioned that a 'large shareholder' intimated his intention to ask the NER to approve an annuity of £200 for Hudson. A nice idea, but one which was likely to receive short shrift. No annuity was ever considered by the NER, nor was it likely so long as the company, through Thompson and Leeman, was still pursuing him in the chancery courts. However, the idea of supporting Hudson did eventually take hold.

In May 1869, at a meeting of the River Wear Commissioners in Sunderland, Hudson's close friends, Hugh Taylor (of Chipchase Castle) and George Elliot MP proposed setting up a subscription to help Hudson in his declining years. Taylor told the meeting that Hudson was nearly starving and in great destitution and that he scarcely had the means of living. He added that, without Hudson, the new Sunderland dock would never have been built and the coal-owners would have to have sent their coals via the Tyne docks at great expense and the people of Sunderland would have suffered accordingly. The fortunes of the Sunderland Dock Company were clearly at a low ebb at this time, as Taylor informed the meeting that one of Hudson's problems was that his shares in the Dock company had depreciated by £30,000.

Taylor said care would be taken to ensure that Hudson's creditors could not obtain possession of any funds raised. George Elliot, who had assisted Hudson in 1865 when he was held in York debtors' prison, told the meeting he had recently met Hudson in Paris and was struck by his destitute appearance and that he was wearing clothes that no respectable man should be seen in. Elliot said it was not likely that Hudson would return to England while there were as yet unsatisfied creditors. Elliot said he had spoken to many wealthy and influential men about a subscription, including Thomas Brassey, the famous railway engineer and contemporary of Hudson's when the latter was at the height of his powers. All supported the idea of a subscription and Elliott said he believed that it would be possible to raise a sufficient sum, especially if Sunderland set the example. At the end of the meeting £500 had been raised including 100 guineas each from George Elliot and Hugh Taylor. Two weeks later it was reported that the Sunderland subscription had reached £1,500.

Noting the subscription that had been set up in Sunderland, the *Nottinghamshire Guardian* wrote that it would be an eternal disgrace to English society, especially those who had made their profit and who had enjoyed the company of the Railway King during the height of his power, should he be left to starve in a foreign city in his old age. The paper noted that Hudson's errors had been fully atoned by the unparalleled punishment he had received in commercial history. Viewed against what the paper described – but did not name – as men who were held 'to be angels of purity and superior in mould' to Hudson, the latter's fate must be considered very hard. Whatever he had done, it was undeniable that Hudson had contributed more than any dozen men who could be named, to the development of the railway system and the benefits that had arisen from it. The North of England in particular owed him a debt it could never repay. All should join with Sunderland in relieving the ex-Railway King 'who is starving miserably in a French garret.'

Even the *York Herald*, at one time one of his most vociferous critics, found room to sympathise with Hudson's current predicament.

In early June, the paper wrote 'We rejoice that such a movement [a subscription] has been started in York.' The paper wrote that, once a household name, Hudson had for a long time been forgotten, but now he was back in the public eye. The paper recalled his career, saying how he had risen from being a draper in College Street York, to devising railway after railway, becoming Lord Mayor of York and an MP and how Albert Gate was once crowded with worshippers and sycophants. Then the wheel of fortune turned, the panic arrived and the bubble burst. The paper wrote that there was much in his railway career that could not be justified, but now they were 'heartily' committed to the movement of sympathy and expressed the hope that the appeal for a subscription would not be made in vain. They need not have worried. Apart from Sunderland and York, subscription committees were set up in Newcastle and Whitby, as well as at the London Stock Exchange and by the Society of Engineers. Despite all the stories to the contrary, Hudson still retained many friends and sympathisers who recognised what he had achieved for the railway industry and for the country. By July, the York committee had collected £1,280 from 173 people, who had contributed between ten shillings and £50 each. Of the eighteen who gave £25, perhaps the most surprising name was that of George Leeman, Hudson's long-time foe, who was still an integral member of the NER team seeking payment of Hudson's debts.

Hugh Taylor wrote to Hudson to tell him about the subscription and the annuity. Hudson was obviously deeply grateful for the trouble that Taylor and others had taken to collect the subscription and arrange for the annuity. In his letter of thanks to Taylor, postmarked Calais August 10, 1869, Hudson wrote:

> [It is my] duty as well as my pleasure to express my grateful thanks to you, and through you to the numerous friends who have so handsomely contributed towards it. I can hardly tell you how I, in adequate terms, can express my gratitude for their recognition of my services in the promotion of public works. I assure you

I am deeply thankful to you, and to the large number of friends in Newcastle and Sunderland, as well as in other places ... [and] thus secured for my remaining days a comfortable competency. I shall ever reflect with pride and satisfaction on my connection with your district; the knowledge that I was enabled to assist in giving to the town of Newcastle its High-Level Bridge, to Sunderland its docks .... And of extending the system of railway to Scotland, is a great pleasure, and fully compensates me for any suffering I may have endured.

In September 1869, at a meeting of subscribers in York, it was announced that £4,400 had been raised, enough to earn an annuity of £512 per year. A board of trustees was then established to manage a Trust and oversee the annuity, which was arranged via the British Assurance Company. The conditions of the Trust were devised to prevent Hudson's creditors claiming or benefitting in any way from the fund. A year later it was announced a further £850 had been invested in the annuity and that Hudson's potential income had increased to £635 per year.

Hudson was, of course, still unable to return to England because of the threat of being incarcerated in a debtors' prison. Charles Dickens, whose father had suffered the ignominy of being imprisoned in Marshalsea debtors' prison in London in 1824, had long campaigned against imprisonment for debt. Eventually, in August 1869, parliament abolished the requirement for all debtors to be imprisoned until their debts were paid. The Debtors Act came into force on 1 January 1870, whereupon Hudson immediately returned to England. One wonders if Dickens enjoyed the irony that this Act enabled a man whom he had despised in years past, to return to England a free man. Interestingly, the 1869 Act included provisions to continue to imprison debtors who could afford to pay but refused to do so. The fact that Hudson felt able to return to England without the threat of imprisonment implies that he did not have the wherewithal to clear his debts.

On his return to England, Hudson moved in to share lodgings with his eldest son, William, at 37 Churton Street, Pimlico in south west London. Some have suggested he shared this address with his wife Elizabeth, but this was not the case. According to the 1871 Census, taken in March 1871, George is shown as living at 37 Churton Street with William, whilst Elizabeth is recorded as living in an apartment at 22 Hornton Street, Kensington in West London. Not only were they estranged at this time, but Elizabeth was in poor health. With this in mind, sons William and George most probably suggested it would be best for their father to live with William on his return to England. George senior was shown as the head of the household on the census and both were described as 'annuitants', suggesting William was not in employment and that he was being supported by his father. The address was divided into two lodgings, the other being occupied by James Bosworth, a cheesemonger, and his wife Mary.

Despite his case in chancery still rumbling on, Hudson was determined to enjoy his new found freedom. Not long after his return, he resumed his membership of the Carlton Club in London and was once again appointed chairman of the Smoking Room; 'my old position!' Hudson is quoted as saying.

On 9 April 1870, he travelled to Newcastle with his close friends James Foster and Hugh Taylor and stayed with Taylor at his home, Chipchase Castle. When Hudson arrived at Newcastle Central station, he was met by many of his friends from the north east and it was recorded that even a gentleman from the NER treated him with great kindness and courtesy. He was described as not being as stout as he was in his 'white waistcoat time' and that he had lost the 'brusque, bustling manner' he had when 'snobs bowed before him as King.' Now he was said to have a rather pensive expression and gave the impression of being a 'nice, canny-looking old gentleman who carries the burden of his years well.' The writer said the coming years could turn out to be the happiest and best of his very eventful life.

On Tuesday 12 April, Hudson, Taylor and Foster visited Newcastle, including the High-Level Bridge, before travelling to Sunderland where they were greeted at Monkwearmouth station by the Mayor of Sunderland, William Thompson, and numerous local dignitaries and old friends. The party left the station in an open carriage to hearty cheers from a large crowd. Hudson was said to have been very gratified to know that he had not been forgotten in the town. The following day they visited the new dock, which 'presented an exceedingly gay and holiday-like appearance' for Hudson's visit, with streamers and bunting flying. They then attended a small reception where the guests 'partook of sherry and biscuits.' In a short speech, Hudson said he was very much indebted to Mr Taylor for bringing him back to the north east to meet scenes of his youth and though many had passed whom he knew, he could meet their descendants and enjoy the good feelings he had on those previous occasions. He heartily expressed his gratification for being there again. It had not left him a wealthy man, he said, and he faltered as he remembered those former times, but went on to thank Mr Taylor and his friends for raising him above want. James Laing, the chairman of the River Wear Commissioners replied to Hudson, saying the new dock would ever remain a monument to him.

The following Saturday, 16 April, Hudson, Taylor and Foster returned to Sunderland to attend a banquet in Hudson's honour at the town's Queens Hotel. Amongst the guests were Lord Vane, John Candlish (one of Sunderland's two Liberal MPs), George Elliot MP and 'many of the principal merchants and traders of the town.' In proposing a toast to Hudson, the Mayor said the north country owed a deep debt of gratitude to Hudson, especially for the construction of the Jarrow and Sunderland Docks and the High-level bridge in Newcastle. Hudson was loudly cheered when he rose to reply. He said it was thirty years since he first came to the area and saw the potential to place the area's railways on a profitable footing. He talked about the original plan to take the railway around the centre of Newcastle, but he persevered and succeeded in taking it through the town. He mentioned the new dock at Sunderland of course, and that he had been in the forefront of developing Jarrow Dock in Newcastle. He claimed to be the first to adopt a policy of 'railway amalgamations', to make railways more profitable and cited the creation of the Midland Railway.

He could not say he had not suffered, but he had kept his courage and in his deepest distress there was always a kind friend to help, and Sunderland had always stood firmly behind him. Speaking of the charges made against him, he said it was no use speaking of them now, but he knew that he never supported a project that he did not believe to be right. He had thousands and thousands at his feet, and he could have made a fortune by buying shares of railways he recommended for amalgamation, but he did not and now 'wondered at his moderation!' This phrase would have been familiar to most of those present as this is what Clive of India in 1773 had said, when talking of his achievements in India. In other words, Hudson was saying he could have made so much more money had he taken the opportunities open to him. He went on to say he had committed some errors but 'they were errors from the head and not the heart.' He said it had been held against him that he had paid dividends out of capital but, Hudson said, he had heard since that this was what other companies had done and added that after all the 'miserable straining of matters against him', out of the £1.75million of dividends said to have been overpaid, only £50,000 could be said to have been actually overpaid. Concluding his speech, Hudson expressed the hope that he could spend the rest of his life in peace and quiet.

Reflecting on his triumphant return to the north east of England, the *Lincolnshire Chronicle* commented that Hudson had suffered severely at the hands of an ungrateful legislature for his originality and the daring of his financial conception. Then, referring to his recent annuity, the writer said it was pleasant in these days of 'self-seeking' to find someone honoured in his own country, especially after being made the 'scapegoat of a whole nation, because he originated the speculations which ended in so wild a panic.'

Chapter 17

Final Days...

In its judgment of March 1869, the House of Lords had agreed that £11,464 of the £33,000 received from the sale of Newby Park could be used by the NER to discharge a debt due to the company that was secured by mortgage. Inevitably this did not go down well with other of Hudson's creditors, including Joseph Wright and George Elliot, who also had mortgages against Hudson's Whitby property. They believed that the £33,000 should have been used in its entirety towards discharging all mortgage debts and not just those of the NER. At a further Rolls Court hearing on 7 June 1870, George Jessel QC put forward the creditors case, whilst Sir Richard Baggallay QC defended the NER's position. The parties had to wait three weeks, until 27 June 1870, before Lord Romilly ruled that the NER were at liberty to allocate the money 'in any manner they thought most for their advantage.' In his summing up Romilly also summarised the state of play with Hudson's total debt to the NER. He said that, as at 30 June 1867 the debt stood at £118,521. Since that date the NER had paid out £29,221 in interest and other costs and had received via rents and sales of property, £29,894. The NER was also holding, since 1861, £21,673 in respect of the sale of 1 Albert Gate. Allowing for further adjustments for interest payable, Romilly ordered that the figure of £118,521 be reduced by £20,673, leaving a balance of £97,848 and that the interest charged since 30 June 1867 should be revised accordingly. At first glance it may seem that Hudson's debt had suddenly increased. However, the revised figure of £97,848 is broadly made up of mortgages totalling £75,000 and the £21,590 still outstanding from the debt of £54,590.

Unsurprisingly, Elliot was unhappy with Romilly's ruling and he decided to lodge an appeal, which was heard on 13 February 1871, in front of Lords James and Mellish. On hearing the case involved George Hudson, Lord James exclaimed 'Is this *the* George Hudson?' When told 'yes', James remarked that it must then be a very old suit, but he was assured it was not Hudson's case directly, just a branch of it!

George Jessel once again made a strong case for the creditors. But, in his summing up, Lord Mellish agreed with Baggallay's argument that payment of the £33,000 formed an essential part of the compromise agreement between the company and Hudson, that enabled Hudson to pay a lesser amount for the settlement of his debts. Whilst the agreement was not set out in writing, Lord Mellish said it was referred to in two deeds (dated January 1854 and October 1854). The £33,000 received from the sale of Newby Park represented the first payment under this agreement. Their Lordships therefore agreed with the House of Lords ruling that the NER could apply the £33,000 'pro rata, first to the payment of interest and secondly to the payment of the principal sums.'

Elliot's appeal marked the last of the hearings in the long history of Hudson's time in the chancery courts. Chancery proceedings often came to an end when the money ran out to pay the legal costs, or when one of the parties died and could no longer take part in the proceedings. In this case it would seem that even Harry Thompson finally had to admit that pursuing the NER claim any further would be a fruitless task, as there was no prospect that Hudson would ever be in a position to pay any of his outstanding debt to the company. So it was that, quite out of the blue, the NER agreed to drop the case, but with certain conditions.

On 1 December 1871, James Foster, Hudson's long-time friend and owner of the *Yorkshire Gazette* newspaper, received a telegram from Hudson to say that the long running litigation between him and the NER had finally been brought to an end. A new agreement between the parties allowed Hudson to retain ownership of his West Cliff estate in Whitby, whilst the NER would take over his shares in the Sunderland

Dock company. The news filtered out and caused great excitement in Whitby, where it was hoped that work on his West Cliff estate, which had practically ground to a halt during the 20-year chancery dispute, would soon resume.

All through the trauma of the chancery court hearings Hudson had displayed enormous inner strength. At no point did he give up, nor did he ever blame anyone but himself for his troubles. Had he done so, he is unlikely to have helped himself and would have caused much trouble for the many people who had helped and supported him through his life and who had remained his loyal friends.

To celebrate the end of the case and his new found freedom, Hudson travelled to Yorkshire to visit friends and family. He firstly stayed with Charles Russell in Malton, then visited family in Howsham and intended to spend a weekend with James Foster in his home at Ogleforth, York. For some time, Hudson had been suffering chest pains and on 8 December, whilst at Foster's, he had an attack of what was described as *angina pectora*. Dr William Matterson was called to attend and provide some relief for Hudson's pain. Matterson was the son of Alderman Matterson, who led the campaign to have Hudson's portrait removed from York Mansion House in November 1849, further evidence perhaps that Hudson did not hold grudges against those who had let him down, although maybe he had no alternative in his choice of doctor. The following day, Hudson returned home to London, where he was attended to by Dr Thomas Watson. He was advised to rest and avoid all excitement and exertion. He wrote to Foster shortly afterwards to say he was hopeful that Dr Watson's advice would help and that he would soon be better again. Sadly, the next letter Foster received was from Hudson's son William, to advise that his father had suffered a relapse and fallen into a deep coma from which he did not recover. George Hudson passed away at 37 Churton Street, in the arms of his youngest son, William, at 8.40am on 14 December 1871.

The train that took Hudson on his last journey to York left London at 11.50pm on Thursday, 20 December. The train is said to have travelled via 'his' Midland route, so presumably went via Rugby, Derby and Leeds. His lead lined coffin had an outer coffin of inch and a half thick French polished oak and weighed half a ton. It was accompanied on its journey north by his sons George and William and the undertaker, Mr Smith of Brompton Road, London. The coffin rested in the railway carriage in which it was brought to York until 9.00am on 21 December, when it was transferred to a hearse in readiness for its journey to Scrayingham, where a number of years earlier Hudson had bought a plot beside the main entrance of St Peter and St Paul's church for himself and his family. At the time he bought the plot, Scrayingham was still the parish church for Howsham and was where all his ancestors had been laid to rest.

At 9.30 the funeral cortege set off from the Station Hotel, York consisting of the hearse drawn by four horses which, in accordance with the wishes of Hudson and his wife Elizabeth did not wear the feathers that 'give pomp to funeral pageantry.' Four bearers walked on each side of the hearse, which was followed by a single mourning carriage conveying Hudson's sons, William and George, and two old friends, James Foster and William Richardson. They were followed by two cabs occupied by various acquaintances of Hudson, including Thomas Cabrey, a former engineer of the YNM, and John Close, his long-time associate since the days of the drapery business. Harry Thompson and George Leeman were notable absentees. Although Thompson's absence was to be expected as he was a staunch enemy of Hudson, that of Leeman is surprising, bearing in mind, despite his enmity, he did show some sympathy towards Hudson over the issue of his portrait back in 1849 and contributed to his annuity subscription in 1869. In their stead, the NER was represented by General Manager Henry Tennant and Passenger Superintendent, Mr Christison.

The cortege passed through York city centre, over Lendal bridge and along Coney Street, High Ousegate, Pavement, Fossgate and down Walmgate and then out into the countryside via Grimston, Gate Helmsley, Buttercrambe and then up into Scrayingham. In Coney Street and some other parts of the city, shopkeepers kept their shutters up and their blinds down as a mark of respect. All the while the coffin made its way through the city, the Minster and the church of St Martin-le-Grand tolled a bell every minute. The man who had done so much for the city of York was sent to his last resting place with as much respect as could be offered. In Whitby, many shops were partially closed during the day as a mark of respect to the town's 'greatest benefactor.'

On reaching Scrayingham, the procession was met by Hudson's numerous family and friends from Howsham, Whitby and Malton, including his sole surviving brother John, who was then 83 years old. There were two significant absentees from the service, his wife Elizabeth and daughter Ann. The *Morpeth Herald* mentioned that Elizabeth was at this time a 'confirmed invalid.' It is no doubt the case that she did not attend on account of her not being able to travel from London to York, let alone onward by carriage to Scrayingham. Ann had moved to Germany following her marriage to Count Suminska in 1854. Bearing in mind that her father's funeral was held just a week after his death, it was probably impossible for her to travel to England in time.

The funeral service was conducted 'free from ostentation and parade' by the Rector of Scrayingham, the Reverend William Douglas. The *York Herald* noted that throughout the day 'the sun shone with a brilliancy rarely witnessed on St. Thomas Day, the shortest day of the year' and that Hudson now rests 'in the substantial vault of his ancestors, overlooking the beautiful sequestered valley of the [River] Derwent.'

Shortly after his funeral, a number of Hudson's friends in Newcastle decided to raise funds to furnish his grave with a simple marble monument. The polished Aberdeen granite tombstone they purchased still adorns his grave to this day. In 2015, a local group of friends of Scrayingham church set about raising funds to restore the surrounding stonework, which had deteriorated somewhat over the previous 150 years. Remarkably the tombstone itself was found to be as level and as solidly in place as when it was first installed in the 1870s. It required no work apart from repainting the faded lettering. To raise money for the restoration, various events in the church, such as 'George Hudson' and 'Brunel' evenings, were held. The funds generously donated by the public at these events were added to grants from the Railway Heritage Trust and the Stephenson Locomotive Society and the stonework restored in September 2019 by renowned stonemason Matthias Garn and his team.

A week following Hudson's funeral, the River Wear Commissioners in Sunderland agreed to rename the town's South Docks 'Hudson Dock North' and 'Hudson Dock South.' Supporting the decision, John Candlish, one of Sunderland's two Liberal MPs, said that whatever anyone thought of Hudson, and he thought him a great man, he was always faithful to Sunderland and it was fitting for the town to honour his memory. Edward Gourley, the town's other MP at the time, also supported the proposal and related a story where he had written to Hudson a few years earlier, to tell him how much was owed to him by the town. Hudson had replied saying it was the first time he had been spoken of favourably since his fall and that Gourley's words had moved him to tears. Then, in sharp contrast to the reaction of York Council following Hudson's fall from grace in 1849 when his portrait was removed from the Mansion House, Edward Gourley set about negotiating with Elizabeth Hudson to purchase the full-length portrait of Hudson painted in 1846 by Francis Grant that was in her possession. The intention, Gourley said, was to display the portrait in a 'conspicuous' place in Sunderland. In latter years, the portrait was displayed at the council-run museum housed in the former Monkwearmouth station, which Hudson used when he visited Sunderland. This portrait was removed from Monkwearmouth in 2017 when the museum closed due to the building being unsafe. It subsequently reopened as a football 'fans' museum, but Hudson's portrait was transferred for display in the Shipbuilding gallery of Sunderland Museum.

Just a few days after his funeral, Madame Tussaud's Waxworks in London dusted off their effigy of Hudson, sculpted at the time of his 'greatest success', and put it back on display. It was advertised in the press along with a new model of the Prince of Wales and of the infamous Thomas Castro, who purported to be the 'Tichborne claimant.' Entrance was 1 shilling for adults and sixpence for children under 10. Madame Tussaud's advertised that visitors could reach their Waxworks by taking the 'Metropolitan Railway to Baker Street' – a railway connection to the end!

In his Will, dated 24 February 1858, Hudson gave his address as the 'Carlton Club' in London, which suggests he may have lodged there when attending the House of Commons in the late 1850s. In his Will he left two thirds of his estate to his eldest son George and one third to William. They were also required, as executors, to 'carry out his views and wishes respecting his daughter Ann', but these are not specified. There is no mention of Elizabeth which tends to confirm that the couple were leading separate lives by this time. He also made reference to his interests in Spain. It is to be hoped that his sons were not too disappointed when it was revealed that on his death his estate was said to be worth no more than £200.

Chapter 18

What They Said

When Hudson died, very many newspapers of the day published fulsome obituaries. Most were sympathetic to Hudson, noting not just his railway exploits but his charitable work in York and his ebullient character despite all the troubles he faced in later life. This chapter looks in detail at what was said about him in the immediate period after his death and how, towards the end of the nineteenth century, those who wrote about him began to establish the reputations that have subsequently been attached to him.

The first newspaper to publish an obituary, was *The Times*, on 16 December 1871, two days after his passing. The newspaper wrote that a new generation had risen since Hudson was at the peak of his powers and known as 'The Railway King' and that:

> those to whom his face and figure and voice were familiar, who added to the crush at his entertainments and listened to, or retailed the anecdotes respecting him, are to be found only among the middle-aged members of the Commons or the most seasoned frequenters of London society. There was a time when not to know him was to argue one's self unknown; now he is only a tradition. It often happens that a man who has been famous in the past emerges from a long obscurity in the newspaper paragraph which announces his death. The first impulse is to exclaim, 'Has he really been alive all this time?' Some such thought will occur to many who remember the George Hudson of the old times, what he did and what was done for him, his wealth, his grandeur, and his fall. His social [disappearance] preceded his political disappearance.

A quarter of a century ago he turned all that he touched to gold; in after years his name was enough to wither the prospectus on which it was printed. The world which blindly trusted him, which cringed to him and flattered him, avenged itself by excessive and savage reprobation. Its anger and contempt were increased by the discovery that he had really nothing left. 'See how ill-gotten gains vanish!' exclaimed these moralists after the events.

It would be ridiculous to apologize for him, and to deny his faults merely because he is dead, but it is fair to notice that to the last he had warm friends, and that these were among the men who knew him longest and best.

The history of the railway enterprise in England is a strange one. This country has the honour of giving birth to that famous invention which has revolutionized the habits of men and the relations of kingdoms. No change in the history of the world is greater than the change which was effected when George Hudson's locomotive first ran upon rails with passengers behind it. Yet for many years this great discovery was but little applied in the country which produced it.

It is impossible to deny that he did great things to develop the railway system in the North of England, and to direct the national enterprise into this channel. The north-country people stood by him for years, and his constituents sent him to the House of Commons till 1859. He was a man who united largeness of view with wonderful speculative courage. He went in for bigger things than anyone else. He took away people's breath at first, but he soon succeeded in persuading them that the larger the project and the bolder the scheme, the more likely it was to pay. He showed his confidence by investing more largely than anyone else, and taking upon himself all sorts of responsibilities. This is the kind of man who leads the world. Let him have one success and people will follow him anywhere. Mr. Hudson was for two or three years looked upon as having the key to untold treasures. The world will court rich men, but there is one whom it will court still more, and that is he who is supposed to be able to make all men rich. This was Mr. Hudson's position.

The *Morning Post, Yorkshire Gazette* and *Railway News* were amongst the many newspapers that carried a similar article about Hudson following his death. These repeated John Francis's assessment that Hudson 'was not a tyrant just because others were sycophants' and added:

when lords courted and ladies caressed him, he forgot not those he had known in less prosperous days. He still remembered the friends of his youth and he was ever ready to aid those whom he could serve.

He rejoiced in being the architect of his own fortune and we could tell anecdotes, very significant to the student of character, confirming the kindly disposition of the man whose broad and massive frame, whose face and figure, characterised by determination and stamped with power, might seem to argue a less genial nature.

He did great good by stealth. He availed himself of his riches to assist the needy. He made loans to many without the least prospect of payment. Much of his benevolence was spontaneous and many a one has benefited who never knew from whom the favour came. Many an afflicted widow and embarrassed family were relieved, who never knew the alms-giver. The public charities of York and Yorkshire found in him a munificent benefactor.

Such was the man for whom future days of adversity and gloom were in store. A fierce revulsion took place in popular feeling towards him. The public believed all the accusations against him; tales were circulated which truth has since repudiated and it was even alleged as a smear against him that he had accepted allotments of shares which his shareholders had forced upon him.

If Mr. Hudson acted unwisely, he paid the penalty; if he erred, he suffered.

Remembering all that he had done, the triumphs he achieved, and the trials through which he passed, he should be thought of as 'more sinned against than sinning.' He was the scapegoat for the sins of many.

[In the House of Commons] he was one of the foremost champions in the defence of British industry, and Hansard records some speeches made by him most remarkable for their deep research for boldness of conception and for frankness of style.

He leaves a widow, two sons, and a daughter to lament his loss and we are sure that they will have the warmest sympathies of the citizens of York and lots of friends elsewhere, who revere the name of George Hudson, which will shine brightly in the history of his time.

The *Bristol Times and Mirror* wrote that the vices of the Railway King had long been forgotten and that it was only the recent raising of an annuity for him by his friends in Sunderland that had brought him to attention again. He was, the paper wrote, but a nine-day wonder and 'if spoken of today, it is as an audacious and brilliant charlatan' but:

despite all his faults, we probably owe more to the Railway King than to many abler and better men, for it was his spirit of enterprise and speculation that led to the country being covered with railways from Perth to Penzance. He led many hundreds of thousands into a career of rough and in the end ruinous speculation. But the ruin of these shareholders gave impetus to the prosperity of the country which is felt today.

For a few years everything turned to gold, he was the 'Railway Midas.' Every line he had something to do with flourished and became prosperous. But he was the dupe of his own imagination. He did not see the crash coming, but when it came, he was one of its first victims. He lost everything and with it his reputation.

In the full flush of his prosperity, he was the most powerful man in England. He was more popular than Sir Robert Peel. His social gatherings at Albert Gate made the proudest Duke blush. In the City he overshadowed the Rothschilds and the Barings. It was even proposed to put a statue up of him in London but Thomas Carlyle put an end to that project. And then the bubble burst. Ruin and desolation was brought to every town and village.

The *Derby Mercury* wrote that Hudson, once a prosperous draper, was identified by the maddest fit of financial gambling since the South Sea Bubble, but he was a remarkable man:

> with very little education, he did what most educated people might have sat down and thought of for a thousand years without doing anything. He had extraordinary practical foresight, boundless confidence in his own calculations and knew that railways would add enormously to the wealth of England. An anticipation which had been justified. When he fell, some of those who

worshipped him most devoutly, reviled their idol with a bitterness corresponding with their previous servility. He bore the loss of fortune and favour with such courage as to show conclusively that he was no commonplace rich upstart. His good humour was as inexhaustible as his courage, whether he felt his fall much or little, no one was allowed to know. During his time in exile he bore himself so bravely as to win not only pardon but admiration.

The *Cumberland Pacquet and Ware's Whitehaven Advertiser* commented that:

If Hudson had done the same as other promoters of public companies prior to 1866, he would have saved his money and died a rich man. But Hudson did not do this. He was a man who believed in what he was doing and who would not ask others to take a risk which he himself would refuse. He put his money where his mouth was, unlike the modern [in 1871] promoter whose object is to run the least bit risk to himself, to act as a decoy duck, to walk off with his ill-gotten gains before the companies he has shares in goes to the wall.

The *York Herald*, at one time no friend of Hudson's, published a long and sympathetic obituary, saying that in his long life he had always looked on the bright side when speaking about himself or his troubles:

His spirit was, to the day of his death, as fresh, sanguine, and life enjoying as a boy's; and when the writer of this notice met him a month or two ago, he was confident that he should once more represent Sunderland at the next general election. 'The happiest part of my life', he said quite candidly. 'was when I stood behind the counter and used the yard measure in my own shop. My ruin was my having a fortune left me. I had one of the snuggest businesses in York, and turned over my thirty thousand a year, five-and-twenty per cent of it being profit, when a relation died and left me a goodish fortune. It was the very worst thing which ever happened to me. It led me into railways, and to all my misfortunes since.' This was spoken with infinite cheerfulness and good temper, and was immediately, followed by expressions of thankfulness to the friends who had rallied round him in his later years.

The *Herald* wrote that Hudson often recalled the social fun he had with 'old George Stephenson, the best of fellows and the best of friends.' He also delighted in telling the story of how he would go to Billingsgate Fish Market in London to buy his fish:

'I do now what I did when I lived at Albert Gate, I always go down to Billingsgate and buy my own fish. I never allowed a servant to do that for me when I could do it for myself, and I never fancied the fish at a fishmonger's when I could see it in large quantities as it came into the market. So, when I was a great man in London, no matter where I'd been the night before or what grand people had been to my house, and nearly everybody was glad to visit me in those days, I used always to get up early and go down to Billingsgate and choose my fish for the day's use. I did it because I liked it then, and I do it now for economy and because I like to.'

This is scarcely the time for dwelling on the fever which beset the nation during the Railway Mania, or for analysing the part played in it by George Hudson. If he was one of the chief offenders, he was assuredly one of the chief sufferers, and it is intolerably notorious now that many of the practices for which he was so heavily punished, have not always been held sufficient to ostracise the commercial people who have been guilty of them.

Hudson never split upon his friends, or there might have been some curious stories to hear about people whose fingers you would think were incapable of being soiled. What he suffered in silence no one knew but himself. He was so miserably poor during the long years he languished on the Continent that there is good reason for believing that he not infrequently went hungry to bed.

Arthur Helps, in his book *Thoughts upon Government*, published in 1872, wrote that, if he were asked to point out the men who had shown the most remarkable competency for the conduct of business, they would, in several instances, prove to be men of very limited education. The *Herald* commented that George Hudson was such a man. His history, and the influence he exercised, without apparent effort, over the hard-headed, money-getting men of his generation, proved the general belief in his competency. You could not talk with him, or note his admixture of shrewdness and simplicity, without finding that his education had been limited. He never lost his broad Yorkshire accent and he never affected greater refinement of manner than was appropriate to the provincial shopkeeper of the old school.

The *Bath Chronicle* wrote that the old days of George Hudson live in the pages of *Punch* and of some of the best known writings of Thackeray, where he was not too tenderly judged. The subsequent misfortunes of the great speculator, however, have caused men to look more leniently on him and his doings than they were inclined to look when they envied him his prosperity or exulted in his fall. It was to his credit, rather than theirs, that he had friends who remained faithful to him to the end. And it must be remembered that the schemes which he favoured and advocated have all, by their success, vindicated the soundness of his judgment.

A 'Whitby correspondent' wrote in the *Morpeth Herald* that Hudson's connection with the town had begun some thirty years earlier and although interrupted, it was never entirely severed. He said Hudson had:

undoubtedly been of much benefit to the town. He it was who opened out and beautified the West Cliff, and gave Whitby its first start as a watering place; and it was also during his reign that Whitby was embraced by the great railway system. Hence, that Mr. Hudson's popularity in Whitby was literally unbounded, and as he himself once remarked, after the battle of life had gone against him, 'Whitby was faithful when other friends had been faithless.'

The *Richmond and Ripon Chronicle* said, despite being compelled to move abroad, Hudson was rarely to be found downhearted, adding there were few men that were better company than Hudson when recalling his stories from the past and one he particularly liked telling was the origin of his title of 'The Railway King':

The Reverend Sydney Smith, the great wit, first called me the Railway King and I remember very well that he made a very pretty speech about it, saying 'while some Monarchs had won their title to fame by bloodshed and by the misery they inflicted on their fellow-creatures, I had come to my throne by my own peaceful exertions and by a course of probity and enterprise.' This was always Hudson's tone. He had been made a victim. There was a great reaction and a great public outcry, and he was the scapegoat; but where were the schemes and enterprises he had favoured most – successful every one!

As evidence of Hudson's probity, the *York Herald* published a recollection from someone who had known Hudson for over thirty years, who recalled an occasion in 1846 when Hudson was offered shares to become a director of a speculative company. The prospectus for the proposed railway was issued which showed that the new line would be a sure-fire success, so much so that people asked why it had not been built in the very earliest days of the railways. The rush for shares was so great, that it was impossible to give applicants the number asked for:

> In a few weeks the scrip, £8 paid, was selling in the market at £16; then came a lull and the speculation hung fire. Mr. Hudson at that time was in the zenith of his fame. A clever rascal who had already pocketed £20,000 clear profit upon his dealings in this particular scrip bethought him of a grand scheme whereby the speculative waters could again be moved; it was to get Mr. Hudson to become a director of the company. An offer of 2,000 shares was made to him at par as the price of his adhesion, or, in plain English, a bribe of £28,000 for the honour of his name. To his credit be it ever remembered that he refused the offer with scorn; he pointed out that the projected line could not be constructed under any circumstances, that the whole scheme was a swindle, and that he was surprised to find any respectable man lending his name to such a manifest fraud. The affront was quietly pocketed by Mr. Hudson's correspondent, he got out of the concern as soon as he could, and the whole thing collapsed, the unfortunate shareholders getting back 5s. per share, and a vast number of innocent people were ruined. If many men took this lesson to heart at the present day it would be well, and this single trait in Mr. Hudson's character speaks volumes for the honesty of the man, and will be remembered when his many failings have been forgotten.

Two articles about Hudson appeared in the *Witney Express and Oxfordshire and Midland Counties Herald*. The first was an account of Hudson's life from someone who had known him. The second was the paper's formal obituary. In the first article, the writer said he had last met Hudson two years previously at a dinner party, given shortly after he had returned to London.

He looked built to live to ninety years; declared that he knew nothing of headaches or indigestion; ate and drank freely of everything good, and with his anecdotes and reminiscences, engineering and political, was the life and soul of a very cheerful party, which included two of his old colleagues in the House of Commons.

By successful management he became an authority as a railway director, and commenced a series of amalgamations on a principle that seemed like coining money. His plan was extremely simple. Every line he wanted, whatever its dividends, he leased at ten per cent, and the public at once dealt in them at that value. By this means the present Midland was formed.

At King Hudson's levees the junior aristocracy of both sexes crowded. Ladies of the brightest fashion treated him with more attention than a rich unmarried duke. He was followed into the City. A stockbroker of my acquaintance pushing suddenly into the King's waiting-room with important news, found something soft resisting behind the door. It was two countesses come to beg for allotments.

The writer concluded by noting that there were two towns that always remained faithful to Hudson - Sunderland, 'which he made with docks and railways', and Whitby and that although Hudson's financial arrangements might have been ruinous to those who believed in him, his principles of railway amalgamation were sound, and were now bearing splendid fruit, 'witness the Midland Railway.'

In a fulsome obituary, the *Witney Express* wrote that Hudson's was a name that was once on every man's tongue and noted that his:

rapid rise and sudden fall might have seemed more natural in America than in an old steady-going country like England, where people are not in the habit of making fabulous fortunes at a bound.

He devoted his energy to developing the railway system in England, and it was mainly through his exertions that the national enterprise was directed into this channel. He continued to prosper, moving in the highest Society, and giving princely entertainments, until the great railway crisis and crash came. Thereafter, George Hudson became involved in so many Chancery suits that his once splendid fortune was swept entirely away.

If George Hudson's life was a failure, the railway system which he did so much to promote, and the splendid dock works at Sunderland, set a-going by his enterprise, have proved great successes.

This 'remarkable man' rose from being behind the counter at his drapery shop to become 'King at Capel Court and greater than a King at his home in Albert Gate', enthused the *Belfast Newsletter*. His rise had no parallel in modern history. He was shrewd, intelligent and enterprising. 'Railwayism' was little known at the time he began his career in railways but:

what he achieved in starting new projects and in guiding and directing some of those already in hand is well known, but the world is yet to give him credit for all that he accomplished and all he sacrificed for creating the comparative perfection of England's railway system.

In 1845 the three greatest men in the House of Commons were Sir Robert Peel, George Hudson and Sir James Hogg MP and director of the East India Company. In some respects, Hudson was ahead of the other two. On nearly all matters of detail with railway Bills submitted at this time, the Prime Minister (Sir Robert Peel), sought Hudson's advice. This was the zenith of his career, when the Reverend Sydney Smith, gave him the soubriquet of the 'railway king.' Royalty sought his advice and the Duke of Wellington, who was not given to sought celebrity, forgot his 'pipe-clayed etiquette' and enjoyed conversations with the oracle of the iron way.

It has been said by some writers that, in the heyday of his glory, Hudson became arrogant. But that was not the fact. Like Napoleon, he proved himself able to deal with adversity. When in prosperous days he was courted and followed by Dukes and Dowagers, when the great capitalists of the City of London gambolled before him as the Israelites had danced around Aron's golden calf and the elite of Piccadilly and Park Lane were proud of his recognition, Hudson never forgot himself.

Next to George Stephenson, the success of England's railway system was more attributable to Hudson than any other living man.

But not every newspaper eulogised about Hudson. The *Northern Whig*, published in Belfast, wrote that Hudson had:

not left many friends. He was, we believe, a poor vulgar creature at the best – very arrogant in his prosperity, and not very dignified in his adversity. But he has gone. His history if properly told would indeed point a moral and adorn a tale. Hudson was worshipped by the aristocracy and he delighted to call them by their Christian names on the racecourse. He almost succeeded in marrying his daughter to the Duke of Buckingham. When he dined at Newcastle the mail train was delayed for an hour to wait for him at the station. He was worshipped as Mammon. But the crash came. And when he fell from his high pedestal, his titled admirers rushed away from him, leaving him in the dust.

The *Spectator* reflected how, now he had died, everyone was speaking well of Hudson, after all his speculations had turned out well but, whilst that was true, that was not the point:

> Nobody ever accused him of stupidity, and the accusation of pocketing money may have been incorrect; but the main charge against him was proved, and was more grave than either. He did "cook accounts" – that is, he, being responsible for accuracy, did sanction the issue of a series of intentionally inaccurate statements to the public, in order that certain schemes might be well thought of. That his figures proved right years after is no excuse for those statements any more than it would be an excuse for a Chancellor of the Exchequer who misrepresented the revenue from sugar in 1870 if in 1880 his figures happened to tally with the facts. Falsehood is not truth because it happens to resemble a truth subsequently realized.

On his passing, *Bell's Weekly Messenger* wrote not about Hudson, but about the 'disgust' it felt for the 'titled reptiles, time-servers, and toad-eaters, who fawned upon, and flattered him in his days of prosperity':

> Many nobles of the land – ignoble in every respect but the accidental possession of a peerage – others, untitled, but still great people in their own estimation and roaring lions of the world of London all condescended to accept invitations at Albert Gate, and there quaffed the King's champagne, whilst they secretly derided him and made cutting jokes at the expense of his *parvenue* wife when they went home. These flunkeys went willingly to Hudson's house – and why? To make money out of him, or through his means. They cared little for the foul source

of the glittering gold – no more than Vespasian when he met the remonstrance Titus with the caustic inquiry – '*Num adore offenderetur?*' Messrs. Pyke and Pluck were not over particular about *their* host, so that they could 'break out afresh' at dessert-time, after a dozen courses, 'as if nothing remarkable had occurred since breakfast.' They rather liked 'a discount dinner', so long as Lord Verisopht, and not themselves, were bound to pay the piper thereafter. 'Where the carcase is, there will the vultures be gathered together.' The parasites scented their prey afar off, and when they had 'made their game' they left him to rot in gaol, or to starve on a pittance in some obscure corner of the wide world. The tale is an old one, and the moral 'somewhat musty.'

The *Messenger* said *The Times* was always ready to patronise successful people but, although it took up George Hudson at first, it soon dropped him. The paper continued:

The geese and lame ducks of the Stock Exchange caught the infection. The Railway Mania in 1845 was at its height, an "iron" age seemed likely at that time to supersede the golden one imagined by the poets. Stock jobbers are a notoriously gullible race. They will always swallow the most startling news, even when *a priori* improbable, if conveyed by a pigeon; and 'pigeoned' they often are accordingly.

The vulgar superstition, which 'has respect of *persons* because of advantage', was illustrated in all these incidents of Hudson's unedifying career. And so now-a-days! Why, we could ask, are the jog-trot majority of common-place people so absorbed in the Tichborne trial just because a vast sum of money is at stake? Were the issue one of pure principle, and not of personal interest, the newspapers might cease to publish their lengthy and most tiresome reports, for they would remain unread.

One feels half inclined, on witnessing in England the sure success *of* success, if only, as in Hudson's case, for time, to seize a spade and rush to the 'diggings.' One might tumble into a devil's dyke in the sequel; but, what's the odds so long 'the world slides along' and one slides through life with it, easily and rapidly! 'Holdfast is a better dog than Brag.' The future is far remote. Who but an angel – or saint – can resist the potentiality of the present?

Three years after Hudson's passing an anonymous correspondent, calling himself *Eboracensis*, wrote to the *Newcastle Chronicle* reflecting on Hudson's career and legacy. *Eboracensis* wrote that he was once a neighbour of Hudson's in College Street York. And, because he never profited from any of Hudson's transactions and was opposed to him in politics, he could not be accused of partiality. Without wishing to excuse Hudson for his faults, *Eboracensis* said that now the excitement of those times [the Railway Mania] had passed, it was possible to discover some redeeming features in Hudson's character. For example, a number of the public works in the North of England could be attributed solely to his enterprising spirit. Sunderland owed him an everlasting debt of gratitude. During the Railway Mania of 1845-50, when nearly everybody dabbled in shares to their cost or profit, when mythical companies were floated for the purpose of gratifying the public propensity to deal in 'scrip' – a state of things unparalleled since the days of the South Sea Bubble – we can hardly wonder that Hudson, who was looked up to as an authority, became elated by success, was tempted and subsequently failed.

Eboracensis continued, saying that it would require a severe stretch of the imagination to conceive that Hudson accomplished all his plans unaided. He was always surrounded by a horde of satellites, ready to take advantage of his policy. But when the day of reckoning came, he was deserted by the well-fed vultures who had fattened in his train, and he was left almost alone to bear the brunt and consequences of their united actions. It is this part of his career which seems to convey the most instructive lesson to posterity. *Eboracensis* ended his letter by asking, how many people are there in this district who date their entrance into 'Society' from King Hudson's reign, but who quietly ignored their former patron in his hour of need? Like Cardinal Wolsey, he learnt what may be expected from the base ingratitude of man – '*Sic transit gloria mundi*' (thus passes earthly glory).

As the memory of Hudson began to fade from popular memory following his death, newspapers of the day would often reflect on the days of Mania 'forty years ago.' In one such article carried by the *York Herald* in October 1889, the writer said that when Hudson fell from grace 'a howl of execration arose from his deluded followers and those who had bowed the lowest during his brief reign, [they then] hissed the loudest when he fell.' The holders of stock following the fall in shares at the collapse of the Railway Mania, were 'all grievously enraged' and they looked about 'for a victim', for someone to blame for their losses. They found their victim in George Hudson. Whilst this article appears to show some sympathy for Hudson's plight, describing him as a 'victim', less than six months later the *Herald* carried a reader's letter which included some of the tropes about Hudson that have carried on down the years. For example, the reader wrote that as:

> success nerved him to greater efforts [Hudson] entered on a career of wild speculation, contrived schemes of a questionable nature, moulded a hundred projects that were not above suspicion.

This description of Hudson is blatantly untrue. There were many charlatans and swindlers who sought to separate gullible railway investors from their money during the Mania years, but Hudson was most definitely not one of them. Such fabrications of the truth have done Hudson's reputation much undeserved harm over the years and there is still, 150 years after his passing, a reluctance in some quarters to recognise his achievements. George Hudson may not have been a great engineer like George Stephenson or Isambard Kingdom Brunel, but he was most certainly the greatest railway entrepreneur of his time and since.

Chapter 19

Elizabeth Hudson

Unlike her husband, very little has been written about Elizabeth Hudson, though she had a very important role in his life. Unfortunately, similar to her husband, Elizabeth's reputation has also been tarnished over the years, by stories and gossip told of her character and reputation. This chapter is an attempt to tell something of Elizabeth's story and the important part she played in her husband's life, particularly when he was at the height of his powers as the Railway King.

Elizabeth was born in York on 16 October 1795 and was the younger sister of Rebecca (born October 1790) and Richard (July 1793). Her parents were James and Elizabeth (nee Wainman) Nicholson, who married at Holy Trinity Church Goodramgate York on 1 November 1789. Apart from these details nothing is known of Elizabeth's early life until the first reference to her comes in George Hudson's story, when he became apprenticed to the drapery business of Bell and Nicholson in 1813.

William Bell took over a drapery shop in College Street York in 1809. He was later joined in the business by Elizabeth's older brother, Richard Nicholson. In April 1813 William married Elizabeth's older sister Rebecca. Sadly the marriage only lasted eight months, as William died in December 1813. Richard and Rebecca then ran the business which continued to be known as Bell and Nicholson. During the same year, George Hudson had joined the business as an apprentice. George evidently excelled in his job and in February 1821 he became a full partner in the business which then became known as Nicholson and Hudson. It is not difficult to imagine that, when George first arrived in York, Elizabeth, who was five years older, took to the boy from the country. Over the following eight years their relationship grew, from being just friends to becoming a courting couple. They were married at Holy Trinity church in York on 15 July 1821 and began married life living above the shop in College Street.

Inevitably, Elizabeth's next few years were dominated by motherhood and the mixed emotions of joy and sadness as her first three children died young. Her first child, James Richard, was born on 15 April 1822, but sadly he died just three weeks later. Her second son, Richard Nicholson, named after her brother, was born on 27 September 1824, but he died in March 1834, aged 9 years, after what the *Yorkshire Gazette* described as a 'short illness of 36 hours.' Her third son, Matthew Bottrill, who was born on 21 June 1827, also died young, aged six months. However, her other four children were all longer-lived. They were, George born 30 September 1829, Ann Elizabeth, 28 September 1830*, John, 15 May 1832* and William, 10 February 1834* (*baptism date).

When George and Elizabeth moved into Matthew Bottrill's house in Monkgate in 1827, Elizabeth assumed responsibility for ensuring the family home was comfortable and for hiring and managing servants. J.A. Knowles recalled an amusing story concerning her coachman, a certain Richard Newsham, whom she found very difficult to manage. Whenever she asked Richard to do something, Richard always did things his way and in his time. On one occasion, when he was having a house built in Lowther Street, Elizabeth asked to be taken for a ride through the centre of York. The weather had been very wet for some time and the streets were in a terrible state, with deep ruts making it very difficult to drive carts and coaches. Richard was evidently irked at being asked to drive in such conditions and rather than take Elizabeth into the city, he decided to take her to see his new house in Lowther Street.

When Elizabeth realized they were going in the wrong direction, she tried to catch Richard's attention by calling to him out of the carriage window, 'Richard, Richard!' But Richard was deaf to all and drove on. The road got worse and the wheels started reeling in the ruts. Elizabeth was now shouting at the top of her voice 'Richard, Richard!'

from within the carriage. She could not put her head out of the window because of the mud splattering up from the road. At last Richard pulled up in front of his new house and with the utmost coolness pointed to it with his whip and said 'See Mum! That's my new house!' then with great difficulty, he turned the horses in the swamp and drove back to Monkgate.

Peacock describes Elizabeth as seeming to be 'incredibly stupid.' This is not only very harsh, it also misses the fact that without Elizabeth, George would not have been able to host the many banquets and balls he and Elizabeth hosted over the years. Nevertheless, Elizabeth's lack of education, her lack of etiquette and particularly her lack of fashion sense did not do her reputation any favours when it came to mixing 'in Society.' In May 1834, George and Elizabeth were guests at a dinner hosted by William Thompson, then MP for Sunderland and the owner of Pen-y-daren ironworks in South Wales. Lady Charlotte Guest was also at the dinner and she was none too complimentary about Elizabeth, noting in her diary:

> Conceive the horror of seeing a fat woman sit opposite to one in a *yellow* gown, and an *amber* cap with *red* flowers, and the still greater horror of that fat lady claiming to be an acquaintance. She proved to be Mrs Hudson, and the only other people in the room that I knew were Major Gore Brown and his wife, with her sister, Miss Buryon. The Browns and the Hudsons were almost the only two families in London that I have taken pains to avoid having any communication with, so that it was supremely unlucky to have met them there.

From Lady Guest's description, it is apparent that Elizabeth had what might be considered an 'individual' sense of fashion! Working behind the counter in College Street, she would have been well aware of changing fashions, but maybe fashion in York took a while to catch up with fashion in London, or possibly her fashion sense was rooted in her Georgian past. Whatever the case, it is evident that Elizabeth's sense of fashion reflected her personality as a fun-loving person who had a good sense of humour. In her eyes, her dress that evening would have been perfectly appropriate for the occasion.

It should not go unnoticed that this incident took place well before George had attained any prominence either in railways or politics in York, let alone anywhere else. However, it is significant that William Thompson was not only MP for Sunderland at the time, he was also a senior partner in the firm of Thompson and Foreman, the principal firm in the iron rails furore of 1845. Thompson also had close business ties with William Crawshay, the South Wales ironmaster. With a railway connection having recently been mooted in York, maybe it crossed George's mind that it would be useful to build relationships with such important suppliers of iron rails.

It has been suggested by some who have written about George that he was not much interested in the fine arts, music or the theatre, but Elizabeth clearly enjoyed such pastimes and even if the arts were not amongst George's primary interests, he often attended events with her. One such was a fancy-dress ball held in York in early September 1835, attended by the future Queen, Princess Victoria and her mother, the Duchess of Kent, as well as over 850 other invitees. The participants' costumes were described as being gay, fanciful, elegant, outlandish and ridiculous. A large crowd gathered outside the Assembly Rooms before the event to admire the guests' outfits. Dancing took place in the Assembly Room and in the Concert Room, where the royal visitors sat in the royal box. The *Yorkshire Gazette* commented that ladies' fashion is open to 'much latitude for fancy' and that it was not easy to be different without being very 'outré.' Elizabeth was described as wearing 'fancy dress.' One can only hope that she was wearing something very outré! For his part, George was described as wearing 'full dress', which probably meant he was wearing an evening suit. Whilst the royal guests left the event at midnight, revellers, including no doubt Elizabeth and George, partied on until the small hours. A few months later, on

19 January 1836, the Hudsons were again partying at the Assembly Room, when they were amongst 353 guests at the County Ball.

Showing their taste for more cultural pastimes, on 5 July 1836, the couple were amongst an audience of around 800 at York Minister for a concert by the York Choral Society, who played music by Haydn, Handel, Beethoven, Niccolò Zingarelli and Johann Hummel. The press report of the occasion mentioned there were two novelties during the evening. One was *The Wanderer's Return*, a Scottish melody, harmonised for four voices by the late Thomas Bridgewater of York, the words taken from *Lyrical Gems*, a popular selection of sentimental poetry published in 1825. The other was the overture from *The Maid of Artois*, then the latest piece of work by the Irish composer Michael Balfe. The performances were met 'with loud applause from the audience.'

William Etty, the famous York born artist, often attended the theatre in York. In the spring of 1838, he was present along with the Hudsons when they were Lord and Lady Mayoress of York. Etty later recorded, he was over 'head and ears in business' and that amongst the paintings he was working on at the time were portraits of John Brook, a York lawyer, and Elizabeth Hudson. In the summer of 1839 Etty exhibited Elizabeth's portrait at the Royal Academy in London, under the title *The Lady Mayoress*.

Etty was used to receiving criticism for some of his portraits, but he was likely quite unprepared for the abuse he was about to receive for his portrait of *The Lady Mayoress*. The critic writing for *The Court and Lady's Magazine* described the picture as the 'rummest thing I ever saw in all my born days' adding, he was 'struck by the true naivete of the [sitter's] expression' which he felt was 'ridiculous.' This may have been a comment about Etty's painting, but imagine how Elizabeth must have felt. The critic's reaction will have been the polar opposite of what she would have been hoping, indeed expecting, after having a likeness portrayed by such a famed artist as Etty. The criticism of the painting did not stop there. The critic for *Fraser's Magazine for Town and Country* wrote that, while the portrait was a very fine painting, it was a 'curiosity in its own way; the expression of the Mayoress being like that of Lady Macbeth.'

Gilchrist, in his *Life of William Etty*, recorded the derision which Etty's painting received from the newspapers. He wrote that Etty himself considered the 'abusive reception' of the painting due to 'personal enmities' both of 'the painter and his subject.' At this stage in his career, Etty was not as popular as he had been in earlier years and whilst the criticism aimed at Elizabeth seems on one level unkind, it reflects the wider perception 'educated' people (for want of a better expression) had of the Hudsons. Gilchrist comments that the reaction of the press to the painting was partly due to the joy critics took in following public opinion ('the herd' he called them), who watch a man achieve success then were ready to pounce when he produced a failure, whether real or imagined. In other words, Etty was suffering that cultural trait of building a man up before knocking him down. The parallel with the future reaction to Hudson was uncanny.

Gilchrist wrote that when Etty's paintings were rising in reputation amongst the art-public, he was subjected to a good deal of disparaging remarks from 'abortive painters, 'stickit' painters mostly ['wannabe' painters we might say today] who palm off their spite as criticism.' Gilchrist says that Elizabeth's complexion numbered among the topics of 'well-bred' ridicule and her 'millinery' was much excepted to – 'a devil incarnate with such a cap' said one 'polite gentleman of the press.' Gilchrist comments it might have been better for Etty had Elizabeth been 'less desirous of seeing herself at the Exhibition.' This remark tells a little about Elizabeth herself, that she was determined to see herself exhibited as much as her portrait at the Royal Academy, but had no idea that her appearance would cause the reaction it did.

Etty was much annoyed by the 'assassins of the press' as he described them and the furore over Elizabeth's portrait remained a 'lasting vexation' to him. This was in contrast to his usual reaction to criticism, which was to ignore what anyone said about his paintings. Etty was clearly a close friend of Elizabeth and her brother Richard, and he was most likely embarrassed for her as much as himself. But, Gilchrist asked, was it not possible for the sitter to hear the clamour of voices 'however coarse and ignorant?' In other words, could Elizabeth have accepted that the portrait would not be suitable for exhibition?

About Elizabeth's portrait, Gilchrist says Etty had done with it as he had done with other portraits of lady-friends, he had met the difficulties of his subject and her costume by 'bold effects of colour and of Painters-picturesque.' However, the same success could not be achieved with this portrait as with others more favourable to his style of art, where beauty and youth could interest his fancy. Such a portrait, of Elizabeth, was not one a collector would buy to display in their drawing room, though most of Etty's portraits *are* that kind of painting. Poor Elizabeth, Gilchrist is saying she was no oil painting!

But, Gilchrist continued, even if the portrait was not so attractive as one of Mr Finden's beauties, a study of colour and effect from the hand of such a great master could not be without merit. Surely, he wrote, it is much better than any of the 'smooth and plausible performances' of most [day to day] portrait painters, that are truly 'Art-less achievements.' Gilchrist concluded that Mrs Hudson's portrait should be judged as an 'Exercise of Art' and that such a description might have prevailed had it not been for the 'foul breath of the newspapers.'

The painting's whereabouts in 2023 is unknown. Is it hiding in a loft somewhere or did Etty or Elizabeth destroy it following the awful comments about it? Within the collection of the York Museums Trust there is a painting by Etty that is titled 'Portrait of an unknown woman.' Although this painting is said to have been painted towards the end of the 1840s, it bears a striking resemblance to the description of Elizabeth's portrait, particularly the sitter's facial expression and the cap she is wearing. It could even be described as resembling Lady Macbeth! Maybe there is not enough colour, but that could simply be down to the age of the painting. Maybe one day the 'Lady Mayoress' will be found and the opportunity given to see what all the fuss was about.

Despite the controversy surrounding Elizabeth's portrait, Etty remained on good terms with the Hudsons. In early September 1847, he recorded a visit he made to their home at Newby Park, when Richard Nicholson was also a guest. At this time Nicholson owned around fifty or sixty of Etty's paintings and Etty said he was very happy that so many of his 'children' were still around him in his old age in York. Any visit to Newby Park would have been hosted by Elizabeth and this meeting is worthy of note as it shows there were no ill feelings on either part about the painting. The following day, Hudson escorted his visitors back to York. Etty noted that Sir Robert Peel was passing through York at the same time and that Hudson introduced the two men.

In March 1844 the *Illustrated London News* published an account of two new buildings being built by Thomas Cubitt at Albert Gate on London's Piccadilly. At the time they were the largest and tallest houses in west London, so big in fact that it was feared that they were too large for anyone to purchase. However, there was one man who could afford to take one and that man was George Hudson, the wealthiest businessman in the country at the time. Hudson paid Cubitt just short of £14,000 for a 75-year lease in January 1846. Added to this was the small matter of ground rent of £150 per annum. Hudson also leased a coach house and stable in William Mews behind Lowndes Square. Having purchased the house, Elizabeth then spent a further £14,000 on furnishing it to make it fit for a king and his queen to live in.

As events turned out, the Hudsons' time at Albert Gate would be relatively short-lived, but while they lived there, they certainly made the most of it. Many are the stories told of carriages turning up at the house with the coat of arms of some noble or other on the side, of the balls and banquets held there, with Elizabeth as the hostess. Whatever Society thought of her, Elizabeth was never short of guests at her various soirees and her experience in arranging similar events when she was Lady Mayoress in 1837 and 1838 would prove to have been invaluable. As at the York Mansion House, Elizabeth also assisted George with arranging dinner parties at Albert Gate.

On 1 June 1847, Elizabeth hosted a concert 'at home' for invited guests at Albert Gate, but she was not only a hostess, she was also invited in her own right to Society events. For example, on 18 June 1847, she was a guest at two events on the same day. The first was a morning party hosted by the Marquis and Marchioness of Westminster at Grosvenor House. Other guests included the Duke of Devonshire, the Duchess of Sutherland, the Duchess of Norfolk and a great many more dukes, duchesses, earls, marquis, marchionesses and lords and ladies. Then in the evening, she attended a Grand Ball hosted by the Austrian Ambassador at Chandos House. Other guests included the Duchess of Cambridge, Princess Mary, Prince George, the Duke of Wellington, Sir Robert Peel, Benjamin Disraeli and innumerable dukes, duchesses, lords, ladies and too many more to mention. Of some surprise, but a measure of Elizabeth's self-confidence in spite of her detractors, is that she attended both events without George.

Undoubtedly the highlight of George's tenure as chairman of the Eastern Counties Railway came on Monday, 5 July 1847, when he escorted Queen Victoria and Prince Albert to Cambridge, for Prince Albert's installation as Chancellor of Cambridge University. The Queen and Prince Albert joined the royal train at Tottenham station. The outside of the royal carriage was described as being 'most elegant' with 'white and gold prevailing.' Inside, the linings were of figured French grey satin with a couch at one end, on which the Queen sat and two chairs on which the Duchess of Sutherland and the Duchess of Desari were seated. At the other end were two small ottomans. The ceiling was draped and fluted with the same French grey satin. In the centre of the carriage was a 'very beautiful little table of satin wood' on which stood a superb bouquet. The carriage was hung all round with the 'freshest and fairest favours of flora.'

It is difficult to imagine that such an opportunity to impress the Queen, and indeed wider Society, would have been passed up by Elizabeth and that she had much to do with the decoration of the royal coach and the ECR's arrangements for the royal journey. If so, it would not have been her first involvement with making arrangements for royalty. In August 1842, Prince George, the Duke of Cambridge, grandson of George III and a cousin of Queen Victoria, visited York. The Hudsons hosted the Duke at Monkgate for what was described as an 'elegant and most sumptuous dinner.' The dinner was in full accordance with the 'good taste and liberal spirit of the worthy Alderman.' Although George may have provided the wherewithal for the dinner to take place, it would have been Elizabeth who ensured the dinner was a success. Maybe the Duke was acknowledging her role in making the arrangements when he 'politely gave his arm' to her in their procession to the dining room.

In May 1848, Elizabeth hosted a concert at Albert Gate which was attended by, amongst others, the American Ambassador, George Bancroft, and his wife Elizabeth. In a letter home to her sons, Elizabeth Bancroft provided an interesting insight as to how the Hudsons were enabled to mix in the highest echelons of Society:

> On Monday evening we both went to a concert at Mr. Hudson's, the great railway 'king', who has just made an immense fortune from railway stocks, and is now desirous to get into society. These things are managed in a curious way here. A nouveau riche gets several ladies of fashion to patronize their entertainment and invite all the guests. Our invitation was from Lady Parke, who wrote me two notes about it, saying that she would be happy to meet me at Mrs. Hudson's splendid mansion, where there would be the best music and society of London; and, true enough, there was the Duke of Wellington and all the world. Lady Parke stood at the entrance of the splendid suite of rooms to receive the guests and introduce them to their host and hostess.

A month later, on 20 June 1848, Elizabeth hosted her first ball at Albert Gate. Reporting the scene witnessed by 'nearly 600 members of the fashionable world', the *Yorkshire Gazette*, noted how Albert Gate had been improved over the previous year and how the most admirable taste had produced 'an effect rarely, if ever, before equalled.' The *Gazette* reported that the four principal saloons on the first floor were all thrown open for the ball and when illuminated they 'presented one of the most gorgeous scenes.' The reporter wrote that Elizabeth greeted all the guests in the centre saloon, after which they passed left or right into a larger or smaller ball room as they wished. The fourth saloon, described as a most elegantly furnished boudoir, was reserved for those who did not wish to participate in the dancing.

Guests at the ball included the Duke of Wellington, who was received warmly by Elizabeth in the ballroom, members of the Spanish royal family, the American Ambassador, the Duke of Buckingham, the Duke and Duchess of Richmond and innumerable earls, lords and ladies; also, Robert Stephenson, MP for Whitby and one of the Hudson's most longstanding friends. Dancing began at 11.30pm and continued through to 1.00am when a superb supper was served, after which dancing resumed until an early hour. As with the ECR's royal carriage, Elizabeth had again been hard at work ensuring that her decorations were not only the best money could buy but were also the best any of her guests had seen before. The newspaper concluded its report by saying 'A more delightful [occasion] in which the noble and distinguished guests appeared to enjoy more completely the princely hospitality of their hostess, it has never been our lot to witness.'

In the week before the Royal Agricultural Show held in York on 15 July 1848, George and Elizabeth hosted numerous distinguished guests at Newby Park, including the Duke of Buckingham, the Duke of Richmond, the Earl of Stradbroke, Lord Ingestrie, Lord George Bentinck. Also, the American Ambassador George Bancroft and his wife Elizabeth. In another letter home, Elizabeth wrote:

Now comes my pleasant Yorkshire excursion. We left London, at half-past three, at distance of 180 miles. This was Saturday, July 8. At York we found Mr. Hudson ready to receive us and conduct us to a special train which took us eighteen miles on the way to Newby Park, and there we found carriages to take us four miles to our destination. We met at dinner and found our party to consist of the Duke of Richmond, Lord Lonsdale, Lord George Bentinck, Lord Ingestre, Lord John Beresford and Lady Webster.

Prince Albert was the guest of honour at the Agricultural Show and he attended a ball at York Mansion House on 13 July. The Hudsons were represented in numbers. George and Elizabeth were joined by their daughter Ann, son George and Elizabeth's brother, Richard Nicholson. In total, there were more than 700 guests. Elizabeth's influence would seem to have been at play with the selection of music for the evening, which included several quadrilles, polkas, galops and waltzes. Supper was served at midnight in the Guildhall behind the Mansion House and the letters V & A and a crown were lit up in gas lights above the entrance to the Guildhall. Toasts were raised to their Majesties and especial thanks were given to George for helping to bring the Royal Agricultural Show to York. Prince Albert and his entourage stayed overnight at the Judges Lodgings in Lendal.

Whilst at Newby Park, the Bancrofts had visited the Hudsons' Londesborough estate, which Elizabeth Bancroft described as 'nobly situated in the Yorkshire Wolds, a fine range of hills, and overlooking the valley of the Humber, which was interesting to me, as it was the river which our Pilgrim fathers sailed down ... awaiting their passage to Holland.'

The Bancrofts were again guests at a dinner hosted by Elizabeth at Albert Gate at the end of July 1848. Other guests included the Marchioness Dowager of Ely, Lady Anna Loftus, Lord and Lady Wharncliffe, Sir James and Lady Graham and numerous MPs, including George Dundas. Then again, on a subsequent evening, the Bancrofts were joined at Albert Gate by a number of diplomatic guests, including members of the Spanish royal family and Ambassadors from

Belgium and the Netherlands, and others including, the Duchess of Leeds, the Marchioness of Ely and the Earl and Countess of Morley.

Elizabeth may have had a reputation for her faux pas and malapropisms but, as Arnold and McCartney note, these stories are the kind that might be told about anyone who was perceived by her critics to be a 'nouveau riche ignoramus.' One such story was when in Paris, Elizabeth particularly wanted to buy some shoes from 'Gauche et Droit' because the name appeared on each pair of shoes she saw. Surely, this sounds more like a schoolboy joke. In fact, according to Arnold and McCartney, William Lennox in his book *Celebrities I have known*, published in 1877, recorded Elizabeth as having a good grasp of French, although she spoke it with a 'pure Yorkshire accent.'

Elizabeth was certainly not as 'stupid' as some might have cared to think; not only was she self-taught in French, she had a good knowledge of music, her organisational skills were legendary and her taste in furnishings, which may have been sneered at by some, always seemed to hit the mark. There is evidence too that she had a sympathetic heart for those less well-off as in the case of Joseph Mason. In 1843 Mason, a resident of Clifton in York, was found guilty of a shooting at the house of Thomas Carr at Hall Moor near Skelton, Yorkshire. He was sentenced to twenty years' transportation in Australia. It was subsequently found that his conviction had been the result of a 'misapprehension' and that he was not guilty of the offence. Henry Yorke MP successfully led a campaign for Mason's sentence to be quashed. He eventually received a pardon on 1 January 1845 and was granted a free passage back home, but it was not until May 1846 that he arrived back in England. Although the government awarded Mason a gratuity of £25, it refused any further investigation into the circumstances of his guilty verdict. Elizabeth took an interest in the case and it can be safely assumed she insisted that George find the unfortunate Mason a job on his return to York as, on 5 May 1846, she wrote to Mason's wife to say her husband had given instruction for Mason to be found suitable employment on his return to York.

In his book *City Characters Under Several Reigns* published in 1922, Thomas Escott tells the story of how a 'big, heavy man, with drab-coloured wiry hair' would travel in a 'carriage gorgeous enough for a Lord Mayor' from Piccadilly to London's Mansion House, with a 'homely lady on a large scale seated by his side.' The man he was describing was, of course, George Hudson and the 'homely' lady by his side was his wife, Elizabeth. Escott wrote that on their drive the couple would be met by curious and admiring glances and at times cheering voices from those they passed. Escott described Elizabeth as the 'Mrs Malaprop' of her day and added that she was 'showy, not over-refined, but by no means bad hearted or stupid.' He says her speech was not all affectation and some of her remarks in her Yorkshire dialect were sensible enough and not without some flavour of mother-wit. For example, of a person she considered untrustworthy she would say 'He is like a pat of butter on a hot plate; you never know when you have got him!'

In September 1848, Elizabeth's only daughter, Ann Elizabeth, became engaged to George Dundas, Tory MP for Linlithgow. Ann was by all accounts an amiable and attractive 17-year-old, with a cultivated mind. Dundas, who was ten years Ann's senior, was born at Dundas Castle in Linlithgow, Scotland. Dundas Castle had been occupied by the Dundas family since the twelfth century. Coming from such an old established Scottish family, Elizabeth and George would have been very happy with the marriage of their daughter to Dundas. The couple were due to be married at Christmas 1848, but rumours of George's impending fall were beginning to circulate and the marriage was postponed and then called off when the rumours became fact. Elizabeth would no doubt have been very upset for her daughter. But fate often plays a part in life. If Dundas called off his marriage to Ann as a result of her father's troubles, then it becomes clear his only interest in Ann was her future prospects.

Whilst with Ann, Richard Lambert related a story of the time when the Duke of Wellington helped George's daughter settle in to a new school in London when the family moved to Albert Gate. The story goes that the Duke's sister had bought some shares in an underperforming railway company and was desperate to sell them. The Duke asked Hudson if there was anything he could do to help. Hudson said he would see what he could do. Shortly after the meeting Hudson bought a few of the company's shares and subtly let it be known that he had done so, to help push the share price upwards. When the Duke next met Hudson, the latter advised the Duke to tell his sister to sell her shares immediately, which she did. The Duke was so pleased with Hudson's intervention, he asked if there was anything he could do in return. Hudson thought for a moment and then mentioned his daughter was finding it difficult to make friends at her new school in London and he asked the Duke if he might pay her a visit to bolster her confidence. The Duke duly agreed and arrived at the school with a bouquet of flowers for Miss Hudson. Seeing that Ann was an acquaintance with no less than national hero the Duke of Wellington, her contemporaries soon forgot their snobbery and became friends.

As if George's troubles and Ann's broken engagement were not enough for Elizabeth to contend with, in early May 1849 came the devastating news that her brother Richard had been found drowned in the River Ouse in York. Elizabeth would have been distraught at this news and must have held George at least in part, if not fully, responsible for her brother's death. The Jury at Richard's inquest returned a verdict of 'Found drowned; there being no sufficient evidence to show how he got into the water.' Despite the coroner court's uncertainty, there was little doubt that Richard committed suicide as a result of the ignominy that was surrounding George. As an essentially private man, who shunned the limelight, Richard would have been particularly fearful that he might be required to account for any part he may have played in George's dealings. In July 1850, George told the Richardson libel hearing that he had made a payment of £35,000 to the YNB against his 'better judgment', saying that his persecutors had taken advantage of distressing events to 'persons nearly connected with me.' This was undoubtedly a reference to the distress felt by Elizabeth and Ann about

Richard's loss. At the time of his death Richard had numerous debts that needed to be met. Bearing in mind George's partial responsibility for Richard's state of mind when he died, it was very likely Elizabeth who persuaded George to clear all of Richard's debts after his death.

Shortly after Richard's death the family retreated to Newby Park to find some peace and quiet and to recover as best they could from the troubles that had engulfed them over the previous few months. It would not, however, prove to be a complete rest. George would still be consumed with having to answer questions posed by the various committees of inquiry and drafting his letter of explanation (published in January 1850).

Then, in July 1850, he was summoned at short notice to appear as a witness in the Richardson v Wodson libel trial. Once the trial was over, the family sought a complete break from the problems they faced at home and travelled to the continent for a tour of Germany. Some biographers have suggested George may have looked for railway opportunities whilst abroad, but there is no evidence for this. It is more than likely the trip was undertaken for all the family, including George, to enjoy some rest and recuperation.

In October 1850, when they returned from Germany, the family once again retreated to Newby Park. In December the same year the family was invited, along with a number of other guests, to spend a few days at Burton Constable Hall in East Yorkshire, as guests of Sir Clifford Constable. This invitation gave some encouragement to Elizabeth to think that things could get back to normal, or at least as normal as they could be after the events of the previous year. But not before they were once again ostracised in York. In January 1851, it was rumoured that the Hudsons were to attend a festive occasion at the city's Assembly Rooms. The rumour was picked up by *The Yorkshireman,* who warned against the York public accepting the Hudsons' 'respectability.' Taking heed of their possible reception, George and Elizabeth decided not to attend the event. It must have come as some relief to Elizabeth that in March 1851, she and George decided to return to London for the summer season.

On her arrival back in London, Elizabeth wasted no time in celebrating her return by organising a grand ball at Albert Gate. Held on 13 March 1851, this 'brilliant ball' was attended by upwards of 300 members of 'the fashionable world', who enjoyed the evening 'long into the following morning.' The ball will have been very much a cathartic experience for Elizabeth and she would have been exhilarated that it proved to be such a success. She and George had not been shunned by Society in London as they had been in York. The following month saw absolute proof of their continued acceptance amongst London's social elite.

On 1 April Elizabeth, George and Ann attended a performance of *Gustav III,* an opera by French composer Daniel-François-Esprit Auber, at Her Majesty's Theatre in London. The performance starred, amongst others, the French opera singer Caroline Duprez and the ballerinas Carlotta Grisi and Amalia Ferraris. Also in attendance that evening were Queen Victoria and Prince Albert and a plethora of titled persons including the Duke of Wellington, the Marquis and Marchioness of Salisbury, the Marquis of Clarincade, the Earl of Essex, Earl and Countess Bessborough, Viscount and Viscountess Villiers, Sir Robert Peel, and Sir Lionel and Lady Goldsmid. Although not known for certain, it can be imagined that the royal couple were introduced to those attending the performance, including Elizabeth, George and Ann.

A month later, on 1 May, George, Elizabeth and Ann attended a musical and choreographic performance at Her Majesty's Theatre, to celebrate the start of the Great Exhibition of 1851. The star of the show was the comic opera singer Luigi Lablache. The performance was attended by the Duke of Cambridge, the Marquis and Marchioness of Westminster, the Duke of Cleveland and many and various earls, viscounts, lords and ladies and MPs. In July they were again at Her Majesty's Theatre, this time attending a performance by a celebrated horn virtuoso, Giovanni Puzzi. And once more they were in illustrious company, with the Duke of Wellington and many other titled and prominent members of society present.

As if to emphasise their place back amongst London's elite, the annual census that took place in April 1851 showed Elizabeth managing the immense household needed at Albert Gate to sustain the family's lavish lifestyle. In total, there were fifteen servants, ranging from butler James Bosworth, housekeeper Elizabeth Roper to three footmen, four housemaids, two lady's maids, a kitchen maid, a confectioner, a valet and a 'still room manufacturer' (a member of the kitchen staff employed to make jams, chutneys and sauces etc). Provided all were still being paid, it is evident that, despite his difficulties, George was still wealthy enough to finance an enormous household. The full census return is set out in Appendix 2.

In June 1851, Elizabeth, George and Ann attended a garden party hosted by Mrs Louisa Lawrence at Ealing Park, a 100-acre estate near what was then described as the rural village of Ealing (now a west London suburb). Louisa was married to society surgeon William Lawrence and was the daughter of a haberdasher – no doubt she and the Hudsons would have found much to talk about. Louisa was a much-respected horticulturalist and her gardens were famed for her collection of orchids and roses. Queen Victoria visited the garden in July 1845, helping to put it and Louisa on the Society map. The *Morning Herald* reported that the garden party was held to enable guests to meet the Duke of Cambridge and the Duchess of Gloucester (though the Duchess was unable to attend on the day). Between 1300 and 1400 guests were present and included the Duke of Wellington, members of the nobility, various ambassadors and numerous notables from Society, including the Hudsons.

Almost exactly a year later, in June 1852, Mary Disraeli, the wife of the then Chancellor of the Exchequer Benjamin Disraeli, held a reception at the Chancellor's residence in Grosvenor Gate London. This reception was attended by an extraordinary array of guests including the Duke of Wellington, ambassadors from Turkey, France,

Austria, Greece, Russia, Brazil and Denmark and many members of the nobility, numerous MPs and the Hudsons. There were more visits to the opera during 1852, including in June for a performance of *Lucia di Lammermoor*, by Bonizetti. Those performing included the Italian tenor Allesandro Bettini and French soprano Anna de la Grange. Amongst the audience were the Duke of Cambridge and the Duke of Wellington (again!), as well as many other members of the nobility.

Bearing in mind that judgment in George's Rolls Court case was due imminently, Elizabeth and Ann showed extraordinary strength of character when, on 30 July 1853, they stepped out to join various members of the aristocracy at a performance of the Royal Italian Opera in London's Covent Garden. The evening would prove to be one of Elizabeth and Ann's last forays into Society. Two days later, the Master of the Rolls dropped the bombshell the Hudsons were fearing, if not expecting, that George must pay the YNM a total of £54,590, meaning that their homes at Newby Park and Albert Gate would have to be disposed of, to enable George to meet his debts.

The Newby Park estate was the first to go. To add insult to injury, George Leeman acted as solicitor on behalf of the buyer, Lord Downe, who bought the property for £190,000 in October 1853. Losing Newby Park would have been bad enough, but losing Albert Gate would have been even more traumatic for Elizabeth, particularly after all the time and energy she had spent making the house a home fit for a king. But in March 1854, it was let to the French government for £1,800 per year for use as their London embassy. The original builder of the house, Thomas Cubitt, was employed by Hudson to make some changes to the building to ensure it suited the French Ambassador at the time, Count Walewski. Unsurprisingly, Cubitt had some difficulty reclaiming the cost of the alterations from Hudson. The leasehold of the house would eventually be sold to the French government and the proceeds put towards Hudson's debts.

The loss of Newby Park and Albert Gate put incredible strain on Elizabeth. Understandably, she found it difficult to accept the shame brought about by her husband's fall from grace, not least because she now had nowhere to live. Nor of course had George and it seems they now began to lead somewhat separate lives. Elizabeth initially went to live with one of her sons in Kensington, most probably George, as John is believed to have been in the Army at the time and William was a student at Oxford University.

The gloom that began to pervade Elizabeth's life in these years after Newby Park and Albert Gate was lifted momentarily in 1854, when her daughter Ann found love and married Jerome Zuminski, a Polish Count. The couple married at St Columba's church, Topcliffe in North Yorkshire on 18 April 1854. St. Columba's was the family's church when they resided at Newby Park. In those days the family had a square pew richly decorated in crimson velvet. George had a lectern in the pew where, it was alleged, he would stand to address the congregation 'with his portly back turned on the vicar.' Members of the congregation later recalled how Elizabeth would put up a fine parasol to protect herself from the sun shining through the windows. After their marriage the new Countess and Count Zuminski moved to live in Germany. There is little doubt Elizabeth would have missed having Ann around enormously.

When George visited Spain in the mid-1850s, to look at possibilities for reviving his railway interests, Elizabeth remained in London. Although it has been suggested Elizabeth did not accompany her husband because of her state of health, it is more probable the real reason was that the couple were by now no longer living together.

In November 1857, the *Morning Herald* reported the distressing tale of how Elizabeth was robbed of some of the clothes she had kept from the heady days of Albert Gate. At the time of the robbery Elizabeth was living in an apartment at 4 Belgrave Road in London's Victoria district. A servant to a lady in a neighbouring apartment, called Elizabeth Griffiths, was found guilty of stealing 'a white satin dress, a crimson velvet mantle lined with white silk, a valuable shawl, five head-dresses and other articles to a value of above £200.' The shawl was said to be worth £100. At her trial, Griffiths admitted to taking belongings from her employer, Mrs Butt. The prosecuting solicitor told the Court that because of Elizabeth's advanced age (she was now 62) and infirmities (a medical certificate was produced), she could not appear in Court to prosecute Griffiths. As a result, Griffiths could not be prosecuted for possession of the items she stole from Elizabeth, but only for those items for which there were a number of witnesses present in court. Concluding the hearing the magistrate, Thomas Arnold, when sentencing Griffiths to two months imprisonment, told her that in normal circumstances (that is had Elizabeth been able to attend Court), she would have been subjected to a much heavier sentence.

The trauma of the robbery was soon followed by even more devastating news, the death of her son John who died in action in India on 14 December 1857. The first report of John's death did not appear in the press until 30 January 1858. The *Yorkshire Gazette* reported that John was a lieutenant in the 6th (Carabineer) Dragoon Gaurds and was killed at Gungaree in East India. John originally joined the 10th Hussars in India and served with distinction in the Crimea and, as a result of his bravery in the field, he was promoted to lieutenant. Elizabeth may have taken some solace from the *Yorkshire Gazette's* comment that 'a more brave and daring officer there was not in the Queen's service.'

The following week the *Gazette* included verbatim a letter her husband George had received from John's commanding officer, C.H. Uniacke. Earlier in the year George had attended a dinner in Marseille with Uniacke and a number of officers from John's regiment before they embarked for India. In a very personal letter, Uniacke, wrote 'I shall wring your heart, indeed, by the sad intelligence I have, alas, to communicate.' He told George that his son was hit in the heart and died almost immediately 'with a cheer on his lip' and that his loss would be deeply felt by all, particularly by those who were his old comrades in the 10th Hussars, to whom he was endeared by what Uniacke described as his 'manly disposition.' A number of other officers were lost the same day Uniacke said, adding that 'we can ill afford to lose such a good soldier as poor dear John.' Uniacke reported that he was now the only one left untouched of the little party who dined at Marseilles. He concluded, 'Begging you to accept my deep sympathy in the irreparable loss you have sustained.'

Throughout most of the 1860s, George had been living in exile on the Continent. When the 1869 Debtors Act came into effect at the beginning of January 1870, he was on the first boat back to England. Contrary to what might have been assumed, he did not return to live with Elizabeth. Not only had his years in exile cemented the rift between the couple, but Elizabeth was now in a such a poor state of health that it would not have made sense for George, who was still very sprightly, despite his own health problems, to have moved in with her, or for the couple to have found lodgings together. Instead, George moved in with his son William at 37 Churton Street, Pimlico, with Elizabeth remaining at 22 Hornton Street, Kensington with her maid, Anne Dallas.

Despite their estrangement, one would like to think, when their 50th wedding anniversary came round on 15 July 1871 they spent some time together particularly as, within five months, George passed away. Elizabeth, sadly, was too poorly to make the journey to Yorkshire to attend George's memorial service and interment at Scrayingham.

George's passing would not be the only family bereavement Elizabeth would endure during the 1870s. In November 1874, she received the tragic news that her only daughter Ann had died suddenly in Dresden. Then in February 1876 came news that her younger son William had committed suicide by jumping in front of a train in London. Reporting the outcome of the inquest into William's death, the *York Herald* carried a graphic description of what happened. Between 12 noon and 1pm on 22 February 1876, William was on the platform of Victoria underground station waiting for a train to come out of the tunnel from the Mansion House direction. As the train approached the platform, William jumped off the edge of the platform, sank to his knees and placed his head on the running track. The inquest heard that William did not appear 'giddy', in other words, he did not fall on the track accidentally. The engine driver, George Squires, saw William jump onto the track and put his head on the rail and then cover his face with his hands. Squires said he applied the brake immediately and put his engine into reverse but could not stop before hitting the deceased. Another witness, Lewis Klein, told the Court that he saw the train go over William and afterwards that he saw his head in one place and his body in another.

William's older brother, George, who was living at 7 Wilton Terrace, Kensington at the time, was called as a witness. He told the inquest that William was 42 years old and 'of no profession.' George said he considered his brother one of the last people likely to commit suicide, as there was nothing he knew of to 'excite' his mind to suicide. He said William was in good circumstances, although he had recently been 'in low spirits' and was in the habit of taking 'chloral' (chloral hydrate), which was used at the time as a sedative. William was most likely taking chloral as a form of anti-depressant; today chloral hydrate can be prescribed as a sleeping pill.

William was a qualified doctor of medicine but, with George describing him as 'of no profession' at the hearing, there is a strong indication that, at the time of his death, William was not in practice. A fact perhaps confirmed by the 1871 Census, which had him described as 'an annuitant.' If William had monetary problems, then having his father come to live with him in January 1870 may have helped to alleviate any immediate financial issues he had, but would not necessarily have helped his state of mind. When George died in December 1871, income from his annuity would have ceased, possibly plunging William into hard times, not just financially, but in dealing with the grief of his father's death. Whatever the reason or reasons for him deciding to take his own life, the inquest confirmed its verdict of suicide, whilst the deceased was in a 'state of temporary insanity.'

Probate of William's will confirmed he was by no means a wealthy man. The value of his estate was registered at below £200. He left all his possessions, such as they were, to his brother George. Probate also showed he had moved at some point from 37 Churton Street to 5 Hindon Street, Pimlico. William's suicide was a truly tragic end to his life and it was no doubt very difficult for Elizabeth to understand and overcome.

Much of the rest of Elizabeth's life seems to have been spent in quiet seclusion. The 1881 Census records that she and Anne Dallas had moved from Hornton Street to a larger apartment at 14 Pitt Street, Kensington. The move was most likely due to Elizabeth, now 85, requiring more domestic help due to her declining health. Anne Dallas was now described as 'Ladies Maid Domestic' and, it would seem, had become Elizabeth's personal help. They were joined in the household by Ann Carthill who was employed as a 'general servant.' For the Census Elizabeth described her occupation as 'dividend widow', which seems a very apt description for the widow of the former 'dividend king.'

Elizabeth passed away at home in Pitt Street on 15 January 1886. Despite her frailties, she had lived to the ripe old age of 91 years. A number of newspapers carried a short biography of the widow of the former Railway King, including the *York Herald*:

> This old lady passing away in a small street in a suburb, once lived in the enormous mansion at Albert Gate which is now the French Embassy, as the wife of the Railway King, who had Royalties for his courtiers, blue-blooded peers for his subjects. In the year '46 he was at the height of his prosperity; by '53 there was left *'none so poor to do him reverence.'* After his fall he lived at Paris and Boulogne and readers of Forster will remember how Dickens saw him at the latter place in the year of '63 – *'a shabby man, standing on the brink of the pier, and waving his hat in a desolate manner.'* Hudson died in Churton Street, Pimlico in December '71 aged 70. Mrs Hudson figured as his *'Mrs Malaprop'* of her day and all kinds of ridiculous sayings were put into her mouth.

Another newspaper recorded that when George Hudson was MP for Sunderland, Elizabeth was well known in the borough and, like her husband, very popular, with many friends in the town. Reflecting her propensity for malapropisms, another recalled an amusing story of when George asked Elizabeth to purchase a pair of geographical globes for his library at Albert Gate. In the evening, the Hudsons were hosting a dinner and Elizabeth proudly told her guests about the globes she had bought from Stanford's but, she added, 'the shopman was very stupid, for he had sent odd ones instead of a pair' (one was, of course, a Celestial globe).

On 22 January 1886, in accordance with the wish set out in her Will, Elizabeth was laid to rest alongside George at Scrayingham. It is not known who else was in attendance, but almost certainly her surviving son George as well as family members and friends from Howsham, Malton and Whitby.

Elizabeth left an estate valued at £3,029. Although nothing like the fortune she enjoyed with George during their days at Albert Gate, this was still a substantial sum. In her Will, dated 3 May 1879, Elizabeth made various small bequests to her friends. To Anne Dallas, her long serving maid, she bequeathed her 'wearing apparel' and all the money and interest in her savings bank account. Almost immediately, Elizabeth must have realised there was not much money in this account because she added a codicil a few days later, on 29 May, in which she bequeathed Anne a specific sum of £70, most likely equivalent to her annual wage. She also bequeathed nineteen guineas to her 'dear son-in-law Jerome Suminska' for him to 'invest in a memorial ring in memory of his mother-in-law.' The balance of her estate, including the sword and scabbard that once belonged to her son John, she left to her 'beloved son' George, who was also appointed executor.

George junior eventually retired from his role as an Inspector of Factories and retired to a house in Sunninghill Berkshire, which he named Newby House in remembrance of the family home in Yorkshire where, for a short while at least, many happy days were spent. He passed away in January 1909 after suffering a cerebral haemorrhage. On George's passing the *Shields Daily News* noted:

> A link with the earliest days of railways in the North of England is severed with the death of Mr George Hudson of Newby House, near Ascot, Berks. Mr Hudson, who was in his 80th year, was a barrister-at-law, but had been retired from practice of his profession for some years. [He was] the last surviving son of Mr George Hudson, "The Railway King." He had associations with the North of England, being cousin of the wife of Alderman G. B. Hunter. Mr George Hudson, senior, was a former Conservative Member of Parliament for Sunderland, and was the founder of the docks that bear his name.

George left an estate valued at just over £17,000. His executors were Sir George Burton Hunter and Ann Hunter (Sir George's wife). Ann Hunter was previously Ann Hudson, George's cousin. Born in Sunderland in 1845, Hunter formed Swan Hunter in 1879 and by 1893 the company was the largest shipbuilder on Tyneside. He bought Wallsend Hall in 1914, which he donated to Wallsend Corporation in 1919.

It is believed that Elizabeth, with the help of her son George, arranged for two stained glass windows in the south west corner of Scrayingham church to be dedicated to her family; one to her husband George and the other to her deceased children, James Richard, Richard Nicholson, Matthew Bottrill, Anne Elizabeth, John and William. Following her own death in 1886, George arranged for a window on the north side of the church to be dedicated to her. As the last remaining family member, there is no memorial to George junior at Scrayingham, nor was he buried there. He was laid to rest at Dorking near his home in Sunninghill in the south of England.

Appendix 1

List of the principal railways opened under Hudson's chairmanship:

York and North Midland Railway

York to South Milford	1839
York to Leeds completed	1840
York to Scarborough	1845
Rillington Junction to Pickering	1845
Seamer to Filey	1846
Hull to Bridlington	1846
Filey to Bridlington	1847
York to Market Weighton	1847
Church Fenton to Spofforth	1847
Spofforth to Harrogate	1848
Selby to Market Weighton	1848
Hull Paragon Station opened	1848

The Pickering to Whitby line, which originally opened in 1836, was taken over by the YNM in 1845.

Other railways acquired by the YNM under Hudson's chairmanship were the Leeds and Selby (1840) and Hull and Selby (1845).

York, Newcastle and Berwick Railway

Hudson was Chairman of the Newcastle and Darlington Junction Railway (June 1842), which amalgamated with the Great North of England Railway in 1846, to form the York and Newcastle Railway (YNR). The YNR was subsequently merged with the Newcastle and Berwick, to form the YNB in 1847.

The railways of the constituent companies of the YNB included (opening):

Newcastle to North Shields	1839
Brandling Junction Railway	1839
Durham to Sunderland	1839
Durham Junction Railway	1840
York to Darlington	1841
Newcastle to Darlington	1844
Newcastle to Tweedmouth (for Berwick)*	1847
Pilmoor to Boroughbridge	1847
Northallerton to Leeming Bar	1848

*Royal Border Bridge was not opened until 1850

Midland Railway

When Hudson became chairman of the new Midland Railway (MR) on 16 July 1844, the MR comprised lines from Derby to Leeds (opened 1840), Derby to Hampton (1839) and Derby to Rugby and Nottingham (1840) and Hampton to Birmingham (1842). Under his chairmanship the following railways were opened:

Leeds to Bradford	1846
Nottingham to Lincoln	1846
Erewash Valley (Codnor Park to Long Eaton)	1847
Syston to Peterborough	1848
Bradford to Colne	1848
Nottingham to Mansfield	1848

Other railways acquired by the Midland Railway under Hudson's chairmanship included Bristol to Gloucester (opened 1844, taken over by the MR 1845) and Birmingham to Gloucester (opened in 1840, taken over by the MR 1845). Under Hudson's chairmanship the two lines were merged in August 1846.

The Midland Railway also took over the Leicester to Swannington railway in 1845. The line had originally opened in 1833.

Eastern Counties Railway

When appointed chairman of the ECR in October 1845, the ECR had already opened lines from London to Colchester (1843), London to Bishop's Stortford (1842), Broxbourne to Hertford (1843), Bishop's Stortford to Brandon (1845). Under his chairmanship, the following railways were opened:

Ely to Peterborough	1847
March to Wisbech	1847
Cambridge to St Ives	1847
Stratford to North Woolwich	1847
St Ives to March	1848
Maldon to Braintree	1848

Other railways leased by the ECR under Hudson's chairmanship included, Chesterford to Newmarket, Brandon to Yarmouth (via Norwich and Reedham) and Wymondham to Dereham, Reedham to Lowestoft.

Appendix 2

Extract from the national census return for 1 Albert Gate, March 1851.

The return gives an insight into the living standards of the Hudsons at this time. It also shows that, despite having given up all his railway chairmanships, Hudson was still able to sustain a large household, thanks to his income from a range of non-railway investments.

Name	Age	Birthplace	Occupation
George Hudson	51	Howsham, Yorks	Income from lands, mines and Manufacture of glass
Elizabeth Hudson	55	York	as above
Ann Elizabeth Hudson	20	York	as above
A.S. Milbank	24	Yorkshire	Land proprietor (Visitor)
Sophia Cranmer	29	Cheltenham Glos	Artist (Visitor)
James Bosworth	40	Mowsley, Leics	Butler
George Pirrot	38	Stravithie, Fife	Confectioner
Edwin Farney	27	Bourn, Yorks	Footman
Lucas Swift	16	Doncaster, Yorks	Footman
John Curlis	35	Kirby Hill, Yorks	Footman
Jane Egard	34	Newbald, Yorks	Housemaid
Mary Proctor	18	Topcliffe, Yorks	Housemaid

Name	Age	Birthplace	Occupation
Jane Proctor	15	Rainton, Yorks	Still room manufacturer
Cecille Corry	35	Scotland	Kitchen maid
Janet Lamont	21	Edinburgh	Housemaid
Elizabeth Roper	50	Beverley, Yorks	Housekeeper
Elizabeth Proctor	20	Morpeth, N'berland	Housemaid
Elizabeth Lanson	30	Idle, Yorks	Lady's maid
John Reynard	33	Mowsley, Leics	Valet
Sarah Miller	30	St James, Middx	Lady's maid

Appendix 3

Popular songs about George Hudson and the Railway Mania

The Monarch of All they Survey
Published circa 1845

I am Monarch of all they survey,
My right there is none to avail;
O'er Great Britain VICTORIA may sway,
I am Lord of the Line and the Rail!

Oh, Pimlico! Where are the charms
Thy Buckingham Palace can boast?
What is sporting proud royalty's arms
Of Railways to ruling the roast!

PRINCE ALBERT to prance on his nag,
And follow the tame deer is free;
But my quarry's a different stag,
And the engine's the hunter for me.

An army our QUEEN may possess,
On the Ocean her navy may roll:
Of the line I have regiments, no less,
And more numerous *navies* control.

My seat of imperial state
I'd not swop for HER MAJESTY'S throne,
Nor for that of my Sovereign vacate
The boiler that serves for my own.

Lords in Waiting are all very grand,
Maids of Honour are all very fine;
But the deft Engineer to command,
And to rule the sharp stoker be mine.

The Railway King
Published approx. 1845

Of Railways and the Railway King,
Hudson the First of England I sing;
A Monarch who's grasped with his Iron Hand
The Land his Electric Nod can command.
Ri too ra loo-ra
Ri too ra loo-ra lay

Nine days to Edinburgh from Town
Our forefathers, they could go down;
Nine hours will just now steam you there
Not wagon'd to death, but cos'y in arm chair.
Ri too ra loo-ra etc

King Hudson, he started with narrow gauge
'Afore he came to Railway Age;
But now it's the narrow, the broad, the wide,
Or any gauge else that he likes beside.
Ri too ra loo-ra etc

King Hudson committees at York at nine,
At twelve committees at Newcastle-Tyne
Committees at Rugby at half-past seven,
And then committees in Town at eleven.
Ri too ra loo-ra etc

At twelve P. M, committees the Commons,
At 1-54, steams a speech at short summons,
At four old Morpheus lets off the steam,
And Old King Hud committees in a dream.
Ri too ra loo-ra etc

King Hudson, he telegraphs health in a trice
With a smack of old port and a gusto of spice;
Newcastle to York - York to Newcastle - Tyne,
You may dine at the Poles, and pledge health cross the line
Ri too ra loo-ra etc

King Hudson, they say - but I can't tell how soon
Is going to Railway it up to the Moon;
He was caught telescoping the man wot lives there,
And asking him if he would hold scrip and share.
Ri too ra loo-ra etc

Then here's to King Hudson, and firm be his Throne,
Who in Iron has found the Philosopher's Stone;
May his frame be long found of true cast iron mould,
And circled his brows with his own well won gold.
Ri too ra loo-ra etc

The Rail, the Rail
Published approx. 1845

The rail! The rail! My own dear rail
As long as it last will never fail, will never fail
Setting no mark or squeamish bound
To scrip that freely flies around
To raise the hopes of flats* to the skies
Swallowing scrip and railway lies
Swallowing scrip and railway lies
I've got the scrip
I've got the scrip
And all I care for is the tip*
I'm board of directors high and low
And stagging* all where're I go;
If a smash should come, no matter, who cares!
For quicker than thought I'll bolt with the paid-up shares

I love, oh how I love to scheme
In mystifying foaming steam
Where spec* as mad as a rail to the moon
Seem whistling to all a pleasing tune;
And telling to all, what's all the go,
And how to raise the wind when low;
I never pass the old bailey door,
But I think of railing more and more,
And onward fly with my scrip to sport;
Like a stag that seeketh old Capel Court,
And a cover it's been, ne'er known to fail
For I was born to live by my own dear rail.

The stocks were low and all forlorn,
In a foggy hour when I was born,
The lame ducks laugh'd and the bears they roll'd
And the brokers clutch'd their bags of gold,
Oh never was heard such a boast and brag;
As welcom'd to life the railway stag;
I've pushed along in noise and strife,
Near twenty summers a dodging life,
More wealth to seek and a court to range,
I'm never or seldom seen to change,
Then the smash, if it comes, let others fail,
I'll cut my friends and my own dear Rail

**flats* – naïve investors; *tip* – inside information; *stagging* – someone who sells for a profit; *spec* – speculation

The Railway Mania by James Bruton
Published 1846

The stirring age we live in now must surely beat the olden one
The present is the iron age the other was the golden one
Our wisdom perhaps is not so great in that there is some failery
But there is no doubt at all that we are much improved in raillery
O Dear O!, O dear O!
Railway speculation now is all the go.

When I was but a tiny boy and did about with granny stir
The only railway travelling then was sliding down the banister
If we got off that inclined plane she'd soundly rate and sermon us
And nothing did we know of rods except about the terminus
O Dear O!, O dear O!
Railway speculation now is all the go.

If I had power to write on rails my manner would be Byron'y
 By laying rods in every part folks will indulge their irony
Some will burn their fingers soon, a pretty mess they'll make at it
The whole country is a grid iron turned and each has got a stake in it
 O Dear O!, O dear O!
 Railway speculation now is all the go.

Bill Brown he talks of shares in the Equatorial and Equator line
And William Brown has been up town on the coal and coke and tater line
 Jack Nokes who dealt in boxes says hisen's a defunct line
So leaves off the portmanteau line and takes unto the trunk line
 O Dear O!, O dear O!
 Railway speculation now is all the go.

 Now horses ride in carriages, instead of flesh tis metal now
Experience proves that little use are cattle [horses] to the kettle now
Calves lean o'er their pens like authors wondering what has got 'em
 Thus 'tis lines of weal we see up top and lines of wheels at bottom
 O Dear O!, O dear O!
 Railway speculation now is all the go.

 Now railways go across the earth enticing many a soul to roll
 Their lines are washer women's quite because they go from pole to pole
Some companies whose rods are bad and who for cash are angling
 Might write up "ironing done here" and very often mangling
 O Dear O!, O dear O!
 Railway speculation now is all the go.

Such moving, grooving, proving, such rounding and such bevelling
A change is coming very fast, a universal levelling
Such pulling down and rising up so that the roads may have no jerk upon
The promoters tell the shareholders that they must have perfect flats to work upon
O Dear O!, O dear O!
Railway speculation now is all the go.

The Wreck of the Royal George
Published 1849 (after Hudson's fall from grace)

TOLL for a knave!
A knave whose day is o'er!
All sunk – with those who gave
Their cash, till they'd no more!

Shareholders grumbled loud,
Directors wroth did get –
Down went the Royal GEORGE,
With all his lines, complete!

Toll for the knave!
The Royal GEORGE is gone;
His last account is cook'd;
His work of doing done!

It was not in the panic,
His credit felt no shock;
The House at Albert Gate
Stood firm as Albert Rock.

> Clerks still drew bated breath,
> And moved obedient pen,
> When the Royal GEORGE went down
> Never to float again.
>
> Cast the tottle up,
> See how the money goes:
> And reckon, railway pup-
> -pets, how much England owes.
>
> The Royal GEORGE is gone,
> His iron rule is o'er -
> And he and his Directors
> Shall the lines no more!

Following his death in 1871, the satirical magazine *Punch* published this long eulogy to 'King Hudson':

KING HUDSON

1

> "He reigned, he died" – the summary
> Might serve for many a king
> Whose reign is void in History
> Of aught that Muse can sing –
> True sovereign gold the coin may be,
> But, somehow, has no ring;

2

But this King, who has passed away
Unmarked, unwept, unsung.
He reigned in quite another way –
Ne'er sovereign louder rung;
Ne'er busier king held sterner sway,
Or mightier mandates flung.

3

O happy ye, whose line of life
Crossed not that meteor's plane,
Whom Fate's allotment spared the strife,
Of great King Hudson's reign,
With Mammon's yellow fever rife,
And spasms of loss and gain!

4

When where King Hudson's sceptre turned –
A true divining-rod –
Pactolus sudden, burst and burned,
In gold, from sand and sod;
Till labour's quiet gains were spurned,
And "scrip" was all men's God.

5

We cried, "Our King of Men appears,
So brassy, brisk, and bold!
Sowing hopes broadcast, spurning fears,
His touch turns all to gold!"
The crown we gave the asses's ear
Was big enough to hold.

6
He moved a Monarch blunt and bluff:
To hear was to obey!
Who of us could bow low enough,
On his gold-paved way?
Lords, Cits,* Respectable and Rough,
Church, Court, all owned his sway.

*Cits – City gents, brokers at London Stock Exchange

7
Pure Nonconformists on his crown
Breathed blessings unawares;
Archbishops put their croziers down,
To write to him for shares,
Great ladies by his smile or frown
Were changed to bulls or bears,

8
"Long live, King Hudson!" was our cry:
No line save his shall be!
As share-quotations ruled more high,
The loyaller grew we.
"His statue let us raise – for why?
Shrined in our hearts is he!"

9
And when he progressed England through,
The struggle was the while,
Who first should lick his royal shoe,
Win most shares in his smile;
Never did England such *kotoo*,
To kingly state and style.

10

What wonder, he we worshipped so
    Bore high that crowned head:
Trod heavy on the necks that low
    Were laid for him to tread;
To hands for bank-notes stretched would throw
    Buffets, sometimes instead.

11

But who that so the seamy side
    Of men 'twas given to see,
Less rough-shod e'er o'er backs did ride
    That bowed at his decree:
Was kindlier for all pocket-pride,
    Than bluff King George could be?

12

And when our fire of straw had burned
    To ash, as straw-fire must,
When the gauds in our hands were turned
    To rottenness and rust,
When our King George, a knave we learned,
    His fairy treasures dust;

13

When all the bubbles we had blown
    Burst with a swift collapse,
And exultation turned to groan
    O'er Stock Exchange mishaps,
And house, crashed, overthrown,
    To earth, in thunder-claps;

14

We too howled out upon the name
   So oft with blessings heard;
Helped pelt with mud of bitter blame,
   The crown we had conferred;
In howls of scorn and shouts of shame
   On our ex-King concurred.

15

So he we'd fawned on so, and feared,
   With curses down was cast –
King Hudson had no statue reared,
   But forth to exile past,
To climb the stranger's stairs, and bear'd
   Penury's bitter blast.

16

Faint tidings of his lot we had
   From far across the main, –
A fat old man, poor, shabby, sad,
   Of casual dinners fain;
Their doubtful recognition glad
   To give men back again.

17

Till some on whom he had smiles when king
   Thought shame that this should be,
And clubbing their alms-gathering
   Bought an annuity;
They said it is a sorry thing
   A Beggared King to see!

18

And poor King Hudson clutched the gift
And grateful was therefore, –
The weight of poverty to shift,
The wolf keep from his door;
His pittance used, they say, with thrift
Till int'rest's fruit it bore.

19

Now for his ups and downs not loath,
He rests, where Kings and churls are one:
He scaled heights, sounded depths, with both:
As basely fawned as spit upon,
Should men who hailed his mushroom growth,
Cast at his humble grave the stone.

Select Bibliography

Arnold A.J. and McCartney S., *George Hudson, the Rise and Fall of the Railway King* (Hambledon and London, 2004)

Bagnell, Philip, *The Railway Clearing House* (George Allen and Unwin, 1968)

Bailey, Brian, *George Hudson, The Rise and Fall of the Railway King* (Alan Sutton Publishing, 1995)

Bancroft, Elizabeth, *Letters from England, 1846-1849.* Project Gutenberg

Baynes, Ken and Kate, *The Railway Cartoon Book* (David and Charles, 1976)

Beaumont, Robert, *The Railway King, a biography of George Hudson* (Review/Headline Book Publishing, 2002)

Brandon, David and Brooke, Alan, *The Railway Haters* (Pen and Sword, 2019)

Burnage, Sarah; Hallett, Mark; Turner, Laura (ed), *William Etty, Art & Controversy* (2011)

Burton, Anthony, *George and Robert Stephenson* (Pen and Sword, 2020)

Byrne, Liam, *Dragons, the Entrepreneurs who built Britain* (Head of Zeus Ltd, 2016)

Clapham, J.H, *An Economic History of Modern Britain – The Early Railway Age 1820-1850.* (First published 1926. Reprinted Cambridge University Press 1959)

Clapham, J.H, *An Economic History of Modern Britain – Free Trade and Steel 1850-1886.* (First published 1932. Reprinted Cambridge University Press 1967)

Crowquill, Alfred, *How He Reigned and How He Mizzled, A Railway Raillery* (J. Harwood, London, 1849)

Davies, Hunter, *George Stephenson* (Weidenfeld and Nicholson, 1975)

Dawson, Anthony, *Yorkshire's First Main Line, the Leeds and Selby Railway* (Railway and Canal Historical Trust, 2020)

Deary, Terry, *Dangerous Days on Victorian Railways* (Weidenfeld and Nicholson 2014)

Fawcett, Bill, *A History of the York-Scarborough Railway* (Hutton Press Ltd, 1995)

Fawcett, Bill, *George Townsend Andrews of York "The Railway Architect"* (Yorkshire Architectural & York Archaeological Society, and North Eastern Railway Association, 2011)

Francis, J.A., *A History of the English Railway 1820-1845* (First published 1851. Reprinted by David and Charles, 1967)

Gilchrist, Alan, *Life of William Etty* (1855)

Glyn, John J., *Development of British railway accounting 1800-1911* (1984)

Gordon, D.I., *A Regional History of the Railways of Great Britain, Volume 5 – Eastern Counties* (David and Charles, 1968)

Greenwood, Marjorie, *Railway Revolution 1825-45* (Longmans, 1955)

Hebron, Chris de Winter, *50 Famous Railwaymen* (Silverlink Publishing, 2005)

Helps, Arthur, *Thoughts upon Government* (1872)

Hoole, Ken, *A Regional History of the Railways of Great Britain, Volume 4 – The North East* (David and Charles, 1965)

Hough, Richard, *6 Great Railwaymen* (Hamish Hamilton, 1955)

Lambert, Richard S, *The Railway King* (First published 1934. Reprinted George Allen and Unwin, 1964)

Lewin, Henry Grote, *The Railway Mania and its Aftermath 1845-1852.* (The Railway Gazette, 1936)

MacLean, John, *Locomotives of the North Eastern Railway* (First published 1923, new edition by Amberley Publishing, 2014)

Major, Susan, *Early Victorian Railway Excursions* (Pen and Sword, 2015)

Miller, Robert C.B., *railway.com* (The Institute of Economic Affairs, 2003)

Mountfield, David, *The Railway Barons* (Osprey Publishing, 1979)

Odlyzko, Andrew, *The collapse of the Railway Mania, the development of capital markets, and Robert Lucas Nash, a forgotten pioneer of accounting and financial analysis* (School of Mathematics University of Minnesota Minneapolis, 2011)

Peacock, A.J. and Joy, David, *George Hudson of York* (Dalesman Books, 1971)

Peacock, A.J., *George Hudson 1800-1871 – the Railway King*, self-published 1988)

Ransom, P.J.G., *The Victorian Railway and how it evolved* (Heineman, 1990)

Robbins, Michael, *The Railway Age* (Routledge and Kegan Paul, 1962)

St John, Thomas David, *How Railways Changed Britain* (Railway and Canal Historical Trust, 2015)

Seymour, William Digby, *Report of the Evidence of George Hudson, Esq., M.P. on the Trial of the Cause of Richardson versus Wodson, York Summer Assizes 1850* (John Hearne, London, 1850)

Simmons, Jack, *The Railways of Great Britain* (First published 1961. Reprinted by Sheldrake Publications, 1986)

Simmons, Jack, *Railways, An Anthology* (William Collins Sons, 1991)

Stamp, Cordelia, *George Hudson and Whitby* (Caedmon of Whitby, 2005)

White, Andrew and Richard, *The Whitby and Pickering Railway, the Horse-drawn Era 1833-1847* (Scriptorium Publications, 2017)

Whitworth, Alan, *Long Live the King! George Hudson and Whitby* (Culva House Publications, 2002)

Williams, F.S., – *Williams Midland Railway, Its Rise and Progress* (First published 1876. Reprinted by David and Charles, 1968)

Williams, Frederick S., *Our Iron Roads* (First published 1852. Reprinted by Frank Cass & Co Ltd, 1968)

Wragg, David, *The Race to the North* (Pen and Sword, 2013)

Index

A

Albert Gate 89, 110, 113, 206, 211, 222, 224, 229, 231, 242-244, 246, 248, 251–254, 258, 259, 264, 272

Albert, Prince 80, 243, 246, 251, 266

Anderson, Robert Henry 20, 25-27, 31, 33, 35, 64

Andrews, G. T. 17, 49, 86

Atmospheric Railways 79-81

B

Backhouse, Thomas 46, 49, 50, 53, 85, 123

Bancroft, Elizabeth 244-246

Barkley, Charles Francis 23-25, 27, 28, 31-33, 35

Barstow, Thomas 23, 50, 84, 86

Bayntun MP, Samuel 22

Beeching, Dr Richard 82, 133

Bell and Nicholson 13, 14, 16, 235

Bell, William 14, 235

Bellerby, Henry 32, 66

Bentinck, Lord George 136, 245, 246

Birmingham and Gloucester Railway 74, 263

Bottrill, Matthew 14-16, 193, 236

Brandling Junction Railway 74, 114, 129, 132, 134, 152, 155, 157, 262

Brassey, Thomas 205

Bristol and Gloucester Railway 74, 80, 81, 263

Brunel, Isambard Kingdom 79-81, 234

C

Carlton Club 106, 199, 208, 217

Carlyle, Thomas 8, 125, 126, 222

Clark, Sir William 60, 62, 67, 68, 104

Close, John 89, 149, 153, 175, 214

Cobden MP, Richard 92, 106, 107

Cooper, William 41, 50, 85

Corn Laws 92-94, 96-100, 104, 105, 163

Crawshay, George 46, 49

Crawshay, William 116, 117, 155, 238

Cubitt, Thomas 242, 253

Cundy, Nicholas 41-44

D

Dallas, Anne 256, 258, 259

Davies, Robert 44, 50, 58, 86, 123, 149, 153, 166

Index   283

Debtors Act 1869 207, 256
Dickens, Alfred 89
Dickens, Charles 136, 177, 192, 194, 207, 258
Disraeli, Mary 252
Duncan, Viscount 99
Duncombe, Thomas MP 180-183
Dundas MP, George 246, 248
Dundas MP, John 23-25, 30, 31-35, 43, 45, 50

E
East and West Riding Railway 154, 155, 167, 170, 175
Eastern Counties Railway (ECR) 82, 102, 106, 111, 117-119, 138, 154, 156, 161, 195, 243, 245, 263
Elliot, George MP 199, 204, 205, 209, 211, 212
Ellis, John 83, 86, 110, 111
Elsley, Charles Heneage 20, 44, 46, 49
Etty, William 120-122, 239-242

F
Fenwick, Henry 163, 180, 184, 187, 189-191
Foster, James 196, 208, 209, 212-214
Francis, John 8, 9, 12, 23, 70, 72, 74, 76, 89, 103, 110, 195, 220

G
Gibbs, Joseph 42-44
Gilchrist, Alexander 121, 122, 240, 241

Gladstone, William 90, 91
Glyn, George Carr 77, 78, 90, 91, 106
Gourley, Edward MP 216
Graham, Hawley 24, 27
Gray, Jonathan 30, 53, 54
Grand Northern Railroad Company 38, 41, 43
Great North of England Railway (GNER) 44, 45, 50, 70, 71, 83, 112, 114
Great Northern Railway (1) (ceased in 1836) 43, 45, 46
Great Northern Railway (2) (incorporated in 1846) 46, 76, 102, 111, 117
Great Western Railway 38, 75, 90, 138
Guest, Lady Charlotte 237

H
Holy Trinity Church, York 15, 235, 236
Hotham, Alderman John 50, 60
Howden, Lord 47, 48
Howsham 12, 13, 213-215, 259
Hudson, Ann Elizabeth (daughter) 15, 94, 142, 215, 217, 236, 246, 248, 249, 251, 252, 253, 254, 256, 260
Hudson, Elizabeth (George's wife) 10, 14-17, 23, 57, 62, 67, 94, 115, 121, 178, 208, 214-217, 238, 244, 245, 235-256, 258-260, 264

Hudson, George
- early years in Howsham 12, 13
- apprenticed to Bell & Nicholson 13, 14, 16
- inheritance from Matthew Bottrill 14-16, 193, 236
- joins York railway committee 38
- appointed chairman of YNM 51
- elected to York Council 53
- elected Lord Mayor of York 55
- elected for second time as Lord Mayor 61
- opening of YNM railway to South Milford 62
- buys Londesborough estate 172
- buys Newby Park 113
- York to Scarborough railway 41, 75, 193, 261
- appointed chairman of Eastern Counties Railway 103
- meets Prince Albert 80
- meets Queen Victoria 243
- elected as MP for Sunderland for first time 95
- first contribution in the HoC 95-97
- re-elected MP for Sunderland 105
- lays foundation stone at Sunderland new docks 107
- answers ECR petitions in HoC 117-119
- resigns as chairman of his railway companies 111 (Midland), 115 (YNB), 116, (YNM), 117 (ECR)
- resigns from York Union Bank 120
- letter of explanation 129-134
- opens new docks in Sunderland 141
- witness in Richardson v Wodson libel trial 143-158
- 'vindication' speech in HoC 181-183
- Lord Mayor of York for third time 104
- sells house in Monkgate, York 124
- stripped of Aldermanic role in York 124
- taken to Court of Chancery by the YNM 165-178
- re-elected for third time as MP for Sunderland 187
- loses Sunderland election 1859 191
- goes into exile 192
- agrees to stand for election in Whitby 194
- arrested for debt before Whitby election 196
- in exile again 199
- benefits from annuity raised by his friends 204-207
- Debtors Act 1869 passed 207
- returns to England 207
- NER abandon their case against him 212
- falls ill on visit to Yorkshire 213

- passes away in London
December 1871 213
- funeral at Scrayingham church
215
- obituaries 218-234
Hudson, George (son) 15, 208, 214,
217, 236, 254, 257-260
Hudson, John (son) 15, 236,
254-259, 260
Hudson, William (son) 15, 187,
208, 213, 214, 217, 236, 254,
256-258, 260
Hull and Selby Railway 155, 167,
168, 173, 261

I
Iron rails 131, 134, 148, 155, 172-174,
238

J
Jarrow Docks 209, 210

L
Leeds and Selby Railway 38, 39, 45,
47, 62, 70, 74, 261
Leeman, George 20, 25-27, 30-33,
35, 54, 59, 63-65, 75, 124, 125,
166, 167, 195-199, 204, 206,
214, 253
Lendal Bridge 175, 177, 214
Lindsay MP, William 190, 191
Londesborough Estate 167, 169,
172, 177, 246
London and Birmingham Railway
38, 43, 77, 138

Lowther MP, John 22-26, 28, 29, 30,
31, 33-35, 43, 46, 48, 49, 50,
57, 67, 91
Lowther, Sir John 28, 86

M
Madam Tussaud's 126, 216, 217
Market Weighton 73, 75, 82, 261
Meek, James 20, 21, 30-32, 34,
37-39, 41, 42, 44-46, 48-54,
59, 61, 64, 85
Midland Counties Railway 43, 74
Midland Railway 74, 76, 83, 86,
108, 110, 155, 156, 195, 210,
228, 262, 263
Monkgate, York 17, 20, 124, 236,
237, 244

N
Newby Park 113, 117, 119, 124, 129,
166, 178, 200, 211, 212, 242,
245, 246, 250, 253, 254
Newcastle and Berwick Railway 74,
79, 83, 84, 87, 129, 130, 262
Newcastle and Darlington
Junction Railway 70, 71,
77, 156, 262
Nicholson, Richard 14, 15, 18, 22,
45, 46, 49, 50, 86, 115, 120,
123, 169, 235, 240, 242, 246,
249, 250
North British Railway 78, 79, 169
North Eastern Railway 75, 178, 198
North Midland Railway 41, 43, 70,
108

P
Peel, Sir Robert 58, 91, 95, 96, 98, 99, 188, 222, 228-230, 242, 243, 251
Petre, Edward 22, 25, 30, 33
Prance, Robert 112

R
Railway Clearing House 78
Rennie, George 39, 40
Richardson, James 9, 18, 27, 31, 45, 50, 59, 86, 123, 142, 143, 147, 148, 152, 153, 157, 157-159, 160, 161, 166, 169, 182
River Wear Commissioners 24, 209, 216
Rolt, John QC 168, 169, 173-176
Romilly, John Sir 167, 169-171, 173-176, 200, 201, 211, 212
Rowntree, Joseph (1801-1859) 18, 19, 26, 27, 41, 46, 49

S
Sandeman, Mr 196-199
Scrayingham 12, 13, 214, 215, 256, 259, 260
Seymour, George 27, 28, 59, 60, 107, 124
Simpson, John, Sir 31, 46, 48, 49, 50, 64, 65, 85, 86, 124
Smales, Henry 60, 61, 64, 65
Smith, Reverend Sydney 226, 230
South Milford 38-40, 45, 62, 70, 261

Stephenson, George 7, 11, 39-41, 43-46, 62, 67, 79, 83-86, 193, 224, 230, 234
Stephenson, Robert 62, 86, 106, 153, 194, 245
Suminska, Count Jerome 215, 259
Sunderland dock 104, 107, 108, 129, 130-132, 134, 136, 139, 140-142, 158, 161, 162, 166, 176, 185, 185, 192, 204, 207, 209, 210, 212, 216, 228, 229, 260

T
Taylor, Hugh MP 204-206, 208, 209
Thompson and Forman 131, 148, 149, 155, 172
Thompson, Harry S 20, 75, 165-167, 193, 195-202, 204, 212, 214
Toller QC, Mr 165, 170, 173, 174
Tuke, Samuel 18, 41, 45, 46, 49

U
Uniacke, C H 255, 256

V
Victoria, Queen 23, 56, 57, 238, 243, 244, 251, 252, 266

W
Waddington MP, David 106, 117, 119
Wellington, Duke of 23, 89, 163, 230, 243, 245, 248, 249, 251-253
West Cliff, Whitby 193, 195, 212, 213, 226

Whitby and Pickering Railway 38-40, 45, 75, 172, 173, 193, 261
Wightman, Judge William 148, 157-159
Wilkins QC, Charles 145, 147, 148, 153, 154, 156, 158
Wilkinson, Bartholomew 148
Wodson, Thomas 143-145, 158
Wright, Joseph 93, 140, 141, 211

Y
York City and County Bank 45
York Debtors' Prison 196, 205
York Flint Glass Company 21, 37
York, Newcastle and Berwick Railway (YNB) 74, 75, 78, 111-115, 117, 123, 125, 129-133, 136-138, 141, 143, 148, 149-152, 154-157, 166-168, 173,149, 262
York and North Midland Railway (YNM) 44-50, 61, 68, 70, 73-75, 77, 78, 82-85, 111, 112, 115-117, 138, 143, 153-156, 160, 162, 164, 165-169, 171-175, 177, 180, 193, 195, 214, 253, 261
York Union Bank 31, 45, 49, 50, 77, 85, 89, 120, 143, 147, 173